Investing in Gold Mine Houses

Investing in Gold Mine Houses

How to Uncover a Fortune Fixing Small, Ugly Rental Houses and Apartments

Jay P. DeCima

New York   Chicago   San Francisco   Lisbon   London
Madrid   Mexico City   Milan   New Delhi   San Juan
Seoul   Singapore   Sydney   Toronto

The *McGraw·Hill* Companies

1 2 3 4 5 6 7 8 9 0   FGR/FGR   0 1 5 4 3 2 1 0 9 8

ISBN   978-0-07-160834-3
MHID   0-07-160834-6

This publication is designed to provide accurate and authoritative information in regard to the subject matter covered. It is sold with the understanding that neither the author nor the publisher is engaged in rendering legal, accounting, futures/securities trading, or other professional service. If legal advice or other expert assistance is required, the services of a competent professional person should be sought.

> —*From a Declaration of Principles jointly adopted by a Committee of the American Bar Association and a Committee of Publishers*

McGraw-Hill books are available at special quantity discounts to use as premiums and sales promotions, or for use in corporate training programs. To contact a representative, please visit the Contact Us pages at www.mhprofessional.com

This book is printed on acid-free paper.

Library of Congress Cataloging-in-Publication Data

DeCima, Jay P.
    Investing in gold mine houses : how to uncover a fortune fixing small, ugly rental houses and apartments/ by Jay DeCima.
    p. cm.
    ISBN 0-07-160834-6 (alk. paper)
1. Real estate investment. 2. Residential real estate. 3. House buying.
4. Housing rehabilitation—Economic aspects. I. Title.
    HD1390.5.D433 2009
    332.63'243—dc22   2008030636

Contents

Contents

Contents

Contents

Contents

Contents

Contents

Introduction

Let me tell you something about myself. Real estate investing truly fascinates me! People often ask me, "Why don't you quit buying more properties? You've already got all the houses you'll ever need for one life-time. Why don't you just sell them and take the money to enjoy yourself? After all, you can't take the houses with you, and you're not getting any younger, you know!"

It's true, I do own more houses than I'll ever need and certainly I could sell out and travel around the world—several times if I wanted to. The truth is that I truly *enjoy doing what I'm doing.* In fact, if I were forced to retire tomorrow and someone asked me, "What do you plan on doing now that you're retired?" my answer would be, "I plan to keep investing in real estate—only slower!"

Real estate investing is an exciting business the way I do it, and it would be very difficult for me to stop doing it altogether. Each new deal is an exciting challenge because every new transaction is different from the last one. Not only are the deals different but my techniques are con-stantly changing too. As I continue to learn more about investing, I'm also becoming a better deal maker, which gives me a lot of satisfaction and enjoyment. Once you get hooked on the excitement that comes with negotiating new deals, it's very easy to become addicted. As I look back now, it was far easier to give up my smoking!

During the past 35 years, I've read dozens of books about real estate investing, and I must tell you that few if any present the ideas and strate-gies you'll find in this book. The reason this book is different is that I practice real estate investing and landlording every single day of my life.

That's all I do, besides write about it! The point is, when you read this book, you won't necessarily find the unanimous opinion of every so-called real estate expert, and you won't find any strategies or techniques that might or could work when the moon is full. But rather, you'll be reading about blood, sweat, and tears. All mine! What I have written for you is based on the details of my own actual transactions: how I set them up, and how I made them work. Obviously, street names have been changed to protect the innocent in case there are any! I will show you how to start with very few dollars in your pocket and acquire cash-producing real estate in less time than it takes the average person to get promoted at a regular job.

I have devoted many years and thousands of dollars to acquiring the knowledge I will share with you in this book. If you are presently working for a salary but would like to become your own boss in the future, I will tell you how to do it. If you wish to earn more income for yourself and family, I will teach you about the highest-paid "part-time" job you'll ever find anywhere. If you're looking for a satisfying new career, as I was, with absolutely no limits on how much money you can make, you need not look any further. This might be your lucky day because I'm about to tell you exactly how you can do it for yourself.

If you're the kind of person who can start something new and stick with it, then you're the kind of person who will benefit the most from this book. Furthermore, *I will promise you* that if you begin using just a few of the money-making strategies I teach in this book, vigorously applying the ones that fit your personality and style, you can become a very successful real estate investor—without any limits!

You can stop investing after four rental houses like my Sierra Boulevard property (see Chapter 18), or you can continue full steam ahead until you own a hundred properties. The choice is yours. However, whichever way you decide, you'll begin to discover that something inside you has changed. Never again will you feel totally dependent on your employer, and you'll come to realize that *you really don't have to put up with a boring dead-end job*. This book will give you an option—an alternative way to provide for yourself and your family. Perhaps even more important, you'll never again find yourself at the mercy of recessions, employer downsizings, bankruptcies, or other economic ills that beset most people.

I've heard many so-called real estate gurus give advice to brand new investors. What you need first, they say, is a team of real estate professionals to help you get rich. To mimic an old TV commercial, *you'll need them when pigs can fly!* In fact, small-time investors are wasting valuable time even thinking about a team. The only person in the whole wide world who gives a hoot about your getting rich is the one you're looking at in the mirror. Would you care to guess how many real estate agents are concerned about your getting rich? How many lawyers, or how many bankers? If you answered none, you can keep on reading!

I'll show you how to put deals together and write 'em up yourself. As for lawyers, most start-out investors have nothing to hide from and even less to protect. And as for bankers, you can easily do without them. Bankers make banks rich, and when times get really tough, they don't even make loans—they just make excuses. I'll show you better ways to finance most of the properties you'll ever want to buy.

Surprising as it may sound, the three things you'll need the most of do not include money:

1. Knowledge
2. Self-confidence
3. Perseverance

Those three important ingredients are all you need to become successful and reach your financial goals.

Know-how—knowledge—is listed first for obvious reasons. That's where I can help you, because my book can be your guide. My personal experiences will be your teacher, and my profitable transactions will provide convincing evidence that my techniques work.

The second thing you must have is *self-confidence*. This will come with knowledge and from actually doing your own real estate deals. When you know how to do something successfully, your confidence level rises by tall leaps and bounds.

The final ingredient you must have is perhaps the most important of all three. It is *perseverance*. Failure to stick to the plan until the goal is reached is nearly always fatal for anyone who can't—or won't—go the distance.

I've watched many investors become discouraged and quit just short of the goal—on the one-yard line. Quite often, someone right behind them will pick up where they stopped and make a fortune by simply running the extra yard for a touchdown! I am so convinced about the importance of this final ingredient that I've included a little ditty below that happened to be the favorite homily of the late Ray Kroc, millionaire and founder of the world's largest hamburger store: the McDonald's Corporation. This man has always been a guiding light and inspiration to me. These words, I feel, have great application here:

Press on: Nothing in the world can take the place of persistence. Talent will not; nothing is more common than unsuccessful men with talent. Genius will not; unrewarded genius is almost a proverb. Education will not; the world is full of educated derelicts. Persistence and determination alone are omnipotent.

—Calvin Coolidge, as quoted in Ray A. Kroc, *Grinding It Out: The Making of McDonald's* (Contemporary Books, Chicago, 1977)

Fixing up downtrodden houses is the best place to start for part-time investors and career changers alike. Both are usually short of money, as well as experience. Buying ugly properties from motivated sellers is much easier and a whole lot cheaper than buying bright and shiny houses. Naturally, the competition will be significantly reduced because the buying public equates value with looks.

Small multiple-unit properties like the ones I recommend often fall between the cracks when it comes to attracting an investor's interest. The big guys, especially partnerships and syndicators, generally ignore them because they're simply too small and troublesome. Most small-time investors rule them out because they've been taught to think in terms of single-family houses. They often conclude that older, dumpy looking properties are worn out, obsolete, and a lot more trouble than they'll ever be worth. Many of these investors lack the vision to search out these gold mine properties covered by dirt and neglect.

Introduction

I often refer to my small multiple-unit properties, both houses and apartment buildings, as "leper properties" because many wannabe investors are simply not willing to touch them. Instead, they fight the crowds, fiercely competing to purchase the nicer looking, sweet smelling houses often called "pride of ownership" properties.

What many investors fail to understand is the value of *cash flow now!* While I will certainly agree that tomorrow's equity is an important consideration down the road, *my top priority has always been getting down the road.* Cash flow production must always come first! You must earn money as you go along to survive. Leper properties are the best cash producers I know of for getting you down the road.

If you will follow my advice from the beginning and acquire the kind of properties that will earn you consistent profits, then one day you'll have enough money to buy any kind of real estate your little ol' heart desires! Making a million dollars is not the least bit unusual. In fact, nearly every wage earner with a decent job will earn a million dollars! The only question is, when? How long will it take to get the money?

In my bestselling book *Investing in Fixer-Uppers,* I tell readers about a mill worker in my town who earned $1,200,000 working at the local sawmill. That sounds like a lot of money until you realize that *it took him 40 years to do it!* Earning a million dollars over a period of 40 years sounds about as exciting as kissing your sister! Even if the mill worker could somehow save or set aside half his earnings ($600,000), which would make him rich by some people's definition, it's still not very exciting because during most of his 40 years at the mill, he would have to live like a pauper, scrimping and going without in order to save half his paycheck.

Most investors, including me, who set out to build real estate wealth or earn a million dollars want to do it while we still have some breathing time left on the planet to enjoy it! In my fixer-upper book, I explained to readers how I fixed up my Hillcrest property and earned a million dollars, same as the mill worker. The big difference was that it took only two years of my time. The key to building wealth and long-term financial security is not only the amount of money you make *but how long it will take you to make it!*

Introduction

In this book, I will show you dozens of practical investment techniques and strategies, ideally suited for small-time, do-it-yourself investors, *both part-time and full-time!* I started as a part-time investor, moonlighting while I was working for the telephone company. Then after 23 years and a string of rental houses under my belt, I mustered up the courage to quit my telephone job and begin a full-time investment career. Without a steady paycheck, it doesn't take very long to realize that **cash flow properties are the only kind you want.**

You'll find my investment strategies work equally well for brand new investors and old salts alike because I recommend only those kinds of properties that will pay for themselves. I'll show you how to earn profits that rise much faster than inflation, even faster than you can spend them and a lot quicker than the tax collectors can snatch them from you!

It is not my intention to show you how to make as much money as Donald Trump—I don't know how! What I can show you, however, is how to make a few million dollars in a reasonable amount of time and enjoy a much richer, more fulfilling lifestyle while you're doing it. If that works for you, study these pages carefully because they truly have the power to unleash the millionaire inside of you.

Investing in Gold Mine Houses

1

The Millionaire's Recipe

Six junky little houses all tucked in together on an oversized city lot. They might have resembled a Norman Rockwell painting if you stood far enough away and had poor vision. They were older, rundown, and somewhat neglected—not much different from all the others I've purchased over the years. As you shall see before the end of this chapter, six little houses like these can make a very powerful contribution to your financial well-being!

My Cherry Street story began a long time ago. In the sequence of time and events, I'm currently living off payments from the promissory note after 26 years of collecting rents from my tenants. In case you might be trying to figure out my age, I can tell you this much: I acquired Cherry Street back when I didn't mind having my picture taken! As it turns out, however, who could have ever guessed how handsome I would look with all my wrinkles.

The Cherry Street Transaction

Beating down the seller to a $145,000 purchase price seemed like a shallow victory at the time. My biggest problem was trying to find the $20,000 down payment the seller wouldn't budge on. A truck driver by day and part-time landlord when he wasn't hauling stuff, he was savvy enough to see that I wanted to buy his houses just about as badly as he wanted to sell them. Back then, I was still teaching myself not to fall in love with properties. The seller finally agreed to carry back financing for $125,000, and he would give me 15 years to pay. But the down payment he said would have to be cash on the barrelhead. I remember thinking to myself, where will I ever find $20,000? I even wondered if there was that much cash in the world. Eventually, I robbed Peter to pay Paul and got the deal closed. That would be the last out-of-pocket money I'd ever have to spend on Cherry Street. My tenants would eventually pay for everything else.

Lifetime Investing

Cherry Street is about making money for life. It's about being a capitalist and living off your assets. That's why I call it *womb-to-tomb investing*. My basic strategy is to acquire the right properties, hang onto them, then harvest the benefits as I go along. My plan is to pay a small down payment and come up with whatever funds are needed for fix-up. After that, all the money starts flowing in one direction: back to me! My tenants will pick up the tab for everything else. As time goes along, I'll eventually be completely mortgaged out. That means every nickel I've spent will have been returned to me. I have often characterized my job as that of an *arranger* or *financial plumber*: I arrange to acquire the right property, I arrange the financing, and finally, I do whatever upgrading is necessary to make the property cash flow.

Today, as I write about Cherry Street, many wannabe investors are worried about real estate values plunging, mortgage funds drying up, and cash flow properties becoming more difficult to find. These concerns are not new; in fact, they are even older than I am. My good friend and investor cohort, the late William Nickerson began investing in properties just like Cherry Street during the country's worst depression, and he did just fine. When Nickerson passed away, his estate was valued in the $16 million range. Pretty good, I'd say, for a do-it-yourself duplex investor! In his now-famous real estate book *How I Turned $1,000 into Five Million in Real Estate* (Simon & Schuster, 1984), Nickerson wrote:

> The opportunity to make a fortune is with us every day. Under the free enterprise system, opportunity knocks not just for the favored few, but for everyone who aspires to better himself. And, opportunity knocks not just once, but many times. Obviously, it's up to you to open the door.

Properties like Cherry Street are the kind of *door-opening opportunities* Nickerson writes about. They are not scarce or hard to find if you learn where to look and adjust your thinking to look for older multiple-unit properties as opposed to single-family houses. Single-family houses are not really income properties in the truest sense. Don't misunderstand me here and think that I don't like owning single-family houses! I do, and I own them myself. They make excellent investments, but they lack what most new investors—especially career changers—need to start with: **cash flow!** Buying in bunches will help you generate cash spending money much quicker. It will also eliminate a great deal of the risk associated with buying leveraged real estate—*namely, going broke!* It's simply a matter of elementary mathematics: depending on six tenants' paying monthly rents is much safer than depending on just one.

Show Me the Money

Cherry Street grossed $10,800 during my first year of ownership. When I sold the property 26 years later, my gross rents had reached $57,240 annually. Some years passed without any rent increases, but during boom times they jumped higher than puffed Rice Krispies. On the day I sold Cherry Street, the books showed a total of $999,010 in rents collected during my ownership.

You might be thinking to yourself, that's a lot of money, but how much did you get to keep for yourself? I'll tell you how much later on, but right now, I will tell you that the rents doubled during my first three years as the owner. They went from $10,800 to $20,560. By then, the green was starting to flow my way. Twelve years down the line, my average rents at Cherry Street had reached $540 a month. When you do the math, you'll quickly see that my annual income had reached nearly $40,000—*roughly four times higher than when I started.*

People often ask me if I think rents will keep going up. My answer is, yes I do! Rents are like groceries: they're a product of the marketplace. In fact, rental houses make the perfect hedge against inflation because rents adjust with the times. When you carry paper or finance your property sales, as I often do, you must always consider the long-term effects of *fixed interest rates.* They are not sensitive to inflation like rental house income.

Is it hard to manage your rentals and collect all the rents? It's sorta like riding a bicycle. When you first start out, you'll most likely crash a few times. But once you get the hang of it, you'll find it gets much easier. Then finally one day, you'll begin to realize that *your tenants are making you rich.* By then, you might even be enjoying it!

The Key to Profits: Sound Economics

To start with, I'm an investor, not a speculator. Don't get me wrong here: when properties appreciate from natural causes or inflation, I'll certainly be the first in line to take my bows and accept congratulations. But inflation profits are what I call *fluff,* or *unearned profits.* I get them automatically without doing anything, just like every other investor whose name gets printed on a deed. True investors never count on appreciation or *inflation* to make a deal work. The deal must work based on sound economics and good negotiating skills.

I paid $20,000 down for Cherry Street, and I'm expecting to receive a very good return on my money. When I made the deal, I also expected to have all my down payment cash, plus my fix-up expenses, back in my pocket by the end of six years or so. Subscribers to my monthly newsletter *Trade Secrets* and the folks who've read my how-to books already know that my average fix-up costs run about 10 percent of the purchase price for the properties I call *light fixer-uppers* (and about

20 percent for *heavy fixers*). My Cherry Street estimated fix-up costs were nearly $18,000, or roughly 12 percent of the purchase price. You must not forget that 70 percent of those expenses ($12,600) were estimated labor costs. But back then, I was doing all the labor myself. That meant that the only cash money I needed was $5,400 for supplies and materials, which, of course, maxed out my overworked Visa cards.

An Ideal Mom & Pop Business

A property like Cherry Street is where every do-it-yourself investor should start. It's much less than a full-time job, yet big enough to give you all the practical experiences you'll need to decide if you're cut out to be a capitalist. Six junky looking houses are about the right size to cause you lots of grief if you attempt to finance them through a regular institutional lender. Five or more units put you in the commercial borrowing category. When your bank officer explains why she won't give you a mortgage, you should immediately jump outta your chair and thank her. She's done you a tremendous favor! You've now experienced one of the most valuable lessons you'll ever learn in this business: it's called *rejection*. Now you have no choice but to begin searching for sellers who are willing to finance their property sales. There's no shortage of these sellers, but most new investors don't try hard enough to find them without the extra push.

Six units are also about the right size for a total family experience. Although they'll scream and holler, the kids can enjoy a boatload of benefits helping Mom and Pop with the family rental business. Several families I've known for years have actually paid for the kids' college with rent money from their houses. With just a little accounting know-how, Billy Bob's new 4×4 truck can be purchased with operating expenses—*completely tax deductible*. One benefit that doesn't get talked about nearly enough is the family involvement part—kids who work with their parents learn more about responsibility. Sadly, this lesson has been lost in the dot-com shuffle in recent years. On a more positive note, what healthy young teenage boy would pass up a chance to cut grass at the family rentals in between video games? Don't forget to mention the 10 to 15 percent maintenance allowance—that might be just the right carrot to dangle!

You needn't lose any sleep worrying about your fix-up skills. At least 80 percent of all the work required is what I call *grunt work*. Even if you can't grunt, you can probably paint, haul trash, hang curtains, fix a fence, or spruce up a front yard. Skilled work, the stuff that needs a contractor or someone who actually knows what he or she is doing, is only a small percentage of the total fix-up cost. Keep in mind that I'm *not* talking about remodeling houses, like moving walls around or ripping out the old plumbing system. That's not the business I'm in. My job is to restore the property and do my best to preserve what's already there. Rental houses must be clean, attractive, and functional to compete in the marketplace, but that's it.

The Magical Power of Leverage

I can think of no other business that offers as much reward for such a small up-front investment. The $20,000 down payment I needed to acquire Cherry Street was roughly 14 percent of the total purchase price. That means that 86 percent of the property wasn't even mine yet—and still, my deed entitled me to 100 percent of all the income. When you divide six houses into the purchase price ($145,000 divided by 6 equals $24,166), you can see that my down payment was $4,166 short of paying for just one house, *let alone all six of them*. This is how leveraging can turn small-time investors into rich tycoons.

When you play Monopoly, you must pay for all your little green houses and your hotel before you can start collecting the maximum "rent" money from the other players who land on your squares. At Cherry Street, my down payment gave me full rights to begin collecting income from all six houses long before I'd have them paid for. Leverage allows you to make phenomenal returns with a relatively small sum of money. In this case, my $20,000 down payment returned $10,800 in rents during my first year of ownership. That's a 54 percent return without considering appreciation, tax write-offs, and the additional value I created with the fix-up.

Folks who have attended my seminars or read my books already know my feelings about selling good income properties. In case you don't, let me shout it loud and clear so there's no misunderstanding: I do not recommend selling income-producing properties!

If you buy properties the right way, and they begin producing a spendable income in a reasonable period of time, there can be very little justification for selling them. That would be like killing the goose that lays the golden eggs. The exception, of course, is when you reach the retirement mode and it's time to kick back and smell the roses. That would be the beginning of a whole new phase of profit making.

Womb-to-tomb investing is my characterization of planning a predictable income from start to finish—or as my probate attorney calls it, "until my case matures." Continuous income has always been one of my most cherished benefits,—you could call it my "old-age retirement fund." The money flow never shuts off with the passing of ownership. After 26 years of collecting rents at Cherry Street, I succumbed to the fragrance of sweet smelling roses in full bloom! I sold my six little money-maker houses for the going rate at the time: $650,000, or roughly 11.5 times the gross rents. (See Appendix C, Figure C-1.)

Switching Horses to Passive Income

I sell properties much the same way I buy them. I offer attractive terms and provide seller financing. I always spend considerable time checking out my buyer to determine if he or she will be able to handle the landlording chores. The key to receiving uninterrupted mortgage payments when you're cruising around the world is directly related to how well your buyer can cope with the tenants. A traveler's worst nightmare is that late-night panicked call to Barcelona from buyer advising you that he or she just can't do this anymore and is *giving you back the keys!*

Pajama money, as I call it, is living off the mortgage payments you receive from financing your property sales. That's about as good as it gets for retiring landlords! Sometimes it gets so quiet, that you almost miss hearing your ex-tenants' voices! Generally that thought passes rather quickly I've found. Still, during my many years as a landlord, the tenants treated me extremely well financially. Looking back, I'm still amazed at my earnings from six little houses. During the last year alone, the property earned me almost three times ($57,240) the amount of my initial down payment.

After collecting nearly $1 million in rent money, I sold Cherry Street for $650,000. I received a $50,000 cash down payment, and I provided seller financing for the $600,000 balance. The buyer agreed to pay me interest-only payments of $3,250 per month for 20 years, with the remaining principal balance due at that time. This transaction worked quite well for both sides. It allowed the buyer to take over the property and immediately begin earning cash flow income. For me, my net income stayed about the same, but as the late Dr. King so eloquently put it, *"I'm free at last!"*

The Final Box Score

From beginning to end, Cherry Street will have earned **121.5 times** the amount of my initial down payment:

$999,010	Rents
50,000	Cash down payment
780,000	Interest income
600,000	Final principal payment
$2,429,010	Total income

2

Beth's Success Story

Millions of folks just like me spend countless hours and huge sums of money shopping in home improvement stores. But unlike me, most shoppers are looking for new ideas and products they can use around the home for improvements and personal enjoyment.

Big Box chain store shoppers are an ambitious bunch, I've found—and many are quite skilled working with their hands. They love fiddling around the house, fixing stuff, and installing new gizmos.

When I was younger, I had the most *overimproved* house in my subdivision. I was constantly redoing everything, and when I finished, I'd start all over again, *improving my improvements*. One day a good friend of mine dropped by to see my house. He suggested, that rather than keep doing the same things over again, why didn't I use my skills on another house? My friend's visit that day would change my life forever!

It wasn't long afterwards that I discovered how easy it was to convert my handyman skills and personal ambition into a *profit-making opportunity*. I can tell you from experience that there's not a dime's worth of difference between working at a hobby *without any pay* and being the highest-paid handyman in the neighborhood.

In my bestselling book *Investing in Fixer-Uppers* (McGraw-Hill, 2003), in the very first chapter, I inform my readers that big money is earned by working **smarter**, not harder! My book explains that with just a little bit of financial training, using the same house fixing skills that most handy folks already have, it's very possible to create a sizable monthly income and *financial security for a lifetime*.

Most people are too busy earning a living to make any serious money. They simply don't take the time to learn about investing or plan any kind of a financial future for themselves. In my first book, I show readers how one small apartment complex earned me the same amount of money as the mill worker would make in 40 years, but the big difference is that I earned mine **20 times faster**. That, my friends, is the kind of financial knowledge you need to know about. The book you're about to read will totally surprise you when you learn that building substantial wealth has very little to do with how much money you start with. And it has nothing to do with what school you went to, your current family obligations, or whether you're male or female. In fact, one of my most successful students was a divorced mom with two small children to care for.

Motivation to Survive

Beth's story is not a whole lot different than many other investor stories I've heard about since I started teaching. She was a divorced mother with two small toddlers to raise, and although she had a college degree, her salaried job left her with less than $10 a day after paying taxes and the babysitter. Obviously, you can't make it very far in the San Francisco area on 50 bucks a week!

Beth had completely renovated the house she lived in before her divorce. So she had some knowledge and experience in firing up and maintaining a property. But like most students who seek my advice, she had very little money to work with. The down payment for her first house came from child support payments. In a way, Beth's child support money was doing double duty!

Beth bought a rundown house where her family could live together, which also eliminated the need for expensive day care. Beth quickly jumped in and fixed up a bedroom, and that's where the kids would stay while she took on the other rooms.

Beth Claims Her 15 Minutes of Fame

Several years later, with four fixed-up houses to Beth's credit, senior real estate editor Corrie M. Anders from the *San Francisco Examiner* heard about her success and asked Beth for an interview. The first question Anders asked Beth was, "How does a single mom, with hardly any money, without a regular job, suddenly become a successful house fixer in the most expensive real estate market?" San Francisco is not exactly the easiest place to buy properties. Beth shared her story with Anders, and the full interview was published in the *San Francisco Examiner*.

Beth admits to pestering the daylights out of local real estate agents, bank loan officers, building inspectors, and anyone else she thought could help her. She attended seminars, joined an investment club, and even took several evening courses at the local college. Somewhere along the line, Beth learned about me and my House Fixer Seminars. I can still remember the first time she called and how impatient she sounded! She told me she'd bought and sold several fixer-upper houses and made decent profits. However, right after her divorce, she said the bankers refused to talk with a single mom who was raising two kids without a steady income. A mortgage would be out of the question, they told her! The banks had stopped Beth's house fixing career dead in its tracks!

Beth Obtains Financing without Money from the Bank

"Welcome to the world of *bankless real estate investing*," I told her. Then I asked her if she had $20 to purchase my book. Well, maybe I didn't ask her quite that fast, but she did agree to purchase my first self-published book: *Fixing Rundown Houses and Small Apartments*.

Before I mailed her the book, I made Beth a promise. Starting right now, *I'll teach you how to buy fixer-upper houses without the bank's money.* She liked the sound of that because the bank had stopped her house buying business cold. Beth had no problems estimating her costs for materials and supplies. Her biggest challenges were financing the properties she bought and finding the money to purchase materials.

Seller Financing Paves the Way to Success

I showed Beth the very same financing techniques that real estate wiz Harry Sonneborn taught Ray Kroc—America's godfather of hamburgers and the founder of McDonald's Corporation. Kroc was struggling along in his early years with never enough money to finance his ambitious plans for building new stores. Then suddenly, *along came Harry!*

Harry Sonneborn assured Kroc that sellers who owned vacant lots sitting there without earning any income would be more than happy to provide seller financing to get the income. Furthermore, he said, we can probably convince them to *subordinate their first mortgage position* to our new construction loans so that we can keep building even more hamburger stores.

I assured Beth that she could do exactly the same thing with *rundown houses.* And by getting the sellers to subordinate, she could borrow her fix-up money to boot! Most sellers with pigsty looking properties will gladly sign a subordination agreement in exchange for part of the borrowed cash.

This simple financing technique allowed Ray Kroc to build the world's largest hamburger empire, and the same technique allowed Beth to purchase junky houses from property owners in south San Francisco. In his excellent autobiography *Grinding It Out* (Contemporary Books, 1977), Kroc admits that he never really understood why sellers were willing to subordinate their first mortgage position after being kind enough to carry back a mortgage in the first place. Beth argued the very same issue with me until I told her, "Don't worry about it! It doesn't matter why. *Just go ask 'em, and see how many will sign.*"

Beth could hardly believe that the owners of ugly looking houses would even think about financing the sale. She just assumed that because the houses were so ugly and rundown, the sellers would insist on having all their money up front for fear they might have to take the property back!

I explained to Beth that there are several important reasons why sellers will jump at the chance to finance their houses. One reason, for example, is that these properties might look so terrible that banks would simply say no to any mortgage! Or even if a bank would agree to a mortgage, the amount would be very low and the terms extremely unfavorable. On top of that, the buyer would need to have an excellent credit rating to start with. Pigsty property owners are pretty much aware of all these problems, so the idea of financing their own property to make a deal work doesn't come as a big surprise to them.

Beth Learns to Use Other People's Money

Beth was quite surprised but extremely pleased when sellers began telling her yes! During her interview with the *San Francisco Examiner*, she told Corrie Anders: *"I never use any of my own money to buy fixer houses. I'm always able to convince the sellers to provide at least 80 or 90 percent of the financing. Money for my down payments and the fix-up costs comes from investors and private lenders,"* she said.

According to the Anders' interview, Beth's profits were $20,000 to $40,000 per house. I'd say Beth got $20 worth of value from reading my house fixer book—wouldn't you agree?

3

Wealth Begins
with a Dream

Gold laboreth diligently and contentedly for the wise owner who finds for it profitable employment, multiplying even as the flocks of the field.

—George S. Clason, *The Richest Man in Babylon*, 1926

What you're about to read is my favorite topic: building personal wealth with real estate. Not just any real estate, mind you, *but the kind that will pay you big money to own it*! It's also the kind that most folks can acquire the easiest, once they learn the ropes! Small rundown houses offer unlimited opportunities for those willing to roll up their sleeves and learn a few new tricks that can turn these properties into personal money machines.

In this book, I'll tell you how it's done. I'll share my profit-making secrets for earning big bucks with small "bread-and-butter" properties. As you read through these pages, keep in mind that you could easily be reading about yourself someday. I will make it crystal clear that all individuals who dream of success can achieve it if they will set their sights on the target and never stop 'til they reach their goal.

The Power of Dreams

Dreams can be a powerful stimulant for your imagination. When you study autobiographies of wealthy people, as I often do, you'll quickly discover that some mighty successful folks started out with little more than their *dreams* and *imagination*.

We all have dreams and imaginations, but obviously not all of us are rich or even close. *So what's the big secret, you ask?* It won't take you a whole lot of reading before you discover that rich folks don't stop dreaming when they wake up like most of us do. Instead, they wake up and immediately begin adding a powerful ingredient to their dreams. It's called **action**. Action causes the imagination to begin formulating a plan. It's this powerful combination of dreams stimulated by action that turns ordinary poor folks into rich tycoons. Let me give you a good example how this happens.

From Bellboy to Empire Builder

Conrad Hilton was a dreamer who added action to his dreams. In the very first chapter of his autobiography, Hilton states:

> When I first saw a photograph of the newly built Waldorf Hotel in 1931, I dreamed that one day I would own it! I read about such luxuries as the special railroad siding in the basement, a private hospital for guests, six kitchens with over two hundred cooks, five hundred waiters, one hundred dishwashers, not to mention two thousand rooms. Back then I was traveling around Texas in my junky old jalopy trying to find work as a part-time bellboy.
>
> It was indeed presumptuous and a totally outrageous dream back in 1931, but I cut out a picture of the magnificent Waldorf and wrote with my pen across the front of it, "The Greatest Hotel On Earth." Later on, when I finally landed a job with my own

desk, I slipped the dog-eared picture neatly under the glass top so it would always be visible in front of me. I never wanted the dream to leave my mind—and I never stopped planning until the day it was mine.

In October 1949, the greatest hotel on earth became a Hilton.

No Dream Is Too Big

Conrad Hilton started out with an *oversized dream and his imagination*. He then began to add some magic to his dream by developing a workable plan. It took Hilton four long years of delicate negotiations, careful planning, a good deal of luck, and a whole lot of praying. In his book *Be My Guest* (Prentice Hall, 1984), Hilton states: "No matter how long we worked into the night, I always started each day down on my knees. I attended church every morning at 6:30 a.m. sharp."

Hilton launched his vast hotel empire with an outrageous dream and hardly any money. Granted, it seemed too big, almost impossible, but Hilton did something else most people are not willing to do. In his book he says, "If you don't dream big, you most certainly won't achieve very much. *It's against the basic laws of nature that govern man*. Unless you can visualize something big, impressive and important, it's almost impossible to attain it."

Strange as it may sound, the large majority of folks today hardly spend any time at all with pencil in hand, planning some kind of strategy to improve their financial future. A successful apartment owner and good friend of mine says: "Most people are too busy earning a living to learn new ways to make big money."

Think about this for a moment; I'm sure you know it's true! Most folks spend hardly any time at all trying to rise above the everyday routine of life, and rarely do they take any action beyond dreaming to improve their financial future. Many people con themselves into thinking that because they have a decent job right now, they are totally secure forever. The truth is that many employees today have little more than the security of two weeks' notice or perhaps a small severance payment should their employer be stricken with tough times.

Real Estate Can Provide Security

People constantly ask me, "what kind of real estate investing do you recommend for ordinary working folks with only a few dollars to invest and
a limited amount of time to do it?" I can answer this question without any
hesitation because that's exactly the place I started from!

I strongly recommend that you invest your money, as well as your
available time, in older residential properties that will produce a positive
income. See how simple this stuff is? Regardless of whether you decide
to invest part-time or jump in head-first the way I did, the properties I'm
recommending will be the same. The only factor that will change when
you're planning is how much time you can devote to investing.

Most everything in life has trade-offs! Early in my investment career,
I made a searching and fearless examination of my financial situation. It
didn't take very long to see where I stood financially. I determined rather
quickly that what I needed more than anything else from my investment
plan was **monthly cash flow**. Whatever else I figured I might need would
have to wait in line behind cash flow. I kept my plan as practical as
I could at the time. With money coming in, I reasoned, I could likely survive and keep growing. And without money coming in, I was absolutely
sure that I couldn't!

It's important to know exactly where you stand financially when you
make your plan. You need to have a good idea of how much cash flow you
must generate to stay alive. Obviously, you'll need to figure out what it
will cost you to get it. Don't make a move until you've played around with
the numbers long enough to make certain you can see a profit.

A Financial Planning Quiz

Time out for just a moment! Let's assume you have **$10,000 cash** that
you're willing to invest for 10 years. You may choose a bank, credit union,
T-bills, municipal bonds, or whatever you consider reasonably safe for
your 10-year investment plan. **Here's my question to you:** What percentage or compounding rate of interest will satisfy you enough to invest
your $10,000 for the next 10 years? Think this over carefully, but be real-
istic. You have my promise that this is not a trick question. We'll use it

only for planning purposes. Besides, your answer will remain your own little secret, so take a minute, and write it in the box below so we can revisit your answer later on.

☐ Percent Rate of Return I Will Accept

Cash Flow Keeps You Green and Growing

Over the years, **planning for cash flow** has always been my number 1 investment priority, and it has paid big dividends. **Cash flow is what** I always advise new investors to think about first. It's a fundamental rule of investing as I see it. When you have cash flow—that is, money coming in—you are growing financially. I call this "green and growing." When you are green and growing, everything is possible, *investment-wise*. Without money coming in, nothing grows except discontentment and the constant worry about financial disaster.

Selecting cash flow as the top priority is one of the most important differences between **investing**, which is what most of us think we're doing when we buy a property, and *speculating*, which most of us should not be doing. I'll be the first one to admit that investing is not quite as much fun or exciting as speculating, but it's much safer financially. Folks who plan to stay in the real estate investment business for the long haul have no good reason to speculate until their bank account can stand a hit—*that means it can take a loss*!

I have several friends in southern California who purchase expensive houses when they think prices are appreciating rapidly. When their timing is right, they make a killing. When it's not, *they end up getting killed*. Sometimes they'll get stuck in a holding pattern! Their mortgage payments and expenses will suddenly zoom up faster than the rents they're able to collect. Vacancies increase, selling prices drop, and all their capital is tied up in a falling market. From a business standpoint, they're effectively shut down.

A good friend of mine has been a millionaire five times already. Every time he hits it big, the market changes and he loses everything! That's the part about speculating I really dislike. **When I get the money in my hands, I intend to keep it.**

Sorting Out Dreams from Reality

Investors who think like speculators often tell me that it takes money to make money. Yet many of these same folks spend thousands of dollars for "No-Down Investment Tapes" and "Easy Street Seminars." Obviously, they need to think a little harder about **planning** and **goals**. "Speculator thinking" often tends to make new investors feel as though they can start right out and enjoy immediate success. Some think they can skip right past the hard work and somehow multiply their investments by big dollar amounts and be rolling down the freeway in a new Mercedes.

That's exactly how my southern California friend thinks, and lately, he's had some serious setbacks. Things are always changing in the big city, and as they say in the used-car business, "He's upside down in several big-ticket properties." He's already owned the Mercedes of his dreams. In fact, he's owned three of them so far! But right how, you'll find him motoring around Pasadena in his youngest son's day-glo minibus.

There are four main reasons why real estate can make you rich—and much quicker than you might think—**but there is a catch**: you must hang on to the property to make it happen. Selling off your golden eggs before they hatch is a cardinal sin. Reaping a small benefit before it fully matures will only short-circuit your path to becoming a millionaire.

Understanding Where the Money Comes From

To get some idea about profits and cash flow, and **more** importantly, about where they come from, let's take a quick look at the four primary sources listed below. We'll discuss each of them individually to see how they work.

1. Appreciation
2. Cash flow
3. Equity build-up
4. Tax benefits

Appreciation: Using Leverage

Paying 10 percent down for a $300,000 property gives you a 90 percent leverage factor. In other words, 90 percent of the property's value is still owned by someone else even though your name shows on the deed as the legal owner. For just $30,000 cash, you now enjoy 100 percent control and all the benefits of a $300,000 asset. This applies to growth, or appreciation, as well.

Now, let's suppose the property appreciates 10 percent during your first year of ownership. That's peanuts where I live (California). Now your property is worth $330,000! You've made a **$30,000 profit** in just one year, but 10 percent appreciation doesn't mean you made just 10 percent. The reason: Because you paid only $30,000 down! You've earned the full down payment back in your first year of ownership. **That, my friend, is a "whopping" 100 percent return!** Remember what Conrad Hilton said about dreaming: *"unless you can visualize something big, impressive and important, it's almost impossible to attain it."* Well, 100 percent of anything is always quite impressive, wouldn't you agree?

Cash Flow

Investing in fixer-upper properties the way I suggest can pump up your cash flow very quickly. My method is not dependent on piddly little rent increases once a year or so. Instead, **my cash flow comes from forcing up the property value.** I say "forcing" because I immediately begin making improvements (adding value) that will increase my rental income. I don't wait around hoping for the economy to get better. In fact, my plan works just fine when there's no appreciation at all!

My adding-value goal is to make selected improvements to the property that allow me to increase my rents 50 percent or more within a period of two years or less. For example, let's say I acquire a rundown six-unit property with rents of $400 per month. My plan will be to fix up the property and make cost-effective improvements that allow me to increase my rents $200 per month. That's 25 percent each year, or a total cash flow increase of $7,200 annually:

$$\$100 \times 6 \text{ units} = \$600 \times 12 \text{ months} = \$7,200$$

Equity Build-up

Equity build-up comes from paying down the principal portion of the mortgage payment. Using our 10 percent down example, we'll be making mortgage payments on the unpaid balance of $270,000. Assuming a 30-year amortized mortgage at 8 percent interest, each mortgage payment will be $1,907.79. It costs $1,800 to pay the interest charge, with the balance going toward debt reduction, or **equity build-up**. You also get equity build-up from normal **inflation** or **appreciation**. For example, let's say the property value doubles in the next 10 years, which is really not uncommon. At that point your $300,000 property would be worth $600,000. That's an average equity build-up of $30,000 per year while you've owned the property, and 30 percent of that time you've been asleep!

Tax Benefits

Government "taxation," observed French Finance Minister Jean Baptiste Corbert, "is the art of plucking the goose so as to obtain the largest amount of feathers with the smallest amount of hissing." Income property investors in the United States can keep most of their feathers intact by taking advantage of lucrative tax laws. The government says that buildings and their various parts begin wearing out and losing their value the very minute you become the owner.

For income property owners, this might be called *tax loss pretending* because, as everyone on the planet knows, the real value of income property keeps going up. How does this make any sense, you ask? The answer is that the government says so. This wearing-out process, or loss of value, is called *depreciation*! For income-producing real estate like the six houses or apartments in our example, Uncle Sam insists that owners deduct this wearing-out expense on their 1040 tax returns, whether the owners like it or not!

The government tells us that residential rental properties will wear out at the rate of 3.64 percent each year. Carpets will be completely worthless in just 5 years, and asphalt driveways and parking areas will be worn out and depreciate down to zero value in just 15 years. The IRS has already determined how long it takes for all this stuff to wear out, so taxpayers don't have to bother figuring it out for themselves. Naturally, the IRS is more than happy to furnish depreciation schedules and whatever other tax information you need. According to their TV commercials, they're always willing to help you!

Although these properties are losing value according to IRS depreciation schedules, we already know that just the opposite is true. During the 15 years of wearing out, most income properties will actually double or triple in value, especially where I live! What this means is that your real estate can be earning a **positive cash flow** all year long, but when you file your taxes (Form 1040), the property could actually show a loss. **This means you'll have no income to pay taxes on.** Figure 3–1 gives an example of what I'm talking about.

As you can see, Jay's rentals produced an annual income of $12,500. The expenses and mortgage payments add up to $10,500 ($5,000 plus $5,500), which leaves Jay $2,000 (**positive cash flow**). However, when depreciation (a noncash expense) is deducted from the Tax Flow column, the property shows a *$2,000 loss* on Jay's year-end tax return.

		Cash Flow	Tax Flow
Annual Income		$12,500	$12,500
Annual Expenses			
Property tax	$1,200		
Insurance	$ 600		
Utilities	$ 460		
Maintenance	$1,400		
Management	$1,000		
Repairs	$ X		
Services	$ 340		
Total Expenses		$ 5,000	$ 5,000
Net Operating		$ 7,500	$ 7,500
Depreciation			$ 4,500
Mortgage Payments		$ 5,500	
Interest	$5,000		$ 5,000
Principal	$ 500		
Cash Flow	Positive	$ 2,000	
Taxable Income	(Negative)		**($2,000)**

Figure 3-1. Jay's rentals: Annual income

The bottom line is this: Jay runs around the property squealing like a wounded little puppy, wringing his hands and telling everyone who will listen, "What a rotten year it's been for us property owners. I've lost $2,000." He sobs, "What's a poor landlord to do? I'm losing my shirt!"

This is what I mean by "tax loss pretending." The reality is that Jay has actually pocketed $2,000 in net earnings—and that's not all! The $2,000 tax loss reported on Jay's 1040 tax return can now be used to wipe out taxes on $2,000 of additional income from another source *like wages or commissions*. From a practical standpoint, this is almost like getting paid twice for doing the same job. Don't ya just love being a tax loss pretender? Who said the American Dream was dead? Certainly not me! I'm livin' it!

Holding versus Flipping Properties

During recent years, dozens of so-called real estate gurus have worn out the carpets in almost every decent-sized motel with a conference room, preaching "How to Get Rich in Real Estate." All but a wee handful who actually know something about the business advise their listeners that it's a sin that ranks right behind adultery to become a landlord and manage screaming tenants. "Skim the money and run," *they advise*. It's un-American to clean up after renters and fix toilets during the middle of the Super Bowl!

On the surface this advice sounds somewhat appealing, but in practice, it's rarely the right path to wealth and financial security. Why is that, you ask? What's the big problem? After all, real estate is still real estate whether you fix it and sell it or fix it and keep it, right? Sorry, my friends, but there's a worm in the apple.

We just finished our discussion about the four primary ways to make money with properties. Put your thumb here to hold your place, and then go back and read them again. Do it out loud this time to help you remember them. **Here's the final test:** add the word *sale* behind each of the four ways to earn profits and income. Can you see what selling would do to each of them? Routinely selling off your properties will effectively reduce real estate investing to a one-trick pony! Take my advice and keep your tenants. In time, they'll pay off everything and make you a **very** wealthy investor.

Combined Returns Can Be Substantial

It goes without saying that real estate investment returns can vary a great deal, depending on the location and the economy. Still, even on the low side, they produce some pretty impressive numbers. Where you end up on the scale depends a great deal on your skills as an investor—choosing the right properties, negotiating the right price and terms, and aggressively pursuing favorable tax treatment. As we've already discussed in the appreciation example, earning 100 percent return with leverage is almost commonplace. The following are the typical high and low ranges I've experienced in the business:

Summary of Annual Returns

Appreciation	20	to	130%
Cash flow	5	to	40%
Equity build-up	10	to	30%
Tax benefits	5	to	50%
Combined	**40**	**to**	**250%**

Where in the range of percentages you end up is influenced by many different factors, as you probably suspect. I can assure you that many investors have achieved the highest returns shown here. Some have even exceeded them. I have personally earned more than 150 percent returns with groups of fixer houses in the early years of ownership. The point is that these high investment returns allow you to soar with the eagles and build permanent wealth much quicker when you learn to maximize their use.

Remember when I asked you what interest rate would satisfy you enough to invest $10,000 cash for 10 years? Didn't we agree that this would be your little secret? Now it's time to revisit your answer. I'm only trying to guess what you're thinking, *but don't you wish you'd picked a much bigger number?* The following chart shows the earning power of $10,000 at various rates of compounding interest over a 10-year period:

5% compounded	=	$	16,288 in 10 years
15% compounded	=	$	40,455 in 10 years
25% compounded	=	$	93,132 in 10 years
30% compounded	=	$	137,858 in 10 years
50% compounded	=	$	576,635 in 10 years
100% compounded	=		$10,240,000 in 10 years

As you can see for yourself, choosing the right investment vehicle can turn your personal dreams of wealth into reality quicker than you might ever imagine! I suggest that the right vehicle is real estate! Not just any real estate, mind you, but the kind that will pay you big money to own it!

4

Looking for Benefits

People who seek my advice and training are generally folks who don't have a pot full of money saved up to invest in real estate. Some are in the same group that high-powered infomercial marketers are trying to attract with their slick 30-minute TV advertising. If you've ever watched these glitzy productions, the first thing you've probably noticed is how quickly the marketers inform their audience that you don't need money, good credit, or even a job. *No-money advertising* appeals to the masses because that's about the same amount of money the late-night viewers have. TV marketers cross their fingers and hope that responders will have enough untapped credit on their MasterCards to purchase whatever product they're pitching!

Most Beginners Have Very Little Savings

The most frequent question I'm asked by investor wannabes is, "How much money do I need to get started?" Most figure it will take from

$10,000 to $20,000, and almost 75 percent of them tell me they'll have to borrow the money, or at least part of it.

Let me point out here that I'm not talking about deadbeats. I'm talking about folks who have jobs and for the most part are out working every day making a living, raising families, and sending their kids to school. If they have a retirement plan with their employer, it's likely to be the only savings they have, which they probably can't touch. As far as extra money set aside or saved for investing—forget it! These folks are working hard and earning a decent living, but there's nothing left over.

No-money-down investing works every day—although probably not for the thousands who call in after watching glitzy TV infomercials. It works for investors who know the difference between a house and a horse. Plainly stated, it works for experienced investors who know how to negotiate deals and are likely have a decent credit standing. These investors are also savvy enough to understand what benefits might be acceptable to the other party. It's highly unlikely that a no-down-payment deal will work for some dummy who just became aware of real estate investing because he stayed up late one night watching TV. If it sounds too good to be true, chances are it is! My suggestion is to check out any offer thoroughly before doing something you may quickly regret.

Planning and Goals Are Most Important

In my opinion, $10,000 to $20,000 is a very reasonable amount for starting out; however, simply throwing the money at whatever pops up won't get the job done. You must first set up a few goals for yourself, including a reasonable time table. For example, do you plan to invest part-time or full-time? Perhaps you wish to supplement your retirement earnings for some future date.

You also need some idea about when you'll be needing the benefits from your investments. These are very basic questions you must answer for yourself before you even think about investing a single dime of your nest egg! If you don't have a reasonable understanding of **leverage** and **basic financing,** you'd be well advised to discuss your plans with someone who can help you with the mathematics. Also, you may need a bit of counseling on the **commonsense** side of investing!

Common sense? you say. That's right, **common sense!** I talk to people all the time who tell me, "Jay, I've got $25,000 to invest right now, but I will need to earn a living from my investments just three years from now when I intend to quit my job. *Do you think that's possible?*" Anything is possible, of course, but in my opinion, your earnings three years from now may force you onto a very strict diet. (As in no money for groceries!) This is where the commonsense side of investing comes in.

As I sit here writing today, *bank certificates* will earn you less than 5 percent annually on your $25,000 in savings. I already know you won't like the results, so let me increase the rate by three times to 15 percent and then calculate your earnings for the next three years. At 15 percent your annual earnings will be $3,750, or *$312 per month.* Can you see what I mean by strict diet? Monthly earnings of $312 is not much money for groceries! By leaving your money untouched for three years and allowing it to earn compound interest, you can do slightly better. At the end of three years, you will have earned $13,020, or *$362 per month.* Either way, I doubt if you'll be asking me if I think you're rich yet. I'm sure we can both agree, there must be a better solution.

Leverage Can Turn a Small Investor into Superman

Earning money in real estate is a whole lot different from earning money with bank certificates. For one thing, there's no fixed interest rate on your earnings. Perhaps the biggest difference with real estate investing is that it allows investors to use leverage. Most folks sort of understand how leverage works. You can lift a heavy object with much less effort by using a mechanical device called a *lever.* The Greek mathematician Archimedes is reported to have said, "I could lift the entire world all by myself if I had a lever long enough—and a solid place where I could stand."

Leverage will do about the same thing for real estate investors. With just a very small down payment, you can acquire large expensive properties that you would never dream of saving up enough money to purchase. This is the principle of leveraging: **a big result for a small effort.** In real estate investing, you can accomplish this task by using *other people's money*, or more often, convincing sellers to extend you credit. With just a small dab of your own money and a truckload of someone else's, you can leap tall buildings in a single bound—something like Superman! Obviously, this is much more exciting than bank certificates, but, like anything else that's a bit out of the ordinary, you must learn how to do this the right way. Speaking of the right way, you won't get much help from the infomercials. Besides, staying up late at night is bad for your health.

Using leverage not only speeds your success but it also allows you to brag a lot. In my early years of investing, I was always highly leveraged. This happens when you pay only 10 percent down or less to acquire a whole bunch of properties. I still remember my first several years and how I bragged about the number of properties I owned—telling folks about the values (my own inflated opinion of course). New investors are a proud bunch, and spouting off big dollar numbers never failed to impress my listeners. As I look back today, it's obvious I was living on cash flow fumes!

When you begin to learn more about leverage, you'll discover, as I did, that it can be your best friend or your worst enemy. It's how you use it that makes the difference. That's the folly of most infomercials I see: they seem to imply that no money down is the ultimate goal. Quite often, achieving this goal ends up in a financial disaster. This is where *common sense* and a bit of knowledge about mathematics is desperately needed.

When you pay little or no money down for properties, it means you still owe someone the full price. Everything looks rosey until the mortgage payment book arrives. It's at this point that many naive investors begin to realize that *they've been had*! Mortgage payments and expenses are often twice as much as the income. In this situation, the maximum leverage has been achieved, but bankruptcy is the direction you're headed!

Negative Income Can't Be Cured with Volume

In my town right now, single-family house buyers (mostly out-of-town speculators) feel like they've robbed our local bank when they can purchase a property for $200,000. To my way of thinking, their only possible motive is future appreciation. Naturally, I like appreciation just as much as the next investor, but I'm totally unwilling to bet the whole ranch on just a single benefit. Especially the kind I have absolutely no control over! Assuming I would pay $20,000 (10 percent down) to acquire a $200,000 house, I'd still owe $180,000 to the bank. Strictly from a leverage standpoint, I'm at the top of my game, but there's much more to consider.

The best possible financing for a non-owner-occupied house in my town is between 6.5 and 7.0 percent as we speak. Using the lowest rate of 6.5 percent, a 30-year amortized mortgage for $180,000 will cost $1,137.72 per month. That might sound reasonable enough until I tell you that top rent is $1,050 per month, which includes a free toaster! Operating costs will drain 40 percent of the rental income, which leaves $630 to pay the mortgage debt. At a cost of $6,100 per year for this "bargain delight," I would ask, how many of these can you acquire before you go broke? Even if you just own one, you had better hope your out-of-town manager doesn't rent to Hell's Angels or their kin folk!

This is the same kind of dilemma I faced many years ago as a beginning investor. That same old argument—that prices are so much higher today—is normally the excuse I hear from the masses! They claim that what I've done in the past cannot be repeated in today's market. Friends, this is the kind of advice that will keep you workin' at the sawmill until they start sizing you up for a box. **It's totally false information!** In fact, the kind of investing I do hasn't changed much during my lifetime, and it was probably around long before that.

When folks tell me they've wandered all over the country in search of good deals, I understand and even agree. I've never yet found a good deal searching anywhere myself. **I have to create my good deals!** Before you can ever be awarded your journeyman investor badge, you must fully understand what I just said in that last sentence. Otherwise you'll never be free of "retail thinking."

Seek Opportunities—Not Houses

In both my seminars and books, I teach that big paydays come from *opportunities*, not buildings. Naturally, buildings are the vehicle, but I'd be a lot less interested in them if it weren't for the benefits they provide me. To say this another way: I do not want my name on the deed or the ownership of any property that won't produce the benefits I want. This lesson must be learned by every investor, *and it doesn't just automatically happen*. You must plan it first, then force yourself to do it!

When I can find a rundown ugly property with low rents because of its condition, I immediately see an opportunity to create the benefits I'm looking for. Obviously, I must be able to fix what's wrong, but in exchange, I'll receive **monthly cash flow** and a **rapid increase in equity**. Both are the kind of benefits I'm looking for. Buying properties for benefits rather than the number of bathrooms or the square footage is a foreign concept to many wannabe investors. Benefit shopping also requires more education and homework, which further discourages the get-rich-quick hopefuls. Investing the way I suggest is not dependent on appreciation or easy-to-get mortgages from the bank but rather on identifying opportunity and creating a customized purchase plan that will deliver the benefits I'm looking for.

Look for All the Right Things Wrong

Building **quick equity** and more **net income** is best accomplished with a plan like the one I used at my Oxford apartments. Acquiring four units (a large house and three apartments) on an oversized city lot, known as the "Oxford property," was my *first step*. I purchased the property from an elderly lady who could no longer maintain the rentals or the main house, which she was occupying by herself. The property was at least 60 years old, and it had gradually fallen into disrepair after her husband passed away. A couple of her elderly friends lived in the two-story apartment, and they were paying about half what the market rents should have been. The third apartment had been vacant for over a year, and it would require some fixing and heavy-duty cleanup before it would be rentable.

My $75,000 offer was acceptable, and she agreed to finance $65,000 if I gave her $10,000 cash for moving expenses. She didn't ask (most sellers don't) for any restrictive terms like a "due on sale" clause in her carryback note. My offer of $500 per month for 15 years was completely satisfactory to her. What had drawn me to this property to begin with was its continuing deteriorating condition. I'd been observing it (driving by) for almost a year. Every time I drove by, it looked worse than before! Lawn mowing had stopped altogether, and a broken-down truck had backed into the rail fence, breaking several support posts. No one bothered with repairs. The big house, where the elderly lady lived, was beginning to disappear beneath the overgrown shrubbery surrounding it.

One day while driving by, I spotted a young man in the front yard. Although he appeared to be in his early thirties, his general appearance matched the ugly property perfectly. I didn't know it at the time, but the young grandson and his "hip-hop" girlfriend had lived in the vacant apartment until Grandma could no longer tolerate the "beat" generation. This unexpected meeting was very fortunate for me because junior was quite talkative, and he couldn't wait to introduce me to his grandmother. Obviously, she'd been thinking about selling for a while, so my timing was perfect. Thirty days after our meeting, escrow closed, and I became the proud new owner of Oxford.

An Oddball Property, Yes—But Benefits Galore

The Oxford property was located in the older section of downtown, which was a neighborhood full of ideal rental units for young working folks employed at our local county courthouse and a large Catholic hospital just blocks away. Looking a bit closer at Grandma's big rundown house, I developed *double vision:* Three-bedroom, two-bath houses are fish in the wrong pond in the downtown area. **Grandma's house would soon become a duplex.** All it took was the addition of a double-spaced privacy wall and a new kitchenette. Like magic, I now had five separate income-producing units! My basic improvement plan for Oxford was to clean up, fix up, and upgrade the units with new Formica countertops, attractive new flooring (carpets), paint both inside and out, and last—*and equally important*—restoration of the once lovely yard to its former condition. I did add automatic sprinklers while replacing a section of the main sewer line serving the property. Six months later, with a shiny new paint job and a born-again yard, the Oxford property had become one of the most attractive looking buildings on the block. My scheduled income was now $1,675 per month.

Oxford Street was a *move-up property* for me. My strategy was to hold it long term (over one year), *then sell it for the highest price I could get, offering good terms with seller financing*! I would then trade my new *seller carryback mortgage* for the down payment on my next deal.

The key to *movin' up* was the sale of my Oxford property. Selling for $100,000 more than what I had paid just 15 months earlier set the stage for my *Creekside purchase*.

Quite often when I discuss dollar numbers, interest rates, and values, folks living in locations like mine (California) laugh and joke, saying, C'mon, Jay, the amount of profit you're talkin' about wouldn't even pay for a small patio or an outdoor toilet where I live!" Yes, I would agree today, but we're talking about years ago when you could still buy a hamburger, fries, and a soda pop for 49 cents. To make these numbers more meaningful, simply think in terms of *percentages* rather than dollars, then apply them to current values and today's prices. You'll quickly be able to see the transactions the way I viewed them many years ago. By using percentages, you'll see just how powerful these smaller deals can be for building wealth quickly.

When I sold my Oxford apartments, I offered the buyer very attractive terms. I always design the terms so that my new buyers (*investors like me*) can operate the property and still make a few dollars every month *managing the property and doing the maintenance work themselves*. By doing this, I get a little more assurance that my buyers will do their very best to make the deal work out.

A Small Profit Can Secure the Deal

To begin with, giving good terms tends to discourage new investors from even thinking about giving the property back to me should they experience difficulties—things like high vacancies, more work than expected, or too many hassles in managing the tenants. When new investors can put a few dollars in their pocket at the end of every month, they tend to overlook how hard they must work to earn it.

People often ask me, "Why sell to new investors in the first place? Why not sell to experienced investors?" There are several reasons, but mostly it's because small properties (six or fewer units) tend to attract the *start-out investors*. That's exactly what I was looking for when I first began investing.

As I became more experienced, I wanted more units with each new purchase. That's because *more units per property normally means less cost per unit*. The price per unit becomes very important for **profit mak-ing**. Obviously, paying $35,000 for a unit that rents for $500 per month is far better than paying $50,000 per unit for the same rent! I've found that selling to *experienced investors* takes more time and effort because they tend to argue and negotiate harder and longer about my selling price. With new investors who normally have very limited down pay-ments to begin with, **the selling price is not nearly as important as good terms**. They would much rather have *lower monthly payments* (better terms) so they can operate the property without going in the hole every month and *having negative cash flow*. Think about this for a moment: which one would you prefer?

Wraparound Financing Allows Me to Control the Terms

My strategy for selling Oxford was to sell the property for the highest price I could get by offering the most attractive terms—pure and simple. My sale price was $175,000 with $15,000 cash down. I offered seller *wrap-around financing* for 20 years with payments of $1,000 or more per month. At 7 percent interest, my new buyer would have a small balloon payment due at the end of 20 years. Understand that this is *not* a fully amortized mortgage, *meaning* that it's not completely paid off in 20 years. With a fully amortized mortgage at 7 percent interest, the payments would have to be $1,240.48 per month. Obviously, with an income of $1,675 per month at Oxford, a mortgage payment that required 74 per-cent of the total monthly income would not be a realistic plan.

With wraparound financing, I remain responsible for the existing mortgage debt on Oxford (approximately $63,500), along with the pay-ments of $500 per month, including 7 percent interest (all due in slightly less than 14 years). Here's how a wraparound mortgage works: every month when my new buyer sends me his $1,000 mortgage payment, I must first pay the $500 payment to the lady who sold Oxford to me. The remaining $500 is mine to keep. It represents the amount I'm being paid monthly for my equity. As you'll recall, I paid $75,000 about 15 months ago, so my equity is about $111,500. *I'm only guessing*, but had there been a standard appraisal for the purpose of acquiring a new bank mortgage, it likely would have come in somewhere between $140,000 and $150,000. (As I mentioned earlier, my estimate of value is often a bit more generous when I do the appraising myself.)

Find Mr. Right—The Motivated Seller

With my *new $160,000 wraparound mortgage* in hand, I struck out to find my next rundown fixer property. My goal was to purchase as many fixer-type rental units as I could, using the equity portion ($111,500) of my mortgage for the down payment. In other words, *my plan was to trade my new mortgage at full face value ($111,500) for the down payment on my next property*. Obviously, you can't make this work with most property owners. However, I'm not looking for most owners! I'm only looking for one who is willing to trade his fixer-upper real estate for my $111,500 equity and $500 a month income. To say this another way, the owner I'm looking for must be extremely motivated and willing to trade the property he now owns for something else—*hopefully my mortgage with $500 monthly payments*.

In my experience, I've found it's not enough for an owner to be merely thinking about selling *or hoping he might sell*. Rather, the owner needs to be dead-set on selling to anyone who shows up and appears to be breathing *and makes a reasonable offer, of course!* People sometimes ask me, "Just how scarce are these types of sellers?" Obviously, they're a lot more scarce than the average run-of-the-mill sellers. However, as you develop your Lieutenant Columbo detective skills, you'll find as I have that there's more than enough "don't want 'er" sellers, like the ones I'm talking about, to make you a very wealthy real estate tycoon.

Creekside Estates Gave Ugly a Bad Name

It was a rainy dismal day when I first laid eyes on the Creekside Estates. It's true: a small seasonal creek actually runs right through the middle of the property (eight cottages on one side, seven on the other), but it's also true that a large regional sewer pipe runs 12 feet below the creekbed.

Sometimes people ask me whether my property has water and sewer available. Yes, I tell them, more than enough of both!

Rainy weather always makes ugly properties look even uglier. I counted 14 nonrunning vehicles scattered around the two-acre property, and it was quite obvious to me that maintenance and repairs were not the highest priority on the owner's things-to-do list. Several roofs were covered with rolls of thin plastic sheeting, but the occupants told me they still had many leaks. "Nothing ever gets fixed around here," they said. *"Rent, rent, rent*—that's all the owner talks about!" Oddly enough, that's the same thing the tenants told me when I purchased Oxford.

Sitting in my pickup, soaked to the bone and *shivering*, I managed to sketch out a freehand drawing of the cottages. I always prepare a field drawing of the property, showing each of the houses, *the addresses, and my guesstimate of how much work might be involved and the cost*. I also try to estimate what the market rents should be once the houses are fixed up and the property starts looking presentable. **I highly recommend this technique to all investors.** For just 30 minutes' worth of drawing time, you'll save yourself hours and hours of negotiating and talking on the telephone with sellers. Naturally I prepare these sketches only for those properties of which I feel there's a good chance I'll become the new owner.

The owner of Creekside was an elderly man who had operated low-income rental properties most of his life. And he was a *milker*: when things broke, he didn't consider replacement until he ran out of duct tape! The temporary plastic sheeting nailed on the roofs of five houses was on its third season. When the wind blew the plastic around, he simply added a few more staples to hold it. Several tenants whose rent was subsidized by the U.S. Department of Housing and Urban Development (HUD) and who occupied the houses covered with the plastic sheeting were moved to other houses because HUD would not pay rent subsidies until the roofs were replaced. And the roofs were just too expensive to replace, the owner told me. After our first meeting at the property, it was clear to me that he was tired of the rentals and just wanted out. It was beginning to look like my timing was just about perfect!

Creekside was listed with a real estate agent—an old fishing buddy of the owner. The agent was not a member of the multiple listing service, nor was he very active, so only a few of the owner's close acquaintances even knew the property was for sale. Apparently no one had much interest until I showed up. Most investment property buyers would have been completely turned off by the looks alone. I was told by the agent that one potential buyer was somewhat interested in the land (two acres plus), but as far as the pigsty looking houses were concerned, he wanted no part of them! Naturally, his lowball land offer was rejected. Since the property was free and clear, *without debt*, the owner had no financial motivation to sell. He simply wanted to be out from under the hassles of daily landlording. He wanted to go fishing forever!

Low Rent Strategy Likely to Reduce Property Value

Like most *milkers*, the owner had kept his rents considerably under the prevailing market rates. This strategy is often used by property owners who have owned the rentals for a long time. The idea behind this strategy is to keep the rents below market rates so the owners are not bothered very often by tenants calling them to fix stuff. Tenants who are renting a two-bedroom house for $100 less than the rent should be will seldom call the owner for fear of triggering a rent increase.

From a don't-bother-me landlord's perspective, this strategy works okay. However, in the long run, the results are often disastrous. *First*, with no calls from tenants to repair things, the property rapidly goes downhill, especially older rentals that need extra tender loving care. *Second*, when it comes time to sell or trade, the rental income is artificially low. Since income properties are valued *mostly* on the income they produce, a lower income means the property is worth less to a potential buyer.

Creekside Estates had many of the qualities I was searching for, even though it looked terrible. There were actually 15 separate rental units—*although* the agent's listing papers showed only 13 units. Two cottages were being used as the owner's personal storage sheds. Rents were extremely low, and the property had no mortgage debt. Obviously, with free and clear properties, the odds for structuring good terms and seller financing increase dramatically.

Another important bit of information I became aware of during my research was that the local county housing authority had free grant money available through HUD for landlords willing to upgrade low-income rental units. This, I felt, could help me a great deal in fixing up the property. But by far the most important factor I had going for me was that the seller wanted out. He wanted to retire. The only remaining question I would need an answer to was, would he be willing to take my mortgage ($111,500 equity) for the down payment? The only way I knew how to get a serious response to that question was to sit down and write up an offer—so that's exactly what I did!

The rents at Creekside totaled $2,160 per month, *assuming all of the rents were paid*. But I had some serious doubts about whether all of the rents were actually paid each month. Three apartments had been vacant for a while, and they needed heavy-duty cleaning and fix-up before they were ready to rent. The listing price of $249,000 was definitely a bit high for the condition of the property. I assumed the fishing buddy agent was being overly optimistic when he suggested the selling price. At any rate, I wrestled with the numbers, even adding in the income for the vacant units after a bit of arm twisting by the agent. If all 15 units were rented, *the scheduled income* would be $2,635 per month. Using the fully rented numbers, I agreed to pay six *times the gross rents* if the owner would accept my wraparound mortgage for the down payment. So my written offer for Creekside was $190,000.

I think the owner was savvy enough to sense that I really wanted his property—and most likely that's the reason he countered at $199,000. He would agree to take my mortgage if I would add $17,500 cash to the deal, so he could pay the commission and other selling expenses. He would also finance the balance of $70,000 for 15 years at 8 percent interest, with payments of $669 per month, *amortized over 15 years*. Even with the slight bump in price ($9,000), these were excellent terms!

I immediately ended negotiations and signed the deal. With three vacancies, my actual rental income was $2,160 per month on the day we closed. That means I purchased Creekside for 7.7 times gross rents:

($2,160 per month × 12 months = $25,920 annual income
× 7.68 = $199,000+)

Obviously, this was slightly higher than my original offer of 6 times gross rents, *but in my view,* it was more than justified because the seller accepted my mortgage at full face value. As it turned out, Creekside Estates would become a much bigger profit maker than I ever imagined!

Don't Try This Offer at Home without Tax Advice

Creekside was purchased with what I call a *lemonade down payment*. That means that the smaller part of my down payment was *sugar* the $17,500 cash and *the larger part was lemons* my equity ($111,500) mortgage trade. Lemons can be anything other than cash money. Lemonade offers work exactly like Hamburger Helper, but they stretch your dollars instead of the evening meal!

Most property sellers won't take a big mortgage for the down payment, especially a *green or unseasoned mortgage*—meaning that the mortgage hasn't existed very long. In this case, I had received only 14 payments from the Oxford sale before offering it as my trade. Most investors would prefer to see a longer payment history—say, three or four years' worth of timely payments—so that they feel more confident that payments will continue. Their worst fear is that they will accept a big mortgage in trade but then, for whatever reason, the payments stop coming in. In that event, they would be forced to take over the property secured by the mortgage via foreclosure. Most investors want no part of taking over a property!

When investors do agree to accept a higher-risk (*unseasoned*) mortgage, they will generally insist on *discounting* the mortgage. That means they won't accept the full face value of the mortgage. With Creekside, the full face value accepted was $111,500. The seller could have easily said, "Jay, I will take your mortgage for the down payment, but I'll allow you only $100,000 for it." In that case, my down payment would have been $100,000 instead of $111,500.

You're probably wondering why the Creekside owner accepted my mortgage at full face value. The answer, my friends, **is for one reason only**: he wanted what I had to offer (the mortgage with a monthly payment) more than what he currently had (his rundown rental units).

It's that simple. He was highly motivated to sell out and retire. He would be perfectly content to get mortgage payments of $1,169 per month and be rid of all the tenant problems forever. *Fishing had now become his number 1 priority.*

Back in the days when I traded my Oxford mortgage, income tax treatment was more liberal. Today, when you trade a mortgage, *it's treated the same as if you had received a full payoff on the balance.* Depending on your tax situation, it may work out just fine, but don't make the trade without getting advice from your tax professional before-hand! Often at my seminars, I'll ask, which is better: making $20,000 profit from fixing up the house or earning $20,000 by making the right income tax decision?" Generally, all I get are blank stares. **This is not intended to be a trick question!** Whether you're fixing houses or planning shrewd tax strategies, its still 20,000 Don't give one away for the other. Take my advice and learn about both and take home $40,000. Remember what I told you earlier: this business is all about benefits and opportunities. Take advantage and end up rich!

One strategy I use today when offering seller financing is **to split up my carryback mortgages or notes.** For example, let's say I sell a property for $350,000, with a $50,000 down payment, and I agree to carry back a mortgage of $300,000. Instead of drawing up a single mortgage for $300,000, I might decide on two mortgages of $150,000 each, or perhaps three totaling $150,000, $100,000, and $50,000. This arrangement allows me to have much greater flexibility when it comes to trading or even selling a mortgage for cash. A 20 percent discount from a $300,000 mortgage would cost me $60,000, whereas trading or selling my fractionalized $100,000 mortgage would cost only $20,000 using the same discount. By having my carryback mortgage split up, I have the option of reducing the full taxable event that would occur if I traded my full $300,000 mortgage.

5

People Financing People

Many new investors are completely confused about seller financing. And adding to their confusion are legions of real estate agents who tell them that sellers don't do that anymore! Sellers nowadays supposedly want to be cashed out, so let's get you qualified for a new loan or mortgage right off the bat. We need to know how much money you have to work with.

That's standard jargon right outta the real estate sales agent's playbook. *But take it from me*, it's far from the only way to buy properties, and, in particular, investment income properties like the ones we'll be discussing here.

Seller Financing 101

To begin with, the term *seller carryback loan* (or *seller carryback mortgage*) is a misnomer. There's really no loan involved with seller carryback financing. It's simply an agreement stipulating the terms of the selling contract or extending credit from the seller to the buyer. The seller agrees to take his or her sale price in payments rather than in one big chunk. In the typical house buying scenario, mortgage funds are obtained from a third-party party lender, normally a bank, which are then given to the seller on behalf of the buyer in exchange for the house. Cash money is disbursed by the bank in the form of a cashier's check, deposited with a designated escrow company or closing attorney. If the check is written for $100,000, that's exactly the amount of real cash money missing from the bank vault to cover the check. The key here is that real cash money is being disbursed by somebody.

With seller financing, or a seller carryback mortgage, no money is disbursed by anyone. There's no money missing from any bank vault, and no check shows up at the closing table. Can you see the difference here? There's simply no real cash showing up from anywhere. The seller who agrees to finance his or her property is merely allowing the buyer to pay over a designated period of time, rather than all at once. See how simple it is?

Financial Advice from a Selling Agent

The discussion between the real estate agent and his or her client often goes down like this:

Agent: Mr. Seller, there's no reason you should have to finance your property for Jay. That's what the banks are for!

Naturally, the seller is listening to so-called professional advice. There's no discussion whatsoever about the benefits the seller might enjoy. With retiring sellers, carryback benefits can often be very substantial. A typical situation might play out as follows.

The elderly sellers have managed their five rental cottages most of their married life. They've long since paid them off, and now their thoughts have turned to retirement. The time for smelling the roses has finally arrived! Their real estate agent has been counseling them about selling, especially about making sure their nest egg (the cottages) will provide the financial comfort they've earned from managing five tenants all these years.

The couple has already informed the real estate agent that the money from the cottage sale will be used to supplement their current earnings from Social Security and their small pension check from the sawmill. They tell the agent, *"If we draw out $700 each month to add to our income,* we can travel and do all the things we've planned with our grand-kids." The agent wholeheartedly agrees with their idea and explains that he will arrange for an all-cash sale to make sure they'll have all their money, *less expenses of course,* when it's time to crank up the Winnabago. He further explains that they should end up with approximately $100,000 cash, which they can deposit in a special bank account that allows them to draw out monthly payments and still earn interest on the balance. This sounds exactly like the plan they have in mind, but of course, it's the only plan they've ever heard about!

The basic problem here is that real estate agents are not trained or skilled in discussing retirement planning or how to fund it. It's not their fault! It's simply not their job! In this case, their job is to sell the five cottages and get the money so the elderly couple can get on with their retirement plans. Naturally, real estate agents love "all-cash deals" where the selling commission is pretty much guaranteed. *As a sidebar issue,* they hate no-down deals where commissions are not completely visible to them. That's why new investors that blurt out "no down" in a sales office are about as popular as a "narc" at a free needle clinic! This is never mentioned on TV.

Real Estate Agents: The Eyes and Ears of Business

At least 95 percent of all real estate transactions are done by licensed agents, so don't even think about going around them. You need them if you plan on sailing your ship beyond the bathtub as a real estate investor. However, you must pick and choose when. *Seller financing* is worth millions of dollars to me, but it doesn't mean "diddly-squat" to most agents. You must learn how to accommodate them when they hold a listing on a property you'd like to acquire. Let me give you an example of how I handle this with my agent, Fred.

To begin with, most real estate agents, including Fred, were taught to keep the buyer and seller apart. They believe that principles will just screw up the deal. As a general rule, it's most likely true, but, as investors, we need to move beyond the general rule. Here's how I solve the problem with Fred.

Jay: Fred, I'd like your permission to meet with you and your clients [the sellers] to discuss the possibility of seller financing. I think I can be very helpful answering any questions about myself, my creditworthiness, and, of course, *the financing arrangement itself*. I promise not to say anything about the deal that doesn't pertain to the financing. Once I've made my pitch, I'll excuse myself and butt out. You guys can finish talking about the rest of the deal without me in the room! If we can clear up this seller financing issue today and nail down the terms and get it signed, I think we're all set to close. We can all go home and get paid for our efforts.

For just a moment, picture yourself as agent Fred: Am I being sensitive to your concerns? The answer is yes! I've asked your permission, and I've agreed not to start blabbing about anything other than financing and terms. And I've assured you that closing is just around the corner if we can settle this today. These are all important issues to any real estate agent, and, obviously, *the mention of closing quickly* is like yelling "strike" in a gold mine. Another important issue worth mentioning is that sellers who agree or are thinking about offering carryback financing will most always want to meet personally with the buyer. They want to talk with him or her, look 'em in the eye, and generally make a personal judgment about whether or not the person is of good character and trustworthy. They need to feel good vibes about the person who'll be mailing them payments during their retirement years.

I have found that most sellers will "open up" a bit if they like me. Obviously, that's one reason I like to meet with them in the first place— to present myself. I've found that if the sellers like me and judge me to be an honest person, they will also confide in me. They will most likely tell me their future plans and what they intend to do with the money from the sale. When I purchase properties from older sellers who are retiring,

I can just about guess the answer every time. The money will be part of their retirement income. They will most likely deposit the money in a bank to supplement their monthly retirement income. That's pretty much what we all do when we sell out, I think.

Many of these retirement-minded folks are simply not educated when it comes to money matters. They need a little coaching! This takes patience and understanding because it's difficult to change how people view their money and its use. For example, my mom and dad both thought saving money was how you ended up wealthy. It was their opinion that investing was far too risky. I seriously doubt if they ever changed their views even after they saw my success. Mom thought I was lucky, and Dad never figured out what I was doing!

You Must Thoroughly Explain Financing to the Sellers

As I mentioned earlier, most sellers don't ever hear about any other plan for selling except what their agent tells them, which is "Get all cash, take your money, and run." I've found there's a better way for me, *and, quite often, it's a much better way for the sellers when it's properly explained to them:*

Jay: To begin with, Mr. and Mrs. Seller, we're not talking about a loan here. **I'm asking you to give me terms instead!** I'll pay you the $120,000 price you're asking for your five cottages. However, I'd like to offer you a $20,000 cash down payment now, then ask you to take the balance of your money in payments of $700 or more per month until it's all paid off. I'll pay you 7 percent interest on the unpaid balance.

It's my understanding, Mr. and Mrs. Seller, that you need $700 each month to supplement your retirement income so you can travel and spend time with your grandkids. I'm also aware that your real estate agent has suggested that you sell for all cash and put the money in a bank account where you can draw out payments every month. I'm here to present an **alternative plan** that might work even better for you.

First of all, I'm willing to pay your *full asking price!* Most often, cash buyers will be asking for a sizable discount when they offer all cash. Next, I don't know if your agent has explained how bank checking and drawing accounts work *or how long the money ($100,000) will last you.* It's true that drawing accounts pay interest, but it's a whimpy amount—something like 1.5 or 2 percent annually, based on the year-end balance. Frankly, that interest rate sucks! Also, I don't know if you have any idea how long your money will last. In other words, how many $700 monthly payments will you receive before your account finally runs dry? The answer, Mr. and Mrs. Seller, is approximately 13 years and maybe a few months! That's how long it takes to use up your $100,000 deposit, plus whatever piddly interest the bank pays you. *In just a smigin over 13 years*, your $700 payments will come to a halt.

On the other hand, if you'll allow me to pay you $20,000 cash down now *and then make payments* of $706.78 per month at 7 percent interest, *amortized*—Can you guess how long your retirement payments will keep coming in? The answer, Mr. and Mrs. Seller, is 25 years! Now let me ask you, **which do you, like better?**

The obvious question is, why the big difference in the number of years? Well, for one thing, you'll be receiving $112,000 interest earnings from me, in addition to your original $100,000 carryback amount. The 7 percent interest I pay you is calculated in your favor while the bank's piddly interest is based on year-ending balances, which is not in your favor. In fact, you'll be earning approximately $100,000 more from me, and of course, your retirement checks will keep showing up in your mailbox for almost twice as long.

For Retiring Sellers, Safety Is Paramount

The number 1 reason that sellers object to *carryback financing* is safety—their safety. When banks finance their deals, they get the money as soon as escrow closes—*it's done.* When they carry back financing for the buyer, *it's not done.* They may have to wait 15 or 20 years before it's done. This is where the sellers' safety comes in. Their main concern is, **will they get their money as promised?** That's the big question you'll need to answer to their satisfaction if you intend to do much seller financing business. Simply telling the sellers that you're an honest, upstanding person won't likely cut the mustard.

I'm always willing to give potential carryback sellers my personal financial information: a *profit and loss statement* plus my current *financial statement*, as well as my *property addresses* (locations), and a *list of mortgage holders, including names and telephone numbers*. This information gives sellers an excellent picture of my current financial status and, of course, the opportunity for them to check me out with other folks I send monthly payments to. I don't give this information out until we have a signed deal in escrow. This is one of the provisions in my offer to purchase:

> Buyer will provide financial records for seller's review and approval within 5 days after escrow is opened at **ABC Title Co.** Seller will approve buyer's credit within 5 days after receipt of documents.

Some sellers will want a bit more assurance that they'll get their money as promised. One of my favorite techniques is to offer what I call **double protection** in the form of additional collateral. *In addition* to the security of the property I'm buying, I'll pledge equity in another property I own. In other words, I explain to the sellers that if I should default on the *carryback financing* with them, they'll be in a position to not only take back the property they're selling me, but also they'll be able to take the *additional property* I'm pledging as well! That gives them *extra protection* to ensure that I will keep my promise to pay them. This **additional collateral** method works very well with even the toughest sellers; plus, *it saves me down payment money*, and doesn't cost me an extra dime. Here's how it typically works.

Let's say I own a beautiful fixed-up property on Sweet Dreams Drive worth $300,000, with a $150,000 first mortgage on it. *In my transaction for the five cottages*, the sellers like my $100,000 carryback proposal, but since they will be traveling the countryside, they know it would be a tremendous hardship on them if I failed to perform as I've said I would. Their only recourse would be to take their property back via foreclosure.

Talking with them, I can sense that they are very nervous about this. It's obvious to me that I need to shore this deal up a bit!

Jay: Mr. and Mrs. Seller, suppose I offer you **double protection** so that if something unforeseen happened and you were forced to take back your property, you would not just be taking back the property you sold me but also my Sweet Dreams property as well! **I call this my 2-fer plan.** I'm buying just one property from you, but if something goes haywire, you'll be taking back **two properties** from me! I'll pay you $20,000 cash down, plus I'll give you another $20,000 deed on my Sweet Dreams property.

This is called **additional collateral.** I won't be paying any extra payments on the $20,000 deed, but it does add an additional $20,000 worth of security, *plus another deed* securing our five-cottage promissory note. I will normally ask my sellers for presigned escrow instructions to automatically remove the extra deed after I've fully performed my obligations for *60 consecutive months.* After five years, most sellers will agree that's enough time to determine if I'm a person who keeps his word *and proves it by making timely mortgage payments.*

Although I haven't discussed taxes, *as in the personal 1040 kind,* installment selling is much easier on retiring sellers because it spreads the tax pain over many years. Obviously, the sellers in this case have owned their five cottages for many years. There's no question that *it's a low-basis property*—that is, it has been depreciated down to land value. Their tax hit, or *liability,* will be a big one! Paying it all up front in the year of sale can be very ugly indeed. The name of the game for paying taxes is **deferral**— keep pushing them out! Remember, if you drop dead, your ghost gets a stepped-up basis—as in starting over! Ain't life grand or what!

Seller financing offers many advantages over conventional bank mortgages because there's no end to the ways you can design them. The bank might have six or more various programs, while I can offer unlimited financing options. Some I haven't even come up with yet, but I can if I'm pressed! To repeat myself, seller financing is **terms**—not borrowing! This is where you'll prove to yourself that successful real estate investing has a lot more to do with people than it does with boards and bricks. If you can figure out how to satisfy the folks you deal with, you'll get all the buildings you want, believe me!

Whether you're a buyer or seller, it will pay you to give considerable thought to what I just told you. **Think people first and real estate second.** By keeping this order, you can avoid wasting a lot of time chasing your tail, looking at properties that have no chance of becoming good investments. By the way, when I first started investing, I had no idea that people (sellers) would play such a major role in financing their properties for me. I'm sure it will take you several deals of your own to prove it to yourself. Meanwhile, you'll have to take my word for it. Don't forget what I've told you many times already: **Good deals are not found; you'll need to create them yourself!**

Mortgage Rates Are Different from How They Might Appear

Interest rates often create stumbling blocks for both buyers and sellers alike. Quite often real estate agents are to blame because they don't fully understand the advice they're giving to their clients. Often the story will go something like this:

Sellers: Mr. Agent, we're seriously considering Jay's suggestion to carry the financing on our property sale. We've already done a credit check, plus Jay is offering us additional collateral for the first five years. It sounds like a winning proposition to us! The only question we have is how much interest should we charge Jay on our note?

Agent: Sounds good, Mr. and Mrs. Seller, but I certainly wouldn't charge less than 7 percent. That's about what most banks are getting nowadays.

The problem with this free advice is that it's worth about what it costs! What the banks are *getting* is not the same thing as what **they're earning!** They've got a whole bathtub full of expenses the sellers don't have.

Just take a peek over yonder at that giant marble-faced building! I'll tell ya one thing for sure, this ain't the low-rent district! And when you step inside, the first thing you'll notice is all the overstuffed furniture and double-thick carpets. We're lookin' at expensive stuff here, and that's not counting all the wages and utility bills! By the time we pay the president and all her helpers, we're talkin' about some big bucks here!

I realize the bank is charging customers 7 percent interest on its mortgages all right, but you've got to consider all the bank's expenses too! The real issue here is, how much does the bank keep for itself? *What it keeps is really not the same as what it earns,* and it's nowhere near 7 percent interest. Typically, the bank's operating expenses will consume 3.5 to 4 percent! That means when the bank charges a customer 7 percent for a mortgage, the bank's actual earnings will be about half that amount.

Creative financing is an overworked term, yet it's still the best description of tailor-made real estate transactions designed to fit the real needs of real people. Once again, being creative takes you beyond Financing 101, and it generally leaves most real estate agents in a state of confusion. *It's simply not the norm,* nor is it the way agents conduct business in the typical home-selling situation.

Serious investors must develop these creative financing skills by themselves in order to construct deals that will provide cash flow. It should come as no big surprise or shock when I tell you that **financing and terms** are the single most important part of any noncash real estate acquisition. *In most situations, the only way you'll ever get even a smell of cash flow is to design the transaction so that you'll have the cash flow built in at the close.* Many newbie investors become quite disturbed (sometimes suicidal) when they fork over 20 percent or more cash for a down payment, then immediately discover they're still light years away from having even a marginal cash flow. This, however, is almost the norm for start-out investors before they learn to use creative financing techniques.

Terms of Sale: An Extension of Credit

When income property owners allow you to purchase their property today and then pay for it some time in the future, they are, in effect, offering you credit just like MasterCard does. The future terms can be whatever both parties say they are or agree to! When sellers are struggling to market their junky looking property, they are forced into being a whole lot more generous with their terms than, say, owners who are peddling their *Sunset* magazine model! This is why I lust and crave for ugly properties filled with foul-smelling bikers. If you can learn to smell more creatively, you'll start smelling seller *desperation* and not the bikers! Desperation creates motivation at its highest level, which in turn makes it much easier for buyers to control the terms. Once again, let me say this loud and clear! **Terms should always be your first priority, and the buildings second!** Use your yellow highlighter on that sentence and never forget it!

I would much rather overpay for a property in order to get the terms I need. I don't mind waiting for profits on my equity, but I cannot survive or pay my monthly bills waiting for cash flow to happen! **I must have cash flow now!** You'll find it's nearly impossible to pay market interest rates for financing income properties and still have any cash flow left over—unless, of course, you pay a huge down payment to start with. Obviously, a huge down payment was out of the question for me when I started, as I'm sure it is for most of my readers as well!

There is no law that says you must pay a particular amount of interest on the unpaid debt you owe. **The amount of interest can be decided between you and the people you owe it to.** Every now and again, someone raises her hand and blurts out, "What about imputed interest? Is that a legal requirement?" The answer, my friend, is yes, but that would apply to the sellers and only if someone can figure out the deal or makes a fuss. Things like imputed interest, spittin' on the sidewalk, and due on sale clauses raise about the same level of concern in my investment business. In the unlikely event of a tax audit, a *no-interest transaction* could be reconstructed to include the current applicable federal rate (AFR) for the sellers. In this example, of course, I'm the buyer!

Lowering the Cost of Debt Is Worth Big Bucks

The interest cost of regular financing can be a real deal killer! Interest rates may be somewhat lower today than they were in previous times, but they can still add up to a ton of money. Looking back over my long investment career, I've always been tickled pink when I could find commercial loans (mortgages) for under 9 percent interest. Naturally, the kind of property I buy, older and ugly, sometimes smelly, is considered higher risk to commercial lenders.

At an earlier time I had 11 Beneficial Finance loans, ranging between 17 and 21 percent interest, amortized over 15 years. They weren't huge loans, but I will tell you, even a $40,000 loan at 21 percent will require a sizable payment of $732 per month at Beneficial. If you can somehow learn to negotiate less interest or no interest at all, you will be surprised how easy it is to own properties that produce cash flow. The interest on mortgage debt is the number 1 reason you don't have cash flow, *and, of course*, that is why dealing with ordinary people rather than stringent banks is so important. People can be flexible; banks can't!

Paying the Full Price and Even More

If you didn't have to pay interest on the mortgage debt, could a property be a lot more valuable to you? Let's examine a typical investor mortgage and see. With a standard bank mortgage of $150,000 at 9 percent interest, amortized over 30 years, the cost is $417 each month to pay the principal back. When you add in the interest, the total amount you'll be paying over 30 years comes to $434,500. The monthly payment, including *interest and principal*, is $1,207. That means that the interest payment alone will cost you almost $800 per month.

If you could somehow convince the sellers to take $100,000 more for their property, *increasing the mortgage to $250,000 but skipping the interest*, you could pay off the additional debt in the same amount of time for just $694 per month. If the sellers took the deal but insisted on the $1,207 monthly payments, *same as the $150,000 amortized mortgage*, your debt repayment time would be cut almost in half *(17 years instead of 30)*.

Creative financing comes in all shapes and sizes. It's whatever you, as the buyer, and the sellers say it is. I will personally pay a lot extra to buy the terms I need. In the example above, I could actually pay $100,000 more to have over $500 per month more cash flow if the sellers accepted. If cash flow were not my goal, the same deal would allow me to pay off the property in just 17 years. Since each payment would increase my ownership at full strength, I would have enough equity build-up to borrow in the shortest period of time should the need arise.

From the sellers' viewpoint, there can be benefits also. For example, interest income can be converted to the much less expensive, long-term capital gain pot. In the example above, the $100,000 higher sales price in the capital gain column might prove to be a nice advantage to a high bracket taxpayer. Also, from a tax standpoint, setting up the books—that is, establishing the basis of an income property for depreciation—is based on the purchase price. A higher price means a bigger tax write-off for the buyer! In order to determine what works out best for both sides, it's necessary to sit down together and discuss these options.

Rich Folks Make Things Happen; the Poor Wonder What Happened

Some may scoff and ask, "What kind of a fool would sell for no interest?" The answer, my friends, is, **"Lots of sellers if you'll ask!"** Naturally, it's not likely to be the normal house owners without any problems. But take a rental house full of bikers, now we're talkin'. Many new investors will read about these different techniques and immediately race out to test them on the very next property they see for sale. They remember the technique all right, but they forget that it's the sellers who make these transactions work. The property's not the key here, folks, **it's the owners of the property.**

The most productive part of any real estate transaction is learning about the sellers *and what they want.* This takes a little time, and you won't likely get the right answers on your very first date. I've read real estate books that suggest I whip out my 20 questions, then ask the sellers for answers to each of them so I know where we stand. As a rule, you won't get truthful answers initially. It takes several conversations and some tactful probing before the truth finally shakes out.

Out where I live, we have snow-covered mountains, giant redwood trees, and hundreds of miles of beautiful Pacific beaches. These amenities cost big bucks when it comes to real estate ownership—even ugly biker properties are priced as if there's oil underneath. Unfortunately, the only oil I've found is dripping from a Harley on the dining room carpet.

Troubled properties are easier to acquire, of course, **but it's troubled owners who must consent to good terms.** Some of my best deals come from owners who have never learned how to manage, much less how to select, decent tenants. Still, even with big problems, they never seem to forget that California properties are supposed to command higher prices.

Here's one technique I've used quite successfully—although I end up paying more than I'd like, I can still make the deal! I'll purchase the property at the sellers' final askng price (normally too high), but I'll pay for only part of it now. This technique amounts to shelving part of the sellers' equity to be paid sometime in the future! This method allows me to pay the sellers' asking price but still end up with cash flow for me right from the start. There are many variations of this technique, but let me show you what works pretty well for me.

Shelving Equity

For this example, let's say I agree to pay $300,000 for five rundown cottages. That equals 10 times the gross rents per month (GRM) of $2,500:

$$\$2,500 \times 12 \text{ months} = \$30,000 \text{ per year} \times 10 \text{ GRM} = \$300,000$$

The sellers have agreed to accept 10 percent down, *but my biggest problem* is that I can't pay what the sellers call *reasonable payments* on their remaining $270,000 equity. The sellers asked for 7 percent interest, amortized over 30 years (roughly $1,800 per month). By the way, these terms are very reasonable where I live, but they're still more than the property can support. As far as the price goes, I've already negotiated with the sellers about as much as possible without their tossing me out of their living room. The property has great potential, so I need to make this deal work somehow!

Jay: Mr. and Mrs. Seller, your rents are only $500 per cottage, which means I have $2,500 per month to work with, even adding in the vacancy you have now. As you already know, fixing this place up is going to cost me big bucks after I pay you $30,000 cash down. I certainly can't afford to pay you much more than 50 percent of my gross rents every month or I'll soon be bankrupt! That means I can pay you approximately $1,250 per month for the balance of your equity. That's really about as high as I can go. Obviously, if your price were lower, then your equity would be less. I suppose that $1,250 would then be a reasonable payment!

Most sellers clam up if you make the slightest suggestion about lowering the price. After a minute or so of complete silence *or dead air*, any other suggestion is generally welcomed with open arms.

Jay: Mr. and Mrs. Seller, I'm willing to pay your asking price, plus I'll even toss in an extra bonus! I'll pay you 11 times the gross rents instead of 10 times the gross! That kicks up your selling price to $330,000, but I need a little help with the terms. I'll pay you $30,000 cash down like we agreed, but now, I'll owe you a $300,000 balance. I'm also perfectly willing to pay you 7 percent interest like you've asked, but I can only pay it on $180,000 worth of debt.

I will pay you $1,198 per month at 7 percent interest, amortized for 30 years. This means the remaining balance of the debt ($120,000) will be placed on the shelf, so to speak, to be paid after the property is fixed up and sold. There won't be any interest on this amount because you'll receive your full payoff balance—that is, *a lump-sum payment*—when the property sells. The $180,000 part of our mortgage *with monthly payments of $1,198* will be assumable; however, the $120,000 portion will be due on sale so **you'll get your full payoff balance** when I sell the property. This way, it shouldn't take forever to get you a lot more cash than you would normally receive if the entire balance had monthly payments for 30 years. *Not only that but you're getting the very top price for your property to boot*!

Valuable Benefits for Me

If I can make this work, I've created a deal that fits my game plan. **My first priority is always cash flow.** Any time I can structure mortgage payments around 50 percent or less of the gross income, *I feel I've negotiated a winner*. Operating rundown properties can quickly consume the other 50 percent, but it shouldn't take very long before my fix-up improvements allow for higher rents. My objective, as Fixer Camp students already know, is 50 percent higher rents!

In this example, that means an income increase of $1,250 per month for five rental units. If I can design a breakeven deal going in, I'll certainly be quite happy with another $1,250 in the pot! In case you're wondering when I might sell, it's just occurred to me I didn't write any time limits into the mortgage documents. The sellers were so excited about selling me their rundown cottages and at the bonus price I paid for them that they didn't even bother to ask. Oh well!

6

Creativity Has No Boundaries

My million-dollar story began when I first learned that an old junky, rundown motor lodge (motel) complex in my town was for sale. I was told that the sellers, two investment partners, were highly motivated. On a scale of 1 to 10, I soon discovered these guys were somewhere near 12. What got them there was a series of nightmarish events, not the least of which was the unholy state of their two-man partnership. They despised each other! One had a good job and was a responsible person while the other was a freeloader who was hardly responsible about anything! Worse yet, he was the on-site manager whose job was to collect the rents from tenants who appeared to be much smarter than he was. Obviously, both partners were on a head-on collision course toward self-destruction. Both the property and the partnership situations seemed hopeless on my first visit to the motel.

This transaction is mostly about creativity. It's about using what you have to get what you want, *or designing a creative offer that might work*! Let me explain what I mean. Almost a year before I heard about Hillcrest (the old motor lodge), I acquired an older three-bedroom house on a large city lot on the far side of town. The property had future commercial potential in the city's newest growth area. I paid $80,000 to acquire the property, including a $20,000 cash down payment. If $20,000 cash sounds like a lot of money, don't forget that back then, I had a legitimate job with the telephone company. The sellers carried back a mortgage for the $60,000 balance.

No Money for a Down Payment

When I arrived at Hillcrest, I was "tapped out," as they say. I had no cash left for any more down payments. After haggling a bit over a selling price, we agreed that Hillcrest was worth $234,000. There were three existing mortgages against the property totaling $143,000. All had delinquent payments, plus late penalties accruing. The sellers' equity was $91,000, calculated as follows:

$$\$234,000 \text{ value} - \$143,000 \text{ mortgages} = \$91,000 \text{ equity}$$

The sellers were looking for a reasonable cash down payment so they could bail out their delinquent mortgages (two had already started foreclosure). There were also two mechanics' liens against the property because the partners had "stiffed" the neighborhood hardware store. Since I had no cash to give, I was definitely not the sellers' first choice as a buyer. Fortunately for me, I was their only choice!

The two partners had simply fiddled around too long, and the mortgage holders were closing in quickly. Besides that, the city abatement committee had the property in their sights, and it was dreaming about a demolition party! The buildings were dilapidated and had already been declared a public nuisance. For two years, the partners had totally ignored repeated fix-it letters from the city building officials. Finally, the day of reckoning arrived, and the sellers knew they were almost out of time. Obviously, I could sense it too.

Earn Big Bucks by Helping the Seller

One of the most important ingredients needed for negotiating a bargain purchase is serious motivation on the part of the sellers. At Hillcrest, you could almost feel the motivation in the air. I had the feeling that almost any concession I asked for, *within reason of course*, would be acceptable to the partners. Sensing this urgency, I sorta stumbled around the property with the sellers following behind me, asking every imaginable question I could think of, much the way Lieutenant Columbo does on TV. In fact, watching Columbo is how I developed my negotiating style.

In case you're not familiar with Columbo, he was that "dumb like a fox" detective who wore the wrinkled-up raincoat on the popular TV series a number of years back. Columbo's style is just the opposite of winning through intimidation! In fact, he's able to solve his homicide cases because the bad guys can't imagine how anyone who looks as dumb as Columbo could possibly be a threat. When people don't feel intimidated, they tend to tell you a little more!

Columbo's technique is to ask a lot of questions even when he knows some of the answers. He gives the bad guys all the time they need to explain the details while he continues to probe. Getting folks to open up, which they do because they don't feel the least bit threatened, gives Columbo a powerful advantage when he's probing for information he needs. Naturally, he keeps his personal views to himself until he learns enough to make his case. Columbo understands that people would much rather talk than listen. He gives the impression that he's a *simple, not too smart, police officer*—when in fact, he's a very shrewd detective who listens while the bad guys trap themselves.

Sellers Will Tell You Everything If You Listen

I have found, like Columbo, that most people love the sound of their own voice. Given the opportunity, they will keep talking as long as someone will listen. Most of us, when we feel we have somehow failed, are compelled to explain why even if no one asks. As a buyer, learning as much as possible about the sellers clearly works to your advantage when you're trying to solve the sellers' problems! **Solving problems** is what makes distressed sellers say yes!

By far, the most important element in negotiating is listening closely to the sellers' problems. Forget momentarily what you want and concentrate on how you can provide a solution to the sellers' problems. If you will make the sellers' problems your first priority, you'll have an excellent chance at getting what you want. Acquiring Hillcrest had very little to do with my negotiating skills and almost everything to do with solving the sellers' problems. And as you shall learn, *solving big problems for sellers can create big paydays for buyers.*

The problems at Hillcrest, taken *individually*, were not all that difficult to fix. My biggest concern was that all the problems needed fixing right away.

My List of Things Wrong at Hillcrest

1. Two of the three mortgages were in foreclosure.
2. The partners were unequal owners: one owned 60 percent. And they were fighting.
3. There was a suspicious looking well serving the property (possibly contaminated). City water was available.
4. The tenants were dope users, small-time dope sellers, drunks, and deadbeats.
5. One owner had his papers ready to file a personal bankruptcy.
6. The city had every intention of demolishing the buildings. Resolution was approved for abatement.
7. Rents were not enough to pay the bills. And there was a poor rent collection policy in effect.
8. A contaminated, nonworking swimming pool was on the property. It needed to be filled in.
9. The outdated power service wires were strung building to building. New underground service was required.
10. The general appearance was terrible—only the corncobs and pigs were missing!

You'll notice my list does not include ordinary fix-up stuff like leaky roofs, falling-down fences, potholes in the driveway, dead lawns, deteriorated paint, leaky pipes, and overflowing toilets. These are the normal everyday fix-up items I expected!

As serious as all this sounds, I've always been somewhat amazed how quickly a property can be turned around when you develop a workable plan and begin fixing the problems one at a time until they're all done. Rome wasn't built in a day, and certainly no one could expect Hillcrest to be fixed overnight.

I've found that most building officials who deal with rundown properties like Hillcrest will generally listen to any reasonable fix-up plan. Since Hillcrest was already under the jurisdiction of the city abatement committee, I invited a local attorney to attend the first meeting with me when I presented my fix-up plan to the members. City officials do not like confrontations with attorneys, and I've found that their mere presence at meetings seems to help any reasonable plan slide through much easier. In this case, the abatement committee would have preferred a much faster completion date than I requested; however, as my attorney pointed out, with the amount of work required and all the money we were spending, my schedule seemed quite reasonable. And the committee members all agreed! The meeting was adjourned.

The Offer Must Benefit Everyone

After I had thoroughly stomped over every inch of Hillcrest's three weed-covered acres and asked about every question I could think of, I decided that Hillcrest had great potential for earning a big profit. Obviously, I could see the property needed lots of tender loving care; still, my gut feeling was that if I could acquire the property without any up-front cash, the most I could ever lose would be my personal labor and whatever it would cost for materials. After calculating the risk,—*my personal labor versus the potential profits I envisioned,*—I decided to charge full speed ahead with the deal. This could be an exciting adventure, as well as a very profitable one!

Basically what I told the partners was this: If we can all put our heads together and come up with a plan that will get you guys totally off the hook—*meaning* that we find a way to get all your debts paid off,—**would you then be willing to sell the property to me?** They said, "yes, just show us where to sign!" I reminded them that we didn't quite have all the wrinkles worked out just yet.

Getting these guys off the hook meant catching up the payments on the delinquent mortgages. It also meant paying off their local trade accounts to satisfy several mechanics' liens. *The total cash required to pay these bills added up to almost $15,000.* That was exactly $15,000 more than I had in my bank account right then! No one ever said this job was gonna be easy, but as you shall see, there's a great opportunity here to be creative and figure out a way to make this transaction work. My offer depended on a bit of *voodoo appraising*, so I summoned the partners together to explain.

"Gentlemen," I said, "I am willing to purchase your scumbag motel for $234,000. That's 100 percent of your asking price, based on what you've already told me. I propose to make you a trade, straight across the board, giving you the equity in my lovely three-bedroom house on Hope Avenue. This trade will qualify as a tax-free exchange under the rules of Tax Code 1031. The house is currently being used as a residential rental; however, it's located in a red-hot growth area with potential commercial zoning. Drive by and take a look."

I had already told the partners that my estimated value for my property was $149,000. It had a current mortgage balance of $58,000, which meant that my equity was exactly **$91,000**. "Gentlemen," I said, "if I'm not mistaken, that's a perfect match for your equity at Hillcrest. *What an amazing coincidence!* This means we have a straight across the board, equal trade, so that no cash is needed to balance our equities!"

No Down Doesn't Eliminate the Need for Cash

The partners went along with the hiked-up value I used for my three-bedroom house. They also agreed with the *no-money*, straight across the board trade, but we still had a serious problem to solve. Somehow we would need to find enough cash to enable the partners to pay off their delinquent bills. Naturally they didn't have two dimes to rub together between them. This is where I used a little extra creativity. I had to find some way to generate the cash to clean up the unpaid bills: Beneficial Finance Company would soon come to the rescue!

First, I asked the partners, "Would you guys be agreeable to borrowing $25,000 from me so that you can pay off all your delinquent bills—*mortgages, foreclosure costs, liens, etc.?*" They were totally agreeable. "Okay, fine. Here's the deal," I said. "I will borrow the money and loan it to you so you can pay off all your outstanding bills, including mortgage payments! From what you've already told me, you owe about $15,000. Obviously, whatever's left over will be yours to keep. The loan will be for a five-year term, with annual interest payments of 12 percent, payable to me once a year. At the end of five years, the entire loan amount will be due and payable. I'll secure the loan with a promissory note and deed of trust against the three-bedroom house I'm giving you in trade."

With the deal written up and signed, I boogied on down to see my friends at Beneficial. I explained that once this trade happened, I would have $91,000 equity at Hillcrest. I was there to borrow $50,000 so that I could fix up the property. They did a quickie house appraisal, and they told me, "Yes, we'll do it if you'll give us some additional collateral." I agreed, and I allowed Beneficial to place a deed on a duplex I owned across town.

When people ask me about this transaction, they always say, "Wow, doesn't Beneficial charge outrageous interest rates? How can you afford to pay them back?" The answer is that *you must earn big profits on your fixer projects!* If you plan to pay 18 percent interest for a loan but you've calculated your fix-up earnings to be 40 to 60 percent, you'll have no problems. On the other hand, if you borrow high-cost money for nonfixer properties that lack the **profit potential** that Hillcrest had, then it's likely you'll crash and burn. As a general rule, **the biggest profits are earned on properties where you fix the biggest problems.**

Fix the Right Stuff That's Wrong

Deferred maintenance is a fancy term that means *the owners never fix anything!* They simply milk the property for income. The Hillcrest owners could have written a how-to book on deferred maintenance. They never fixed anything, and they had years of practice at doing it!

Besides the big-ticket items that needed to be done, like installing a new underground electrical system, filling in the swimming pool, and hooking up to the city sewer system, *there were dozens of smaller chores* that needed immediate attention. Almost every water pipe leaked, most everything needed painting, and almost the entire three acres of Hillcrest's once beautiful lawn had died and was full of weeds. These are the kinds of repairs that most anyone can do. You really don't need any special skills. It's mostly labor, with very little money needed for materials.

Deadbeat tenants don't hang around very long when they begin to see fix-up work and improvements being made. For one thing, just being in the vicinity where work is being done makes them jittery and nervous. Loud hammering and the screaming sound of skill saws at 9 a.m. are certain to interrupt their normal sleeping pattern. Deadbeat tenants are a lot like snails when exposed to the sunlight. They become irritated, and they just slowly crawl away. If the screaming power saws don't chase them away, you can be sure the first rent increase will finish the job!

It took nearly two full years of fixing, plus the balance of my $50,000 Beneficial loan, to turn Hillcrest into a handsome looking property. When it was done, I had 21 rehabbed cottages located on what might be best described as a three-acre park, completely surrounded by *my signature white picket fence*. The rents had more than doubled in just 24 months. I was quite proud of my accomplishment, to say the least. But the most exciting part was still to come. That would happen when I sold Hillcrest for a tidy profit!

Selling is not my favorite thing to do. I much prefer keeping my properties! However, this sale was done out of necessity in an effort to achieve my two most important goals: **staying in business and paying my grocery bills.** As you shall see, the Hillcrest sale helped me a great deal with both!

There Comes a Time for Selling

The buyer who purchased Hillcrest was a local doctor who fell in love with the property. He was also typical of many well-healed investors who earn tons of money but are reluctant to part with it for a down payment. For me, this deal was completely acceptable. What I needed most was more monthly income. We basically agreed to a **no-money-down transaction,** *with higher monthly payments*. At the time we made this deal, the doctor was able to save quite a bundle on his personal income taxes. He also insisted that I manage the property, and he agreed to pay me 7.5 percent of the monthly gross rents. The management fee would boost my earnings about $700 every month, which at the time was very helpful to me. As far as the doctor was concerned, he was quite pleased with the arrangement. Who could better manage your property than the person who did the fix-up in the first place!

There are lots of folks who tell me, "You really don't make real profits unless you sell your property for cash!" When you sell on the installment plan, your profits are eroded by inflation—Washed away just like good topsoil, they say. It's the time value of money, versus its present worth, that hurts you, they claim.

I will certainly agree that **a dollar in the hand is worth two in the bush.** But what about three or four in the bush? Interest income spends just like any other income at the supermarket. And there's another important point worth mentioning: when you offer good terms, you seldom get much of an argument over your selling price. As I'm sure you can already guess, mine is always set near the limit.

When I sold Hillcrest, I carried back a promissory note for $594,000, with payments to me of $6,000 or more per month. The deal was basically a no-money-down purchase for the doctor; however, he did agree to give me additional collateral in the form of a second mortgage on his medical building. We also agreed that I would remain responsible for paying the existing mortgages. To accomplish this, we used a wraparound mortgage, secured by an all-inclusive deed of trust. With wraparound financing, I receive a single payment ($6,000) every month from the doctor. Then in turn, I pay the existing or *underlying* mortgage payments. By not allowing the doctor to assume or take over the private mortgages, I remain in position to buy them back at some future date, should the note holders need emergency cash and offer me a respectable discount.

Installment Sale Treatment Okay with Me

From the standpoint of *eroded profits*, I've always been quite pleased with the way my sale turned out. My equity at Hillcrest, on the day I sold the property, was $260,945. That's what I earned for making it look nice. My interest earnings, or the carrying charges for financing the deal, were more than 3½ times that amount. Altogether, my net earnings were $1,200,022 because I agreed to take my payments over 26 years.

7

Benefits Keep the Wolves Away

Taking a quick drive past Creekside Estates, the average property looky-loo might easily conclude that if there is any value here at all, *then it must be in the land!* However, since average property lookers rarely end up wealthy, it's best not to put too much stock in their hasty opinions. When it comes to making big money in real estate, most first impressions by inexperienced investors often overlook a number of profit-making opportunities. Naturally, this is almost always the case when properties are unsightly and rundown. Right now it's time to grab your highlighter pen and get ready to *underline* my next sentence, 'cause it's most important for your financial well-being.

Wealth does not lie with the property but rather, with the investor's knowledge and the skills that he or she possesses. To say this another way, almost every property I've ever acquired was purchased from sellers who had exactly the same money-making opportunity as I had. But more importantly, **the sellers had the opportunity first**, before selling and passing the property along to me! I'm certain that most people in their right mind would not walk away from a gold mine if they had the knowledge and skills to retrieve the precious contents inside. So *it's not the mine that will make you rich*; it's your ability to **uncover and benefit** from the hidden treasure inside.

Line Up Your Ducks and the Benefits Will Follow

When I write or lecture about building wealth, I often use the expression *going with the flow*. To me, this means avoiding confrontations and burdensome restrictions that hamper my ability to reach the goals I've set. Another way to say this is that *going with the flow* means moving forward and making continual progress. For me, the very first ducks that must line up are sellers who are eager and willing to participate in the sale. If this part is missing to begin with, you'll find yourself swimming upstream, which is *exactly the opposite* of my going-with-the-flow strategy.

I'm looking for sellers who can immediately visualize the benefits of dealing with me. *Conversely*, I will cease negotiations when sellers have too many reasons why my offer is not acceptable. Early on in my investment career, I would often try too hard to overcome seller's objections. Almost without fail, I ended up *as the stuckee!* I gave in on the price and paid too much. Sometimes I would allow a due on sale clause in my private contracts, and quite often I agreed to higher monthly mortgage payments than I should have—all because I wasn't firm enough. My basic problem and my weakness was that I wanted the property more than the sellers wanted to sell it.

Seller motivation must always be present; when it's not there, lining up your ducks will be off to a very shaky start. This is especially true when you deal directly one-on-one with sellers, as I did. Nearly 80 percent of all my purchases are financed *all or partly* by the sellers I buy from. I had to learn how to stand my ground and not give in too easily. Seller motivation is extremely important to me. So when I find owners who are still quite proud of their property, I've learned to thank them for sharing their time with me, *then I walk away*. If you can visualize motivation on a scale of 1 to 10, I won't spend much time with any sellers whom I judge to be less than a 7. I've found there's more than enough sellers in the

7 to 10 range to find all the properties I need. With Creekside Estates, I felt very fortunate indeed that *I had found myself a perfect 10.*

Trading Depreciating Paper for Real Estate

When the Creekside seller accepted my Oxford carryback mortgage in trade for the down payment *and agreed* to finance the balance of the purchase price himself ($70,000 for 15 years), his total income from both mortgages would be $1,169 per month. Obviously it was work-free income, which allowed him to go fishing—*and that's exactly what he wanted.* From my standpoint, I now owned a property with scheduled rental income of $2,635 per month on the day I closed the deal. *Granted*, three cottages were vacant for a short period, but once they were cleaned up and rented, my total income was still substantially below current market rents because of the property's rundown condition.

Looking back at the deal once all the dust had settled, I had given up $500 income when I traded my Oxford mortgage for the down payment, *in addition* to $17,500 cash. I also agreed to pay the seller $669 per month on his $70,000 carryback mortgage. The mortgage cost to me was $1,169 per month. Subtracting $1,169 per month from my rental income of $2,635 left me $1,461. I don't know how you might view this transaction, but from where I stand, *it was the kind of transaction I lust and crave for*! Trading a depreciating mortgage (Oxford) for an appreciating asset (Creekside Estates) is an *award-winning play* straight out of the Millionaire Maker's handbook.

My going-with-the-flow strategy enjoys its finest hour when I'm fixing up pigsty looking properties like Creekside. House fixers can make dramatic changes *and improvements* with almost no outside interference whatsoever, as long as the overall look of the property begins showing improvement. I had no idea just how *bold and aggressive* I could be until I began fixing up *ugly houses* in the nicer neighborhoods.

Some years ago, I became involved in fixing up a small junky duplex surrounded by well-kept custom homes in a very attractive neighborhood. One foggy morning I set fire to a huge pile of old wooden *tarpapered* chicken coops in the backyard, sending huge billowing clouds of smelly black smoke skyward. Instead of neighborhood panic, as in picking up the phone and *ratting me out* for being an unscrupulous air pollutor, the neighbors brought me lemonade and cookies. They even wished me well and prayed for my health! Don't try this in your neighborhood working on *regular nonfixer* houses. You might very well end up reading my next book in the cross-bar motel!

Going with the flow means doing things that everyone around you would like to see done. I have found that when you provide the initiative, they'll bring you the lemonade and cookies! Years ago, I discovered that most people will simply stand back if you act as if you know what you're doing and where you're going. When you clean up an ugly pigsty property or rehabilitate a local crash pad that attracts only *transients and druggies*, most folks will appreciate your efforts. Seldom will anyone even think about reporting your fix-up activities *for fear you might stop*. Never has a building department official ever stopped me to ask me about my *overlooked building permit* when I'm ridding the community of an ugly property or public nusiance.

Uncle Sam Helps Owners Preserve Housing

No sooner had I become the new owner of Creekside then I received an official looking letter from the county housing authority. The first paragraph said that if my buildings had at least $1,000 worth of "qualified fix-up," I could apply for a free grant for rehabilitation. I met the qualifications quite easily. In fact, looking at most of my houses, one might question whether there was $1,000 worth of stuff that didn't need fixing! Like most highly leveraged property owners, the very fact that I'd received a letter promising **free money** was cause for celebration!

Housing rehabilitation programs differ from state to state and county to county, and they differed even between my town (city) and the rural area outside the city limits. Each jurisdiction has its own set of rules for administering federal grants and fix-up loans with the ultimate goal of providing affordable rental housing. But unlike my city HUD program, the rural program would allow me and my *fix-it crew* to do the rehab work ourselves. In the nearby city program, only licensed contractors would be permitted to do HUD rehab work.

At Creekside Estates, I qualified for just slightly under $4,000 per house, based on the unit size, number of bedrooms, and the amount of qualified fix-up work. To gain approval, I was required to prepare hand-drawn sketches and submit my cost estimate for fixing each house. The county reviewed my plans; the officials made only a few simple changes, and within three weeks they approved my plan. The one condition the officials insisted on: *no tenants would be required to move from their apartment.* It would be my job to coordinate the work around them.

Grant payments would automatically come to me as I completed the qualified rehabilitation work and submitted material invoices to the county housing authority. Building permits (when required) were my responsibility; however, most of the work was fix-up and repairs. As it turned out, the only permits I needed were for new gas heating systems and several electrical meter box replacements.

As a general rule, the replacement of a complete system such as a heating and cooling system, an entire roof, or an electrical meter panel will require building permits. Do you recall those roofs with the plastic sheeting stapled to them? Since leaks can damage the interiors of buildings, I elevated their status to *emergency repairs.* We simply didn't have time to wait for permits so we fixed them during the weekend *with all new shingles.* Repairs and maintenance work can often slide through without permits if there's an emergency. *But don't forget,* everything must be done according to building codes!

Grants Are Far Superior to Loans

Back in the days when I fixed up Creekside, $57,000 was a truck full of money, *but most importantly,* it didn't require any payback! *It was gift money* as long as I kept my promise to HUD. The promise was that I must keep the property available to low-income tenants for 15 years. If I sold the property, the new owner would also have to follow through with my promise. If I violated the promise, I would be required to pay back the otherwise free grant money or at least some portion of it. In my opinion, this was a very lucrative program. These types of HUD grants, *and sometimes loans*, are known as forgiveness grants (or forgiveness loans). As a landlord, I've always enjoyed this type of forgiveness!

Quite often folks will ask me about various Section 8 programs and rehabilitation grants. Are they a good deal. What's the scoop? Fix-up investors who intend to provide affordable housing for renters should pay a visit to their local HUD offices. In my town, the HUD office is located in the city hall, next to our building department. But remember, Section 8 housing is not administered by the building department, even though they sometimes work together for common objectives. Housing money for Section 8 rental assistance, as well as housing fix-up grants, are federal monies allocated to each qualified community in the form of **rehabilitation block grants**. The funds are administered by local cities, counties, and/or states.

As a rental property owner, you'll be welcomed with open arms. If you're a real estate agent searching for information about HUD monies available *to* assist with property sales, you may encounter a cold shoulder. HUD folks are more than happy to explain their various programs to landlords and property owners, *but not to sales agents*. If you happen to be a real estate agent trolling for money, you best wear a wig and talk like an owner. Obviously, don't wear your gold C-21 jacket on your visit.

A Higher Rent-to-Value Ratio Improves Cash Flow

Impossible, many say! You can't possibly find houses that rent for 1 percent of their value *per month*. To which I reply, yes you can. Examples would be a $100,000 house that rents for $1,000 per month and a $50,000 apartment that rents for $500. In those cases, the *rent-to-value ratios* would equal 1.00, using my definition. I agree that houses in this category are not hanging on trees like overripe plums waiting to be plucked. You must search diligently to find them, and of course, you must negotiate well when you do. Also, these numbers won't likely work with single-family houses. It takes more units to drive the rent ratio down. For example, in my town, at this moment, a $200,000 house rents for $900, which equals a 0.45 rent-to-value ratio—*that's not even close!*

My actual **rent-to-value ratio** at Creekside was a shade over 1.00 on the day I closed escrow—and that's not counting the three vacant cottages being used to store the seller's junk. Once the vacant units were fixed up and rented, my total income was $2,635 per month, raising my *rent-to-value ratio* to little over 1.30. I have written a great deal in my books about the kind of properties that generate cash flow for their owners. As you can plainly see, cash flow has little to do with the looks, foundations, future potential, availability of bank financing, school districts, and whether or not you think the property will appreciate. When I evaluate each one of those categories or **rank their importance**, there's not a single one with more value to me than cash flow. *Having spending money at the end of the month is my top priority.*

With my HUD rehab work completed, Creekside Estates became a magnet for subsidized tenants with Section 8 certificates and vouchers (only the voucher program exists today). My *rent-to-value ratio* would soon shoot up past 2.00. Even a blind landlord smokin' dubbies can make a profit when you achieve this level of return. What this means is that *each unit or cottage* is earning about 25 percent of its original purchase value **annually**. In other words, it's like receiving rents of $25,000 each year on a house that cost $100,000! At my seminars, someone never fails to ask me about *repairs*. Don't older houses require more repairs than newer ones? Of course they do, but as you've probably guessed, *I can afford them!*

With a Little Help from My Friends

Besides that warm fuzzy feeling I get once a month when I receive my rent check from the local county HUD office—*guaranteed money rain or shine*—my friends at HUD also help me in a number of other ways. Obviously, preserving affordable rental housing is our common goal. One day, with hardly any notice whatsoever, I learned that my county building department was headed out to Creekside to conduct a sewer leak test.

After learning about the test from my tenant who called in, I quickly drove out to see how things were going. About a mile from the property, I began to see my answer. A dark green spiral of smoke was rising above my houses like a huge atomic cloud! Horrible thoughts began racing through my head. Suddenly I felt sick! But when I arrived, there stood my local county HUD officer who had also been called out. Both he and the county smoke blower had already negotiated a plan. Thankfully, it would not be necessary to disturb any of my tenants. Leaky vent pipes were causing the big problem, and my only requirement was to notify the building department when I finished plugging all the holes.

At my Fixer Camps, I often tell students that properties like Creekside will earn their owners a ton of money over 15 or 20 years of ownership **without a dime's worth of appreciation!** Obviously, *no appreciation* is not likely to happen; still, it's nice to know that you can operate investment real estate without counting on appreciation for profits. After qualifying for free rehabilitation funds at Creekside, my out-of-pocket expenses turned out to be a lot less compared to my normal fix-up jobs.

My cost estimate for doing regular *nonsubsidized* fix-up work averages about 10 percent of the purchase price for *light fix-ups* and roughly 20 percent for what I call *heavy fix-ups*. Creekside ended up costing about 10 percent more than my heavy fix-up jobs, so needless to say, I was indeed very thankful for free grant money from my rich uncle HUD. Looking back now, I can say with reasonable certainty that the free HUD fix-up money saved my overloaded Visa card from a serious plastic meltdown!

Love Will Surely Conquer All

About 6 years shy of my 15-year HUD contract, *a very anxious buyer* showed up on my doorstep asking if Creekside might be for sale. Ben had recently scored a big payday on a land sale, and he was rushing around quickly to trade his windfall profits for residential income units. He had already acquired several local apartments before setting his sights on Creekside. Ben told me right up front that he liked my property very much *and that as long as my price was fair* he would be willing to pay it! As most of my readers know, I'm a long-term, no-sell type of investor. But when I sense that there might be a love affair developing between my property and a potential buyer, I reserve full rights to change my spots! **Paying my price as long as it's fair**—now there's a most intriguing proposition, I thought.

I don't claim to be an authority on what other sellers might think, but when a buyer confesses to me on our very first date *that he's willing to pay a fair price for my property*, I begin thinking of him as part of my inner circle! Almost like a long-lost uncle who suddenly shows up on my doorstep with my name printed on his will! Ben and I definitely became a whole lot closer.

Selling properties like Creekside generally means that I'll be selling to other investors who think the same as I do. They are hoping to pay a small down payment to maximize leverage *and then negotiate terms* that will allow them to operate the property without going in to their pockets every month. Obviously, these are the very same terms I want when I'm the buyer, *so I completely understand both sides of the deal.*

Fair Prices and Terms for the Buyers

Eight times the gross monthly income was about the right price for the times. My rents had more than doubled even though our local economy had turned sluggish, with vacancies running about 20 percent. Even so, I managed to keep the Creekside property rented up. With monthly rents of $4,510, I calculated the value as follows:

$$12 \times \$4,510 = \$54,120 \text{ annually} \times 8 = \$432,960$$

Ben's offer of $350,000 didn't seem quite fair enough, so I *countered* at $395,000. I told him that it was the very best I could do. Without hardly batting an eye, Ben accepted! I was now thoroughly convinced that *Ben had fallen in love with Creekside.*

With a cash down payment of $45,000, I agreed to finance the $350,000 balance using a wraparound mortgage (a trust deed and promissory note in California). Ben signed the HUD agreement, and he officially became responsible for my 15-year contract covering the free rehabilitation grant. Everything seemed just fine with the deal except that I still had concerns about *Ben's management experience.* When you agree to carry back financing for buyers, you should always get their approval to run a credit report on them just as you would for a tenant. However, obtaining a credit report is only the first step. *You must also investigate a bit further to protect yourself!*

I always ask for a **current financial statement** along with a **profit and loss sheet**. These documents can be informal, *prepared by the buyers in longhand,* as long as they provide all the information I need. Most often, the buyers I deal with don't have a full-time accounting service. I'll furnish samples of what I need and even help them get the information together as long as they fully cooperate in the effort.

I also want to know about **other investment properties** the buyers own so that I can determine how leveraged they might be. This information is important to me so that I can determine if the buyers have the **financial capacity** to pay my monthly mortgage payments. Research should begin immediately following your agreement on the price and terms. Any buyer who is asking me to carry the financing, *or essentially be the banker,* should have absolutely no problem whatsoever furnishing this information. If there are any objections, I immediately become highly suspicious, **and so should you!**

Managing the Tenants and Toilets

When I agree to carry the financing, by far the most serious concern I have is, **Can the new buyers manage the property and handle the tenants who live there?** Bad management or the lack of management skills can quickly drive new owners to the bottle! One of my *best-kept secrets* over the years has been my ability to detect woozy buyers who have never learned how to manage tenants. At Creekside, more than half the occupants were subsidized (Section 8) tenants. HUD regulations require annual inspections and prompt responses to all service calls. Failure to comply will put any manager in deep *doo-doo!*

Quite often, new investors will acquire a substantial number of rental units much faster than their management skills develop. When this happens, they often find themselves having serious problems with their tenants. In extreme cases, tenants have been known to withhold rents until these problems get fixed. Situations like these could easily jeopardize my carryback mortgage payments. I call this the *domino effect.* The best way to protect yourself from becoming a domino is to thoroughly check out a **buyer's management experience** *at the same time that you* *check out his or her financial capabilities.* Both are equally important when you agree to accept monthly payments from the buyer.

The successful operation of any income property will depend greatly on the owners' ability to manage the people living there *and collect the rents every month.* Buying, negotiating, and writing up killer deals will all be for naught if you can't manage the tenants. It's for this very reason that the new breed of no-money-down and get-rich-quick seminar gurus usually urge their listeners not to become landlords. Instead, these gurus recommend flipping properties, options, sandwich leasing, and whole-saling—*anything in which tenants are not part of the mix*!

I soon discovered that buyer Ben had rapidly acquired 72 rental units in less than a year's time. And although he had paid cash for two apartment buildings, several other properties were leveraged like Creekside. I must admit, Ben's buying frenzy made me just a bit nervous. I was concerned about his **management experience** for the reasons I've just discussed. Ben's potful of money had come from land sale profits, which meant that he was likely unaccustomed to the joys of managing tenants. The thought of Ben's becoming a landlord with 72 tenants in less than a year *with another 15 in the pipeline* was somewhat disturbing to me. That's a whole bunch of tenants for even the most experienced managers! For this reason, I decided that Ben's small down payment (11 percent) was not quite enough security for me. I would need a little more protection to make this deal work!

As Lieutenant Columbo Says, Just One More Thing

The quickest way I've found to solve any problem is to spit it right out to all the parties involved—*so that's exactly what I did*! I said, "Looky here, Ben, you're a wonderful chap, and you're very smart acquiring good income-producing properties. I understand you plunked down all cash for several properties—but not for Creekside! I'm more than happy to 'carry the financing,' and I'm certainly agreeable to your small down payment of $45,000—*but here's my big problem*: what do you suppose would happen to me if for some reason you had trouble managing my wonderful group of tenants? Let's say, for example, they don't like your management style, or they don't feel loved enough, and suddenly without much warning, they rebel, and they just stop paying rents! *Where would that leave me?* I'm concerned that if your income should suddenly dry up, you might not be able to keep sending me my $2,400 mortgage payments for the next 20 years."

Sometimes new owners discover the hard way that tenants don't always do what they're supposed to! Eventually the pain of managing becomes so unbearable that giving the property back seems like an excellent option. Generally, by the time this happens, the most rebellious tenants have been evicted while others have simply disappeared in the middle of the night taking appliances or whatever else they can pry loose. Needless to say, by the time the mortgage holder (someone like me) gets the property back from foreclosure, it's in shambles, and it requires a total rebuild! Obviously, the property will have been *milked* of all advance rents and security deposits, meaning that the mortgage holder—me—would need to pony up a substantial amount of cash to get the place up and running again. After explaining all this to Ben, I told him, "I'm still completely satisfied with everything else about our deal. This is really my only concern."

Tightening Up: It Won't Cost a Dime Extra

I said, "Ben, here's one way we can solve this problem. You recall that list of properties you gave me showing all the real estate you own? This is where your shrewd investing skills can really help you out! If you will allow me to select one of your mortgaged properties that we can use for **additional collateral**, that should give me all the *added protection* I need. I'm sure you agree that it's far better to use assets you already own, than it is to cough up additional cash for a bigger down payment. This way it won't cost you one extra dime, and of course, your mortgage payments will still be the same amount—*$2,400 a month, just as we agreed!*

"Also, I'm completely satisfied with a mortgaged property for collateral. This way, it doesn't tie you up in case you need to use one of your *nonmortgaged* properties for future borrowing. Also, I'm perfectly willing to make this a *temporary arrangement*. After five years of timely payments, I'll feel secure enough to reconvey (remove) the additional collateral from our Creekside mortgage. We can even make this an **automatic reconveyance** if you wish, by presigning the documents and providing instructions to a local escrow company."

The property I selected from Ben's list consisted of the Harmon Street houses. *Seven rental units* in total, consisting of one large two-bedroom house, several smaller cottages, and a duplex, all situated on a large city lot. At the time, I estimated their value to be $140,000. The mortgage debt was $95,000. It was a private seller carryback mortgage that had originated when Ben had purchased the property about a year earlier. The mortgage payments were $950 per month, and the scheduled monthly income was $1,900. It took a little arm twisting, but Ben finally agreed that the Harmon Street houses would be the **additional collateral** for my Creekside carryback mortgage.

What I now had was two properties (Creekside and Harmon) providing security for my $2,400 monthly mortgage payments. I call this *Jay's 2-fer sale*. I'll sell you one property, but should you renege on your payments, **I'll be taking two properties back**. This technique is an excellent way to acquire real estate with smaller down payments. I have used it many times, quite successfully, buying properties from retiring owners who don't need or want cash from their sale. They are more than happy to receive monthly payments and earn interest income. The catch is that they must feel secure. Providing additional collateral will often do the trick!

When the Creekside escrow closed and the dust finally settled, Ben was the proud owner of 15 more rental units producing $4,510 per month income. I received $45,000 cash less my closing costs and a promissory note in the amount of $350,000—designed to pay me $2,400 every month for 20 years. The security, or collateral, for my promissory note and the payments consisted of both the Creekside Estates and the Harmon Street houses. *Combined*, there were 22 separate rental units with a total income of $6,410 per month. Even though the down payment I accepted from Ben was small, *I felt very secure*.

Are We Millionaires Yet?

When I was a small boy, my mother would often tell me, "If you pay close attention to how you spend your nickels, your dollars will take care of themselves." Tall skyscrapers all begin from a lowly position, mostly hidden in the dirt. Gradually, they begin to rise until one day you can barely see the top. *Investing* in small income-producing properties works about the same way. Buying the right properties, one at a time, making sure to search out the benefits you need, will allow you to grow just like a giant skyscraper! Eventually *one day*, you'll suddenly end up a millionaire real estate tycoon. I have students who have already reached this level, and they can't even spell *millionaire* yet!

The Creekside Estates property was well on the way to producing million-dollar profits. Although I had no plans for selling when it happened, I'm always ready when the **right opportunity** presents itself. Paul Masson winemakers religiously claim in their popular TV commercial, "We'll sell no wine before its time!" But just pop in their winery some day and offer to pay double for a green bottle. You'll get a real quick lesson on the meaning of *selling at the right time*!

Counting Up the Beans

Installment selling (carrying back a mortgage) is a bit more restrictive today because of *depreciation recapture*. At the same time, Section 1031 of the IRS tax rules are much easier to use. Today using *accumulated losses* might very well dictate the best strategy for selling a property like Creekside. Just remember that it's most important to keep current on real estate tax laws yourself. You must never depend on your accountant to make you a millionaire; he's simply not that interested!

Creekside was a property "chucked to the brim" with benefits for me. To begin with, the down payment was my large seller carryback mortgage from my Oxford sale, which I traded at full face value (no discount). The balance of the purchase price ($70,000) was seller financing at 8 percent interest, amortized over 15 years. I had no mortgage restrictions like a *due on sale clause* or *a prepayment penalty* to deal with. I cannot overemphasize the importance of dealing with people rather than banks.

To me, seller financing is one of the highest-priority benefits that I look for when I'm negotiating a purchase.

After selling to Uncle Ben (he's now thought of as a family member), my paydays from Creekside Estates have been simplified to making the short jog down to my mailbox on the fifteenth of each month to pick up my check. *Do I miss collecting rents from the tenants?* I'll save my answer for another time! Meanwhile, I quickly "rat-holed" Ben's $45,000 cash down payment in my rainy day account and moved on to other deals. Waiting for the fifteenth every month is not very hard to get used to! By the time Ben finally pays off the mortgage, I'll have walked to my mailbox 240 times. "Have your trips been worthwhile?" you ask. Perhaps you should judge for yourself: in round numbers, I'll have collected $39,271 in principal payments and $536,729 in interest payments, and of course, I'll collect that one big balloon payment of $310,800 at the end. Remember, I did pay $17,500 in *out-of-pocket cash* when I bought Creekside, but it looks like I've got all that money back with a little extra to boot!

For almost nine years before the sale, I netted an average of $2,100 per month in rents from Creekside ($215,000 total). Uncle HUD most graciously gifted me almost $57,000 for fix-up costs, paying most of my labor and materials. And last but not least, the Creekside books (my accounting records) were set up before the current modified cost recovery system of depreciation (MACRS) was enacted. When the Creekside books were set up, the estimated life of real estate was much shorter than it is today—meaning that larger depreciation expenses for Creekside reduced my taxable income. You can begin to see why I refer to Creekside as "my million-dollar baby!"

8

The Real Estate Ski Bum

Folks who know me are fully aware that I don't ski. In fact, I only enjoy seeing snow when it's on a postcard. When I was not yet out of my teen years, I worked on a pole line construction crew for the local utility company. During the freezing winter months, high-voltage lines crossing the snowy mountain peaks would topple to the ground, and my crew was called out to restore the power. My cold, wet feet and my body's freezing like a human Popsicle have never faded from my memory. Today, I won't even buy snow chains for my car because I never intend to drive near the stuff!

The Image of an Entrepreneur

When I use the term *ski bum*, it sorta conjures up an image of how some folks in my town view my existence today. They never see me on the freeways going to work. In fact, most people who know me only by sight don't figure I even have a real job. Every so often, some brave soul will ask me, "What exactly do you do?" Most 9 to 5 working stiffs are totally baffled when they see a person they recognize who doesn't seem to have any particular purpose or place to be.

Being a real estate entrepreneur is completely different from working at the saw mill. To start with, I'm my own boss. There's no one else to please except me. There is no alarm clock in my life, no freeway commutes, and no specified time for me to take trips because I can juggle my schedule on a daily basis to fit whatever I'm doing. For goodness sakes, don't get the idea that I don't work or that I sleep all day! I work plenty, but I work only at things I choose to do and only *when I want to*. Obviously, you couldn't operate 200 rental units without having responsibilities. However, being responsible doesn't mean I'm doing all the work myself. My biggest responsibility is making sure my "helper-bees" do what they're supposed to be doing *so I can do what I choose*! Can you see that my having total control over all my affairs allows me to enjoy the freedoms most people can only dream about?

Years ago when I had a legitimate 9 to 5 job, my boss controlled my schedule. Like most jobs, mine was totally structured. I had to be there at 8 a.m. every morning, rain or shine, five days every week. I eventually earned five weeks' vacation time, but as a rule, taking it required choosing the date many months in advance. The biggest problem I always had with my five weeks' vacation was that it always lasted too long for the amount of money I had. Looking back, I remember telling my friends, "I've got five weeks' vacation time but only two weeks' worth of money to enjoy it!" This problem is not the least bit uncommon among employees of the big corporations.

Working for myself is a whole lot different from working for the other guys. *For starters*, even though I earn a good deal more money now, I get to keep most of what I make. At my corporate job, I lost almost 40 percent to taxes and a bit more to various charities sponsored by my company. The phone company believed that management employees should donate a portion of their earnings to worthy causes. Naturally, *they* decided what causes were worthy. Also, managers were required to dress the part. White shirts, suits, and ties were the standard dress code. Image is very important to big corporations—still, I don't recall any special clothing allowance to help me promote the company image.

Control Creates Financial Opportunity

To achieve wealth, you must control your time and, of course, the amount of compensation you're willing to accept for your services. Working as a W-2 employee for most corporations, these controls are pretty much in the hands of others. If building personal wealth is your goal, as it was for me, you must take these controls back for yourself. In Chapter 1 of my best selling book *Investing in Fixer-Uppers,* I explain to readers how I was able to earn $300 per hour fixin' up Hillcrest. You simply can't get rich by working more hours on a regular job. The answer lies in earning more money for each hour you work. In practical terms, the best way to accomplish this is **working smarter**—not longer or harder.

Control, by itself, can help you only when you select the right vehicle that can pay you the additional money you seek. For example, when I fix up houses, which adds more value to them, there's actually no limit on how much I can earn. **Earning $300 per hour at Hillcrest is a perfect example.** It would be an absolute impossibility to earn that much money working for the phone company no matter what I did. Even robbing the company pay phones wouldn't pay that well!

My High-Paying Vehicle Is Houses

When you work for the corporation as a W-2 wage earner, you cannot work at building your **personal net worth** the way I'm able to do as a full-time real estate entrepreneur. You simply don't have enough time. Wage earners are not just slaves to their bosses but to the IRS as well. Working full-time for yourself *by building your personal net worth* allows you to escape both masters and chart your own course toward much bigger earnings.

Let me pause here for just a moment to say that you must *gradually* build up your real estate holdings before thinking about becoming a full-time investor. I strongly suggest that you don't walk away from your day job in hopes that real estate investing will set you free and end all your financial worries. Without a well-conceived transition plan, you can easily find yourself on the welfare wagon instead of the financial freedom train.

Entrepreneurs Must Develop Many Skills

I'm a strong believer that every do-it-yourself real estate investor should learn a variety of different ways to earn profits with real estate. I don't believe you can reach your full potential as an entrepreneur until you learn many different **income-producing strategies**. These should include buying single-family houses, foreclosure properties, and rundown apartments; using option techniques and wraparound installment sales; buying discounted mortgages; *and of course, you must learn landlording*. Just in case I missed anything, add it to the list because as time goes by, you'll need all the extra knowledge you can get! This might seem like an impossible task at first glance. However, because these strategies and skills I've mentioned are all closely related, you'll find that learning this stuff is much easier than you might think. *Knowledge is what makes you* a **complete investor** It's also knowledge that keeps you a few steps ahead of your competition!

Before I unintentionally mislead anyone, allow me to say this loud and clear: I feel very strongly that **successful investors must develop their own specialty**. I define *specialty* as a strategy or technique that you can do better than anyone else in your town. It's sorta like your ace-in-the-hole money plan. It's a *special skill* or *technique* that you can always count on to earn money when everything else quits working. For example, I specialize in fixing ugly rundown properties generally occupied by ugly tenants. I've learned how to quickly turn *ugly duckling houses* into handsome swans, and at the same time, I can generally resolve most problems with the tenants who live there. This specialty always works for me. I can almost smell the money on the day I start!

When I first began buying investment properties, there was absolutely no question in my mind about where I might find a few extra dollars to tide me over in case my properties didn't generate enough cash flow. The answer was *nowhere*! Even though I was successful at keeping my cash down payments small, they took all the money I had. I knew very well there was nothing left over in my bank account to make up for any cash flow shortages. The only funds I would have available to pay my mortgages and my operating expenses would be the rents I received from my tenants every month. Buying properties this close to the belt can be both challenging and rewarding at the same time. Obviously, there wasn't much wiggle room in estimating my fix-up costs. I also had to make certain that my mortgage payments did not exceed what I was collecting in rents. When you're investing this tight, you had best make sure your cash flow plan is not a "pie in the sky"! *And do it before you sign the deal!*

Predictable Cash Flow Is Number 1

What I'm strongly suggesting here, especially for new investors itchin' to get their feet wet, is that it's a much smarter strategy and it's a whole lot safer to acquire a property with a somewhat uncertain future *(but with a predictable cash flow)* than to pay top dollar for a property with *more potential* but not enough cash flow to pay the bills. Don't misunderstand what I'm saying here: future potential is great, but the future is still the future! It's still a pie in the sky! In my opinion, the first three reasons for owning income property in the first place are **income, income,** and **income.** All the other reasons must start at number 4!

Acquire the Most Units Your Down Payment Will Buy

Nearly every investor I've met has paid too much money for an income property. It happens more frequently when they first start out. There is almost no defense against paying too much, at least once or twice anyway! I've done it more times than I like to admit. However, in most cases for me, buying the *multiple-unit fix-up properties* has allowed me to **add value and improve the income** much faster than if I had *overpaid* for nonfixer properties.

Fixing up properties and adding value quickly has given me the opportunity to increase rents and recover from paying too much! The best training in the world for speeding your education along is to learn true values and what the real expenses are. You'll learn very quickly once you start buying and operating your own properties. Remember, I'm not recommending single-family houses to start with. My recommendation is to acquire just as many units as your down payments will allow you to purchase.

When I first started buying, I quickly discovered that multiple fixer units can often be bought in bunches for the same down payment it would cost for a nonfixer house. As you might guess, the cash flow potential is many times greater. Also, there's an extra-special bonus involved: many fixer properties can be purchased with seller financing to boot!

Inexpensive Rentals Provide Greater Cash Flow

Althought I have diversified my portfolio over the years, my primary investment property has always been affordable rental units. *I want properties that my customers (tenants) can afford to pay for.* These properties provide me with "eating money," or what most folks call **cash flow.** Affordable rental houses are still my biggest source of income today. Lower-end rental units provide a much higher profit return for investors, but there are some trade-offs for more cash flow up front. My kind of properties don't appreciate quite as fast, nor would there be as many buyers if I decided to sell them. I do not consider these trade-offs to be a disadvantage, however. The reason is that I'm a firm believer in first things first: **to me, that's always been cash flow!**

Let me say this another way: investors like me who start out with hardly any money in their pockets need a crystal-clear vision of who they are (**poor investors**) and what their buying capacity is (**not much**). Once you can focus and clearly visualize where you stand—*a struggling investor trying to acquire real estate with very little money*—it should come as no big surprise that **cash flow must be your number 1 priority** if you intend to be an investor very long.

Much of my own success has come from keeping my investments as simple as possible **and paying particular attention to the basics.** That means that I thoroughly analyze all the expenses (money going out), and

I make certain there's enough money coming in from the rents. You don't need to be a brain surgeon or need to know what the *internal rate of return* (IRR) is on your duplex to make a profit. You're far better off knowing whether both toilets flush or not. *Later on, when the money starts rolling in*, you and your accountant can have a powwow and figure out your IRR. Meantime, you might ask him or her to help out with the plumbing in between fiddling with the books!

Personal Skills Can Produce Fast Equity

The most important reason for buying the ugly rundown houses is that you can quickly add to their value using *sweat equity*. Investing in these kinds of properties means you should buy a lot cheaper and sell for a profit in the shortest possible time. You will also be able to increase the rents and generate a positive monthly income much faster with these types of properties. This is much different from buying *pride of ownership properties* at top market prices where your only chance for profit is appreciation. Often that can be a very long wait! A big difference with fixer-upper properties is that you can immediately start making obvious improvements, *the kind that will force the value up*. By forcing up the value, you won't be stuck waiting for appreciation in order to make your profits. **Controlling profits** is a much more predictable strategy than trying to figure out when prices might go up on their own.

With many fixer-upper properties, it's not the least bit uncommon to do a quickie cleanup and paint job along with bringing in new tenants and increasing rents almost immediately. As you increase the income, you're also making the property more valuable. Several of these deals can pump up your equity quickly and allow you to build wealth much faster than you could otherwise. I call this *fast-track investing*

Most investors will never develop these *quick equity-building skills* because they incorrectly believe they're not handy enough to deal with fixer types of properties. Many new or inexperienced investors are reluctant to tackle jobs they've never tried before. They're afraid they might ruin something they can't fix and make a bad situation worse. For this reason, I strongly encourage do-it-yourself investors to acquire at least one rundown property for their own personal "guinea pig." *With fixer-upper properties,* I've found that most investors are not nearly as afraid to experiment.

I can promise you this much: if you will muster up the courage and at least make the effort, you will learn to do things that you never thought you could do! Even more important, *you will have proven to yourself that you really can do this stuff.* The best way to find out what you are capable of doing is to jump in the water and see how far you can swim!

Finally, there's another extremely valuable benefit you'll get from working on your own property. This one is quite possibly the most important benefit of all. It's called **confidence in yourself.** Once you actually experience additional cash flow, you suddenly step back and realize that you are doing some pretty powerful stuff! *Having confidence in yourself is worth more than money!* Yet, strange as it might seem, money builds confidence faster than anything I know of.

Seek Advice from Skilled Practitioners

In his timeless classic *The Richest Man in Babylon,* author George S. Clason writes, "Gold is reserved for those who know its laws and abide by them." The fourth law of gold states:

> To the man who has gold, yet is not skilled in its handling, many uses for it appear most profitable. Too often these are fraught with danger of loss, and if properly analyzed by wise men, show small possibility of profit. Wise, indeed, is he who investeth his treasures under the advice of men skilled in the ways of gold.

Often when I counsel students, I'll ask them why they have decided to invest in real estate. While they're thinking, I'll ask, "How do you propose to do it? Tell me about your investment **plan or strategy.** *Are you using it already,* and if so, how is it working for you? Is it producing a cash flow yet? Tell me more about it, *and let's take a close look at your numbers!*"

Most people have great difficulty trying to explain their investment strategy to someone else. But if you can't explain what you're doing, you need to hold off until you can. The biggest problem I encounter is impatient investors who don't do nearly enough planning before they close the deal. *That's a big mistake*, which generally accounts for overpaying. As a rule, overpaying means there will be no cash flow. *Even worse*, you can end up having to feed the property from out-of-pocket money every month because it doesn't earn its keep from rental income.

Let me emphasize that investing in real estate *the way I suggest* does not require perfection. There is ample room to make a few mistakes. Most are fairly easy to fix. As time passes, you will become more skilled. What's most important is that you learn from each mistake and *do better on your next transaction*. Mistakes are natural, and they provide some of the most valuable lessons on the road to success. When you read the autobiographies of successful people as I like to do, you'll find very few people who became successful without making their share of mistakes as they honed their skills.

Don't forget what I told you earlier about your wealth-building education. It will pay you big dividends to seek out and learn from successful investors who are already established *and have verifiable track records* doing the same kind of investing you wish to do. Stay away from gurus who talk it *but fail to walk it*. After all, a teacher who doesn't use his or her own advice is not very credible. *Wouldn't you agree?*

Investing Rules Remain Unchanged

Many folks have told me that they can't see much **long-range potential** in the types of properties I've been discussing here. *First, let me say* that there is no need to worry about long-range investing potential unless you first get a handle on your short-term investment needs The most important in my view is **positive monthly income**.

Over the years, I've transitioned from small multiple-unit fixer-upper properties to larger properties with 21 units. I've owned a 100-room hotel with commercial storefronts. I still own many single-family houses and two-family duplexes. I've converted World War II motels to monthly apartments, and along the way, I've made some very profitable sales and carried back the financing using wraparound mortgages. The most important part of my investment strategy has always been that *I buy only those properties that will pay me to own them.*

Bargains Don't Change—Your Knowledge Does

Finding *the right properties* with good potential for profits and cash flow is the first step in developing a successful investment plan. It's also important that you break away from the traditional thinking of the *amateur investment crowd.* Serious money is made by those who study their marketplace and develop the ability to spot bargains that others never see. I don't suggest that you purchase rundown properties below your comfort level, but I can promise you that investors who have the courage to step outside the box and push the limits *generally earn the biggest rewards.*

During many years of investing and working to help others get started, a somewhat interesting fact pops out: it seems that investors who have the least amount of resources to begin with tend to have a lot more success with fix-up properties. *They also end up with cash flow much faster.*

In short, it's the poorest folks who follow instructions well and who tend to reach their investment goals much faster because they have fewer opportunities to stray from the target. Being about half smart, and having a few extra dollars to play with, often gives a new investor a false sense of security—and too much time to think! It also gives the investor time to make up lame excuses for not accomplishing anything. **Action is what it takes to become a millionaire house fixer.**

Switching Jobs Requires Much Discipline

Frequently I'm asked, "How long will it take me to start earning enough money from real estate so that I can quit my regular job?" Unfortunately, there is no single answer. The reason, of course, is that investors are people and people are all different. Most folks are in a big hurry to hit a home run!

The truth is that building real estate wealth must begin with a solid foundation. After that, you can start adding more bricks as you learn more, *at a pace you can handle.* Naturally, the more bricks you can lay, the wealthier you'll become. **You must never forget step 1 of any plan is** to achieve positive cash flow. Getting rich will take care of itself as long as you keep cash flow as your main objective.

In my bestselling how-to book *Start Small, Profit Big in Real Estate* (McGraw-Hill, 2004), Chapters 10 and 11 discuss two properties (good examples) that generate cash flow in the shortest period of time. *Both properties* are the kind I recommend for creating long-term wealth. Both properties provide spendable cash flow, and you can quickly add bricks to increase their values. I suggest you study both of these excellent examples during your own planning and preparation.

Building Personal Net Worth Beats a Regular Job

Folks who attend my seminars and Fixer Camps know how much I emphasize the value of *multiple real estate benefits*. These are the benefits that make real estate investing so rewarding. There are many different ways to extract profits from the kind of properties I acquire. Many of these benefits allow investors to take home big profits without sharing with the IRS. Earning money in a way that allows you to keep 100 percent for yourself is a mighty powerful wealth builder. Uncle Sam does not require you to pay taxes when you spend all your time working on your personal net worth.

For example, let's suppose I use my buying skills to acquire income-producing real estate with an appraised value of $500,000. As you already know, I happen to be an accomplished Lieutenant Columbo–style negotiator, so I'm able to convince the owner to sell me his property for $400,000. "Why in the world would he do something stupid like that?" you ask. Because he was dumb enough to allow his property to become rundown and ugly and now he's having big problems keeping it rented. I've purchased property from sellers who were absolutely frightened to death of their tenants. There's always a reason for selling out cheap, and it's up to you to find it! If you swallow what the sellers tell you, then you need to practice your interrogation techniques in front of a mirror before you try it on the sellers. Otherwise, you'll own the famous Brooklyn Bridge!

Obviously, this purchase has made me $100,000 richer, because I have the knowledge to fix the sellers' problems. **Who pays the taxes on my $100,000 profit?** The answer, my friend, is nobody! *I'm building my personal net worth, and it's not a taxable event, even though I'm now $100,000 richer!* Knowing how to build personal equity while steering clear of the IRS is one of the best kept secrets to why the rich get richer! I call it *working smarter!*

On the other hand, let's suppose you happen to be a real estate agent working for commissions or a 9 to 5 wage slave earning the same amount. I can guarantee that you'll pay Uncle Sam taxes on your $100,000.

Using this powerful technique is merely one of the many wealth-building benefits available to *real estate ski bums* like me, who have discovered gold in the houses: *the way you earn money is just as important as earning it!*

Working the Beneficiaries

One of the most rewarding of all my **profit-making techniques** is buying back my own mortgage debt for big discounts. For over a year, I didn't buy or sell one single property. To the folks around me, it might have appeared that I was slowly going broke. The truth was that I was busy as ever negotiating another kind of benefit. Like most landlords, I have monthly rent checks coming in. But to the casual observer who doesn't see me buying or selling, it might appear as if I were headed in the wrong direction. *In reality, nothing could be further from the truth!*

One of my most profitable specialties is buying rundown properties from sellers who agree to finance *all or part of the sale*. Over time, I've accumulated quite a number of carryback mortgages (or *promissory notes*). I generally negotiate long-term monthly payments. Frequently, when I purchase properties, I'll inherit or take over the existing seller financing from previous sales. It's not the least bit uncommon for me to purchase a property and take over two or three existing seller carryback mortgages on the same deal. This sets the stage for one of the most profitable opportunities in my business.

Many sellers who own rundown, dumpy looking properties must provide *seller carryback financing* in order to sell their properties. Most banks want no part of financing "junk yard" rental properties, so sellers must finance the deals themselves. Obviously, most sellers would much prefer to have cash! Sellers who finance their own deals and carry back mortgages or notes are called *beneficiaries*. They're the folks who receive my mortgage payments every month. *We have contact every month in the form of my mortgage checks.* By now, you're probably wondering, "Where's any benefit to sending out mortgage payments?" **Pay very close attention here; I'm about to tell you!**

Many beneficiaries would rather have a fistful of dollars all at once than my mortgage payments dribbling in month by month. This is even more so when the beneficiary is 95 years old and the *promissory note or mortgage* still has 26 years worth of payments left! Quite often an elderly beneficiary will pass away long before a mortgage is paid off, and my debt gets inherited by family members who don't value future payments quite as much. There's no secret to what they want, and they want it now! Many of these *secondhand beneficiaries* will take a lot less cash rather than standing around the mailbox waiting for my payments. *How much less*, of course, depends on their personal financial situation at the time. Naturally, I'll employ my Lieutenant Columbo detective skills to figure out exactly the right time to dangle a potful of cash in front of their nose. **Timing is everything** when you're trying to buy back your mortgage debt for cash.

For example, let's say you offer to buy back your $100,000 mortgage debt from a beneficiary you haven't taken the time to investigate. Had you done a bit of homework, you could have easily discovered that the beneficiary had just won the "big spin" lottery the day before. *Suggesting a big discount for a cash buyback now*, he'll likely tell you to stuff it! On the other hand, if your cash offer arrives smack-dab in the middle of a nasty divorce, or the beneficiary has just been layed off at the pretzel factory, **now $50,000 to $60,000 cash** might easily buy back your $100,000 debt.

During my quiet year, when I didn't buy or sell any properties, many folks around me thought I'd given up real estate investing. Most observers think that if they don't see you wheeling and dealing properties, you can't possibly be making any money. However, here's what observers can't see.

During my quiet year, three separate mortgage holders (beneficiaries) accepted my cash discount offers,which reduced my mortgage debt by $109,000. Besides earning more than $100,000 with cash discounts, my cash flow increased by $811 a month, *or almost $10,000 annually*. And finally, my net worth was improved by $109,000 from the debt reduction. Close observers thought I slept through the entire year. They had no idea I had generated more than $100,000 in earnings because they didn't see any action!

Selling Fixers for Full Price—Extra Full

Most buyers who purchase my "nice-n-clean" fixed-up properties are tickled to death when they discover I'm willing to accept their 10 percent cash down payments **and also provide seller carryback financing.** Assuming my potential buyers are creditworthy, I'm happy to offer very attractive financing—with payback terms up to 20 or 30 years, often with *interest-only* payments. Easy payback terms are far more important to investors than the selling price— *within reason, of course!*

I always tell my potential buyers right up front, "I'm willing to give you easy payback terms, but I won't discount my selling price. I get my full price, and *you get great terms!*" My definition of *full price* is what some folks might call "extra-full"—sometimes up to 20 percent higher because of the easy payback terms I'm offering. Since good terms are always top priority for most buyers, rarely has my **extra-full price** been much of an issue. Buyers want monthly mortgage payments they can afford to pay without reaching into their pocket every month to make up for cash flow shortages.

Naturally, when I sell for top price, easy payback terms, and seller financing, my buyers have no idea that my future plan is to trade their mortgage or promissory note for a down payment on my next fixer-upper property. Sellers of ugly fixer-upper properties, *the kind I'm looking to make offers on*, will often take my carryback mortgages in trade as part of their selling price. Many times they would much rather have the hassle-free income from my mortgage payments instead of trying to collect rents from their deadbeat tenants. As you can obviously see, selling my property for the highest selling price in exchange for giving liberal payback terms gives me a bigger mortgage for my trade. Those liberal payments I gave to my buyer, they're now transferred to someone else.

For example, let's say I own a $500,000 property, which I'm able to sell for $595,000 (20 percent extra) because I gave my buyer excellent easy payback financing terms. *This means I'll have a $95,000 bigger mortgage to trade for my next purchase.* And I'll gain an extra $95,000 worth of equity on my next deal too. Obviously, it means less new financing will be needed, *and chances are*, I'll have a much better cash flow on my new property.

Right about now you're probably thinking, "Okay, I understand, when Jay sells his property and gives his buyer special easy payback terms, he can then jack up his selling price by $95,000. *But is that really legal?*" The answer, my friends, is, yes, yes, yes! Buyers are happy to pay more for *good terms* and *seller carryback financing*! Think about the last car you bought: Were you concerned about terms? If you could own a brand new shiny Mercedes for the same monthly payment as a dull green Chevy coupe, which would you choose? The Mercedes cost twice as much, but the payments are exactly the same! I'll bet I can guess which way you're leaning. Terms work exactly the same way with real estate investing. As for legal, well, I'm not a cop, but I can tell you that everyone I've ever sold properties to is happy with the deal. I call this *Creative Money Making 101.*

Use Small Loans to Acquire Properties

As you begin to stack your financial bricks higher, *building your personal real estate wealth*, chances are that you'll begin accumulating a few extra dollars that are not earning their keep. Real estate entrepreneurs, as well as we ski bums, don't put our extra money in bank passbook accounts or low-paying CDs, and we certainly stay away from buying stocks! One solution I've found for investing a few extra bucks is to offer small **hard-money loans** to other investors who purchase the same types of properties I do: *fixer-upper properties that I wouldn't mind owning* *myself!* Quite often, folks who have to borrow hard money against their ugly properties are on a downhill slope *financially*.

My loans never exceed the $15,000 to $30,000 range, and I will never loan money when the total debt (including my loan) is over 60 percent of the property value. I simply do a personal drive-by appraisal, *and the value is what I say it is!* For example, let's say my drive-by appraisal indicates the value is $100,000. There are two existing mortgages secured by the property: a first of $40,000, and a second of $10,500. My loan offer, in this case, would be $9,500—which added together with the other two mortgages equals 60 percent of the property value.

I realize my mortgage will be a third loan and that it's a bit risky, but don't forget what business I'm in! Let's say that 30 days wiz by and the first payment fails to show up in my mailbox. Should I go looking for the borrower? *No sir, I've never been very good at finding someone I don't want to find!* I'll simply begin foreclosure and take the property instead. Where else can I purchase a property these days for only 60 percent of its value? Can you see how powerful my $9,500 loan can be? In reality, this feels almost like I purchased a $100,000 property for $9,500 cash down— **at a whopping 40 percent discount!** I don't think you need to ask me if I considered my third mortgage too risky or not. If you do, you need to reread this part a little bit slower!

My lending terms are generally for three years, and most likely I'll ask for monthly payments of interest only, *at a respectable rate, of course!* If usury laws are involved, you can avoid any problems by making these loans through your licensed real estate agent to be on the safe side. This is yet another way we ski bum investors stay afloat. Can you begin to see why observers can't figure out what we do or how we survive?

9

Looking for Golden Houses

Many folks like the idea of investing in real estate, but they can't quite decide where to start or what type of real estate to invest in. Without experience, it's difficult for most start-out investors to know whose advice to follow (especially with so many seminar companies criss-crossing the countryside and so many professionally staged infomercials braggin' how easy it is). If it sounds too easy, take my advice and run away as fast as you can because easy is one thing it's not. Talking about real estate and doing it are not the same thing.

The good news is that almost anyone with near average intelligence can become a successful investor—*even a rich one!* "What does it take?" you ask. The answer is quite simple: it takes a combination of getting some education first, and then jumping in and doing it. It's my personal belief that both ingredients should be used in about equal portions. There's very little value in cluttering up your mind with a boatload of information you ain't ready to use yet. You're far better off to learn what you need right now to start, **then get started!** Once you've started, you should continually keep adding to your education as you go along. On-the-job training is always much better than waiting 'til you know everything because you never will.

Starting Small with Inexpensive Houses

Starting with small rundown houses will work for most people whether they're handy or not. Being a bit handy can help, but if you're not, it's still much cheaper to make your early mistakes on small fixer houses than on expensive properties. Cheaper houses are also less expensive to repair, and they're much easier to rent if you keep them the way I strongly suggest. "Why small houses?" you ask. They're much more affordable to a greater number of people. Common sense will tell you that there are more poor renters than rich ones. Also, poor renters won't be nearly as critical of your crappy lookin' sheetrock repairs!

Inexpensive houses are generally older houses built many years ago. Many are desperately in need of rehabilitation, plus a whole lot of cleanup. About 80 percent of the effort needed is what I call *grunt work*, or *unskilled labor*. New investors normally have a lot more grunt power than financial power. Obviously, doing all you can to save money should be a big part of your early learning experience.

Fixing up or *adding value* to older properties takes a few special skills. But at the same time, these older rundown houses offer a wide range of practical do-it-yourself training lessons for new investors. I have always shared my opinion that operating inexpensive fix-up properties is the fastest way to learn the real estate investment business. Perhaps even more important, fixing rundown houses provides the quickest path to profits and cash flow. This is always the top priority for new investors.

Adding value to properties tends to level the playing field when it comes to investor competition. Almost everyone starts out equal regardless of where they come from. High school dropouts, jailbirds, and lifelong geeks fare just about as well as real estate professionals, Ph.D.s, and even experienced building mechanics. The reason for this is that the serious money comes from financial skills rather than hammering on boards or fixing the toilet. Obviously, it's helpful if you possess a few hands-on skills and know the difference between a *grant deed* and *Grant's Tomb*. But regardless, that's not the stuff that makes you rich!

Investing with Minimal Risk

Lots of small-time investors go out of business and lose everything they have when the market stops appreciating or when bank financing dries up. To me, dependence on appreciation or bank financing is speculating—*not investing*! I want more control when I own the property. So my first rule of investing has always been **to control the profits and cash flow.** That's almost impossible when you're dependent on the economy (appreciation) or available bank funds (mortgages). My investment strategy is to earn money year-round regardless of mortgage funds or appreciation. When they're available, I consider them the icing on the cake—but never the cake itself. Minimizing risk is part of becoming rich. It makes very little sense to make a bundle of money, then lose it to circumstances beyond your control.

Education is your map to the gold mine. There are two ways to learn about making money with rundown properties, and both will cost you a few bucks. The first is to start out on your own using the trial-and-error method. I call this the *no-money-down technique*—that is, there's no money down until you make a costly mistake. Obviously, if that happens, any savings would certainly be lost. Then there's the question of time— as in, "How long before I'll be rich?" This requires some serious thought: how many years do you plan to practice real estate investing? You need to know the answer for yourself.

The second method is hire someone who knows the business and can teach you how. Seminars or special group training will be the least expensive. Don't expect to learn this business in two or three days of classroom instruction at a single event. Remember what I said about **on-the-job training:** The best way to learn is to mix formal education (seminars) with doing actual work on your fixer property at the same time. For learning, that's about as good as it gets. Naturally you'll need to pay a few dollars up front for your training, but you should learn enough to avoid the most expensive mistakes. Soon you will realize that your time equals money.

Paying a few extra dollars up front may be cheaper in the long run. Young folks can keep starting over for a while, but when you're older, you must move more quickly and avoid the big mistakes.

Searching for Gold Mine Houses

Much like the gold miners of yesteryear, today's investment house seekers can always use a few good tips about where to look, what to look for, and, of course, the reasons why. Your search for houses, much like a search for gold, is easier accomplished when you have a good idea about where to dig.

Older rundown houses are found in the older sections of most cities, so don't waste your time driving through modern-day subdivisions. In rural areas, they might be scattered almost anywhere, but generally you'll find that, these properties were built surrounding the main commercial areas, close to stores and other retail activities. You won't find the houses I'm talking about in the newer tract developments. Nonconforming properties like a group of single-family houses or cottages on one large lot are often found in commercially zoned locations—even in R-1 zoning. These properties can make excellent investments, and as long as the houses are kept in decent repair and occupied, their current usage will be "grandfathered in" regardless of current zoning laws.

Gold mine houses can best be described as properties with all the right things wrong. These are things that can be fixed or repaired that will automatically increase the value and/or rental income. They are also the kind of houses that provide investors with special profit opportunities not normally found with regular houses—for example, **seller terms for the purchase**, most often called seller financing. This valuable benefit alone can translate to big bucks for *savvy* investors. With seller financing, you can avoid having personal risk beyond the property itself if something goes haywire. You can also skip past the standard due on sale clause, which is automatically written into all bank mortgages. Naturally, the most important benefit of all is that **purchase terms** allow you and the seller to decide the terms of the sale to make the deal work for both sides. Setting up lease options and selling the property with wraparound financing are two more valuable benefits available when you have seller financing.

Reviving Obsolescent Properties

We live in an age when everything operates with the flip of a switch. Even the television shuffles through 75 channels, leaving hardly any reason to get off the couch except for a beer. We have automatic icemakers and special pots that cook dinner before anyone gets home. Today's high-tech houses must be designed and built with every imaginable convenience or they simply won't attract buyers. Sixty-five years ago, no one ever heard of a garage door that opened all by itself without anyone's touching it. The only way it would open is for you to reach down and pull it up—or back through it with the family car.

Times have changed, and houses without all the push buttons are no longer attractive to home buyers. However, home buyers aren't the only folks who pay money for housing. At least 43 percent of the folks in my state live in rental housing at all economic levels. The great majority, however, are young families and seniors who must live on very restrictive budgets. These folks are my primary customers, and the high-tech push-button technology doesn't rank at the top of their housing needs. They want clean, safe housing they can afford. For many young couples and seniors alike, two bedrooms with one bath, a single-car garage, and a small backyard make an ideal rental property that fits their budget. The problem is that they don't build these kinds of houses anymore. And the only thing comparable is apartment house living with a lot less privacy and a long list of can't-do rules.

The good news for do-it-yourself investors is that there are oodles of these older properties around, but you'll need to search for them much like the '49ers searched for gold. My favorite type of property has any-where from 4 to 10 separate houses, cottages, or duplexes nestled together on a single oversized lot. There are several important reasons why I like these properties, but the main reason is that my customers (renters) like them best! This is very important because many investors buy properties without even the slightest notion about what their customers really want.

I've always felt that since my renters have made me a wealthy landlord, I owe them this much: to understand what they want.

Finding Gold Mine Houses

Once upon a time, many years ago, before our present-day zoning laws, home buying families would often build or purchase their home on an oversized lot with the idea of building a few rental houses in the back and sometimes apartments above the garage. Their plan was to supplement their retirement income. Retirement 401(k)s and today's lucrative service pensions were not in the picture back then, so families had to provide their own retirement incomes. Most of these properties are at least 60 years old today, and many are tired, sagging, and generally worn out. These houses can be hidden gold mines for smart investors willing to breathe new life into them.

Forget looking at multiple listings on the computer screen, and don't be waiting around for your real estate agent to call. The few agents who actually understand this business know that even if they found one, disclosure laws would be a can of worms and the financing would likely end up a total nightmare! Naturally, sellers want all cash because most agents have told them that cash is the way it's done today. Back away from this nonsense; it's totally depressing.

Finding these properties is much easier if you take on the task yourself. What you'll need is a good pair of walkin' shoes and a car that runs long enough to get you there. In average-sized cities, begin looking in the downtown area. Start looking for five or six junky houses between the old theater and the RV sales lot or perhaps a few blocks away from the downtown mall. In the old industrial area, you might find a group of cottages hidden in the brush near the soup factory. The idea here is to find these kinds of properties on your own—stompin' through the weeds yourself. Notice, I've never once mentioned slums or the hood. Stay away from the well-established slum areas. You might find a bargain price, but you ain't gonna like your tenants. Worse yet, you'll never get to increase the value regardless of how many times you fix the broken windows or repaint the buildings.

Folks often ask me, "How would I ever find out if there are more houses in the backyard? All I can see is the main house on the street; everything else is covered by trees and overgrown shrubs. I can't even see what's down the driveway."

Look for groups of mailboxes and addresses with A, B, or C after the number. I always look for multiple telephone service wires and more than one electrical service—even lots of TV cables. When you see a bunch of wires, it's obvious that they're going some place! When you suspect that there's multiple units on a property but you can't quite tell for sure, draw yourself a little sketch of the property. Take a measurement (stepped off) to the nearest street intersection. Go to your county tax and map department to find the *APN parcel number* (tax ID number), and then take a look at the assessed property value (tax bill). With multiple units on one lot, the tax assessment will be much higher than assessments for comparable houses in the neighborhood, so the higher figure will indicate that there are more houses (improvements) on the property.

In bigger cities, select an area you feel might be productive. There's no need to drive all over the entire city. In rural areas, groups of houses, duplexes, or combinations might be found just about anywhere. Remember, you won't find older properties in newer tracts or subdivisions. And high-price seacoast towns are tough for new investors breaking into the business. The basic problem in these communities is that there is *too much money chasing too few properties*! Competing investors drive up the prices, and many will pay all cash for fix-up properties. My suggestion is to drive out of town a ways 'til you no longer smell the salt air! Fifty or sixty miles can make a big difference in terms of prices and buyer competition. Whichever location you choose, you must learn the local customs in addition to the prevailing **rent prices** and **property values.** *Local customs* meaning, where do the majority of tenants in your rental price range choose to live? Learning this information to begin with will keep you from buying an investment property in a drug-infested neighborhood that no one told you about. You must know the amount of rent you can charge and how much you can pay for a property and still earn a profit for yourself.

Golden Economic Benefits

I love real estate with all my heart, but there's nothing more distressful than a rental house that won't earn a profit after I buy it, fix it up, and rent it out. This happens to investors all the time with average single-family houses. Buying too many of these will almost guarantee that you'll eventually need help from AA. Although they don't always smell so good, gold mine houses have major financial advantages over most regular houses. The biggest advantage is that they're much cheaper when you buy them in bunches. The *cost per unit* is an extremely important measurement when you're trying to buy houses that will generate cash flow.

For example, not long ago in my town, seven detached houses on a single lot were bought for $629,000. Any one of these houses alone would have cost $149,000, by itself! Renting for $795 per month, *the group houses* would all have cash flow, but one single house wouldn't. The seller took 15 percent cash down and carried the balance of the sale price for 7 percent interest, amortized over 30 years, all due in 15 years. Had a new commercial bank mortgage been required, the best the buyer could have negotiated was 7.75 percent amortized at 5 years fixed, and then 15 years, variable-rate interest. Added to expenses were 2 points on the loan—plus an official Member of the Appraisal Institute (MAI) appraisal costing $3,200. Quite obviously, doing business directly with the seller (terms) is like finding pure gold!

Saving Investor Ryan

Making mortgage payments to the person who sells you the property can have an unexpected benefit every so often. Years ago, I acquired 11 units that for some reason I had trouble renting at the time. My $1,375 mortgage payment to the seller was more than I could pay with 45 percent vacancy. I contacted the seller (by letter) explaining that I could make payments of only $800 for the time being. If that was not acceptable, he could come and pick up the keys without any hassle from me. Since he had sold me the property, he had retired and moved to the coast a couple of states away from me. He grumbled a little, but then agreed to $800 per month 'til I reached 90 percent occupancy. Being able to work this deal out with the seller saved my bacon by giving me the time to turn things around.

Using No Down When That's All You Have

Every now and then when I'm counseling folks about investing, people will convince me that they really don't have two nickels to rub together. Even a small down payment would mean stealing the kid's milk money or going without toilet paper. Trying to save money for a down payment is totally out of the question for some folks. Still, as I often explain, if you have a burning **desire to succeed** and the **willingness to do whatever it takes,** you can even overcome being broke.

Not too long ago, a young family asked my advice about investing. Bob and Susan said they wanted desperately to get started investing but they didn't have a nickel to spare. Bob worked full-time; Susan did babysitting in their home. That way she could earn a little extra money and still take care of her six-year-old twins. Susan said their biggest problem was that they couldn't seem to save any money for a down payment even though she knew her $900 rent payment would be better spent on a mortgage payment instead. Credit card problems and other debts from their past were mostly cleared up, but the banks and mortgage companies weren't totally convinced they were out of the woods yet.

Seldom do I recommend buying a single-family house to live in as the best way to start investing. However, in Bob and Sue's case, it seemed like their best choice at the time. My plan was to convert their $900 rent payments into something that would start building equity. I knew about Bob and Susan's financial dilemma after Sue took me through several hours of "true confessions" about their past credit history. They'd be in deep doo-doo if they had to borrow from any conventional lender. In fact, they still didn't have pink slips for their six-year-old twins: a big part of their unpaid debt was to the local hospital where the twins were born six years ago.

Bob and Sue were financially obligated to the hilt as far as their present income was concerned. They couldn't scratch up an extra dime if their lives depended on it! To begin with, I told them to start searching the local newspapers for a seller who might be both motivated and flexible. Look under the headings. "For Sale," "For Lease," "For Trade," and even "For Rent." Also, gather up all the little freebie booklets with real estate advertising—the kind you find in the paper racks at supermarkets or in front of the post office. These include the "penny shopper" and the popular "deals-on-wheels" paper, which has a real estate section in the back.

Painting Your Way into Ownership

I described to Bob and Sue what kind of property we should be looking for. I told them to start making ad calls and talk to people on the phone. There's no use driving around until we find a seller who shows some interest in what we have to offer. I explained that our strategy would be what I call the *paint for down payment plan*. Obviously, it's not just limited to painting. In fact, the only limits I can think of would be the capabilities of Bob and Sue to fix up the property. "Painting for the down payment" works something like this.

First, I estimated that Bob and Sue could afford $700 per month mortgage payments if they bought a house. That's $200 less than the rent they currently pay each month. The extra $200 will be needed to fix up the house we find. Then $700 will pay off a $105,000 mortgage payment at 7 percent, amortized for 30 years. Obviously, $700 could pay a bigger mortgage if the interest were less than 7 percent.

Here's how the plan works: We begin looking for a rundown house that looks something like a pigsty. It will likely need paint everywhere, and the yard will probably look like the site of the annual auto dismantlers' convention. If gutters exist, they're probably falling off. The property will be a total mess. We'll also look for an owner who lives out of town—someone who is perhaps recently divorced, has just gotten married, is elderly, has transferred jobs, or has tried, and failed, at being a landlord. Don't worry about whether the house is vacant or occupied. Just remember, you're calling a fixer-upper ad that says "For Sale," "For Rent," or "For Something"! The ad wouldn't be in the paper if everything were peachy-keen!

"You need to know a little about market values." I explained. "Real estate agents or perhaps a friend could help if you're totally in the dark. It you want to learn values on your own, I'd suggest you start driving around in residential areas matching comparable houses and prices in several different neighborhoods. Remember, this job is not like building precision watches. Being exact is not required here. Being in the ballpark is close enough.

"Once you know a little something about values, you're ready to start looking at rundown houses selling for about $120,000 in as-is condition. I figure a $120,000 house in rundown condition should easily be worth $145,000 or more after it's all fixed up. Don't forget, the highest mortgage we can afford to pay at 7 percent interest is $105,000. We'll talk about finding a $15,000 down payment in a minute, but remember, **The key to this strategy is finding a seller who wants what you can offer more than what he or she has right now."**

Dialing for Dollars (Houses)

Here's how I talk to sellers on the phone: "Mr. and Mrs. Seller, I'm calling about your classified ad I read in the paper. I'm a family man, and I currently rent the house we live in. I earn a good income. My wife works part-time babysitting at home because we have two small children. Our biggest problem right now is that we can't seem to save any money. According to your ad, the house needs quite a lot of work. What caught my eye is that the ad sounds like I can save a lot of money, and that's exactly what I need—Bring your paintbrush—Sale or trades considered—$120,000—Good terms.

"Both my wife and I can do almost any type of fix-up and repairs to a house. We'd be very interested in fixing up your place if you would let us buy it. We are willing to pay your full asking price of $120,000 for the property if you would carry back a note (mortgage) for $105,000 at 7 percent interest. We would pay you, $15,000 down payment, partly in the form of work credit on the house. We'll do all the work at no cost to you, and all we ask you for is a little extra time to pay our share of the down payment. We can begin immediately paying you monthly payments of $700 on the $105,000 mortgage.

"Since the house is vacant right now, we'd like to move in and start fixing it up immediately. We won't ask you to spend a dime on repairs! We'll buy paint and pay for all materials, and we'll do all the labor ourselves. All we ask from you is a 50–50 split on the $15,000 down payment. *In other words*, we're asking for $7,500 credit for all our labor and the materials we provide.

"If you agree, we'd like to write up a contract to buy the house, spelling out exactly what work we intend to do to upgrade the property. You'll be fully protected because if we should fail to live up to our promise, obviously, you wouldn't be required to follow through with the sale to us. Chances are, you'd end up with a much better house because of the work we've done. Obviously, we have a very strong incentive to follow through with our promise since we're spending our own money for materials and doing all the work ourselves!"

Doing the Paperwork Right

There are several methods that can be used to protect both parties, depending on the situation and sellers' motivation. You can either purchase the property with a contract or use a *performance option*, which allows a purchase to take place only after specific promises are kept. For example, the promises could be that all the painting is completed or a new yard is planted. My choice would be to purchase the property using a *contract sale,* sometimes also called a *land contract*. The title remains with the sellers until you do certain things. For example, the contract might specify that you must complete certain fix-up items, such as those discussed above. Also, it could require you to pay the full down payment before the sellers would transfer title by a deed. These are the two common ways to acquire the property, but whatever the parties agree to will work. It's always best to keep things as simple as you can.

At this point, we tell the sellers, "Once we get the place all fixed up as we promised, all we ask for is a 50 percent work credit from the down payment, or $7,500. Regarding the other half ($7,500), we'll begin paying that as soon as the fix-up is completed. We can afford to pay you $100 per month until it's paid off. Of course, the $100 will be in addition to the $700 payment you're already receiving for the mortgage payment. The only other request we have is that you give us 12 months to complete all the fix-up. By then you'll know how we pay the mortgage payments, plus you'll be able to see the quality of work we do."

Keeping a Clear View of the Big Picture

The strategy I've suggested here can work very well if both parties are motivated to improve the situation they're in. *One party wants in, the other wants out!* Also, there are as many different variations to this technique as your own imagination will allow! Once you start making telephone calls and begin talking with potential sellers, you'll be pleasantly surprised to find how creative you really are. Over the years I've designed transactions in which my total down payment was a ski boat or an old pickup truck. There are many ways to acquire real estate besides using hard cash when you start thinking creatively.

Seller motivation and the **rundown condition of properties** are the most common factors that determine *how weak* or **how strong** your offer needs to be. As you gain more experience from making these deals, you'll look back from time to time, as I do, wondering if you didn't give too much away. Don't dwell on these thoughts too long: *Even if you did give too much away, so what?* You'll end up filthy rich just the same. In the overall scheme of things—the big picture, if you will—paying a few thousand dollars extra won't hurt you very much. What will hurt you a great deal is not taking advantage of these opportunities in the first place.

The Final Score

For Bob and Sue, their days of stacking up worthless rent receipts are over! They are now owners, making equity payments instead of paying rent to a landlord. As property owners, they've automatically taken one giant step up. Their accomplishments look pretty impressive for renters who didn't have a dime to start with.

Here's how their numbers look: They now own a house worth $145,000. You'll recall they paid $120,000 in its rundown condition. They currently owe a mortgage balance of $105,000, payable at $700 per month—plus the $7,500 delayed down payment balance, payable at $100 per month. *The bottom line is* that they now have equity of $32,500, and their monthly housing payments are **$100 less than when they were renters.**

For folks like Bob and Sue, it's tough to beat this no-down starter plan. Acquiring a property with **no up-front cash**, then painting your way into ownership, can be the start of something big: using what you have (*personal labor*) to get what you want (*ownership*) is the ideal poor person's path on the journey to wealth!

10

Doubling Your Money Fixing Houses

The classified ad read:

> True Fixer-Upper. Bring Your Hammer and Paintbrush—It Won't Last Long! Oozing with Ol' Fashioned Charm, It's a Downtown Original.

The temptation was more than I could stand. I had to see this property immediately!

It was located on a main thoroughfare in the middle of my town. The listing agent I called had made me promise not to disturb the tenants. When I got there, it was obvious that she should have told the tenants not to disturb me either! A broken "For Sale" sign posted on the property had long been trampled over and was completely hidden by the overgrown weeds. In fact, the houses were barely visible from the street because of the high weeds and all the brush. There were no address numbers on any of the houses, but as the agent had already told me, I had no trouble finding the property. *It's the most ugly group of houses on the block, maybe on the whole street!*

I Was Thrilled When I Found My Pigsty

Overgrown brush, wild bushes, and all sorts of trees provided constant shade and almost totally hid the junk cars scattered between the houses. Some were perched up on wood blocks with fenders and doors missing. But on a positive note, there were lots of spare parts and transmissions lying around in case restoration was part of some master plan.

The first thing I always notice with these kinds of properties is the occupants' peering out the windows. On this property, they tried to stay hidden as they peeked through dingy knotted-up curtains and the dirty oil-stained bedsheets. In all my years of carefully planning my visits, sneaking around these kinds of properties to get a peek, I have never yet figured out the highly sensitive "security system" these tenants seem to employ. Somehow they can always tell the very minute when someone that doesn't look like them shows up!

The newspaper ad was right! It didn't look like the property would last long. Pecan Street was one of the ugliest properties I'd ever laid eyes on. Even the tenants peering through dirty windows were ugly. Four run-down houses and two junky sheds, all crammed full of junk on one large city lot that was almost completely overrun with wild-growing bushes, uncut weeds, and dismantled cars. Household garbage and empty tuna cans were everywhere. Not a very pretty picture, to say the least! Remembering what most fix-up experts advise—"Always look for the ugliest property on the block"—there was no question in my mind that I had definitely found it!

Sometimes the Agent's Advice Is Correct

Pecan Street was listed with a local real estate office. The agent explained how she had been instructed to sell by the *four elderly sisters* who had owned the houses for many years but who had long since moved from the area. They had inherited the rentals from a family estate, and they had no interest whatsoever in spending any money for upkeep. They did share the rental income, but that was the extent of their interest in the property. They were genuine "milkers" and that was it! Somehow they sensed it was time to sell before all that remained was a pile of lumber and a lot full of rusting auto parts.

The agent had properly advised the sisters to offer **seller financing**, suggesting that they might obtain a higher selling price. Bank financing, she told them, would be far too restrictive. She said the appraisal would likely be quite low and the bank might even require that some funds be set aside for termite work and other repairs since the need for the repairs was clearly visible. Expensive roof replacements might even be required by a bank lender. Not one of the sisters wanted to hear anything like that. *Sell for the highest price you can get, but don't fix anything!* Those were their instructions to the agent.

Low Rents Greatly Speed Cash Flow

The rents were extremely low, so I felt an increase would be possible within three or four months. I offered **$70,000** with a **$7,500 cash down payment**. The sisters flatly refused, saying there's no way anyone should expect to purchase four separate houses for just $70,000—*even junky houses!* they said. They countered my offer with a $90,000 offer and asked for $25,000 cash down. The sisters were trying to net about $5,000 apiece after paying all their selling expenses, which included the $5,000 sales commission. **I refused their** counteroffer—I didn't have $25,000 cash even if I had wanted to sign the deal!

The four sisters constantly argued about everything—and not just between themselves but with their real estate agent too. The sisters would call their agent separately because they didn't trust each other. I've often found that sellers who have inherited properties to start with are always the toughest owners to deal with. Perhaps it's due to Murphy's law or something, but sellers without a dime of their own money invested always seem to want the most money when they sell, *just as if they had earned the money to begin with!*

Low Monthly Payments Are My First Priority

Finally, after spending hundreds of dollars on long-distance telephone calls, the sisters agreed to accept my counteroffer of $80,000, with a cash down payment of $12,500. It was all the money I had at the time! They agreed to carry the mortgage (seller financing) for a period of 10 years with payments of $600 per month at 9 percent interest. The 9 percent interest was quite reasonable for seller financing at the time I purchased Pecan Street. Still, I will now concede that I was not at my peak as a skilled negotiator back then!

Thinking back now, I honestly believe my original $70,000 offer would have eventually been accepted because no one else, to my knowledge, was even the slightest bit interested in this rundown junky property. In other words, **I had no competition!** In hindsight, I would have also tried a bit harder to keep my mortgage payments at no more than $400 per month. I'm certain that with my $80,000 purchase price, the *$400 monthly payments* would have been completely acceptable to the sisters.

I'm always happy to pay a little more for a property if I can negotiate lower mortgage payments. *In case you're wondering why*, additional cash flow is my highest priority. I'm less concerned about a higher purchase price, which of course adds to my basis and ultimately gives me more depreciation (tax write-off). The biggest problem for me when I purchased Pecan Street was that I wanted to buy the houses just as badly, *perhaps even more*, as the sisters wanted to sell them. Over the years, however, I've learned that you cannot fall in love with these properties and get the best price.

Low Rents Are Key to a Bargain

One of the top benefits for buyers of properties like Pecan Street is that your competition is greatly reduced—often nonexistent! When there is competition, you'll find it's mostly the lowballers who make ridiculously low offers that most likely will insult the sellers. It's quite easy to beat your competition if you use your time to figure out how to solve the sellers' most pressing problems. The Pecan Street transaction is a good example: I solved the sisters' problems and at the same time I negotiated a good deal for myself. You must never forget that if you can give people something they really want, you'll find it's much easier to get what you need.

Rents were only $650 per month at Pecan Street, which I had calculated to be about half of what they could be with not much more than cleanup! In situations in which the owners want nothing to do with the property or the tenants, you'll often find that low rents are the owners' *don't-bother-me strategy*. Most tenants know very well when they're getting bargain rents. They also know that if they call for repairs or gripe about anything, it might just trigger a rent increase or even worse, a termination. Tenants who are willing to live in a pigsty environment to begin with are fully aware of how risky any telephone call that bothers the owner could be; therefore, they don't call!

Low rents are one of the most prized ingredients to find when searching for bargain opportunities. Therefore, you must know your local rental market and what comparable *fixed-up units* will rent for. Research this information before you purchase a property. If you're not sure, check out your area by pretending to be a tenant. Call classified rental ads, and visit the units that closely resemble yours. After 15 or 20 visits, you'll have a good idea of what units like yours should rent for.

Meeting New Tenants Is Exciting

Meeting my Pecan Street tenants would make a pretty convincing argument for becoming a "house flipper." If there's one truism in the house fixing business, it's that *yucky houses always come with yucky tenants*. Distressed properties are generally home to distressed (often stressed) occupants. You might say that the property and the folks who live there are generally a perfect match. I quickly learned that each of my new renters was unique and quite different from the others. For example, two were paying rent, *but the other two were not*. One couple was getting by with a single automobile that ran most of the time, but the two young men living in the front house had seven cars between them that mostly didn't run.

And although they were different in many ways, they were alike in many other ways. For example, none of them had what you might call a steady job, although HUD paid the biggest share of rent for three of them! They also shared about the same level of enthusiasm for general cleanliness, yard work, and timely rent payments. I couldn't help but marvel at the individual ingenuity that one tenant displayed. Kevin had a wild rose bush with sticky thorns; the bush had grown so large that he couldn't enter the house through his front door! To solve the problem, he simply built a wobbly ladderlike ramp and began entering and leaving through the side window. During the first two weeks of my ownership, not one single tenant came outside the house even though I was working on the property almost every day. I learned that trust would not be developed overnight with these tenants.

Folks often call me after reading about my tenant landlording stories. "Why," they ask, "would anyone of sound mind even consider doing your type of business?" Regarding the sound mind issue, let's just skip that for now! The serious answer has to do with **money** and **cash flow**. Even the flipper gurus and the folks who buy "American dream houses" will tell you that there's no way you can produce income any faster than you can from fixing up properties and adding value.

Most people who seek my advice need money and cash flow more than anything else. A necessary part of owning real estate and keeping it for very long means you'll be meeting your own "Kevin" type of tenants when you acquire fixer-upper properties. The good news is that landlording is not all that difficult to learn. And it's important to remember that the skills you develop while you're learning will increase your chances of becoming financially independent many times over. Many of the bargain properties I've acquired over the years became mine because my competitors (would-be buyers) were frightened away by the people who occupied the houses.

Fixing Pecan Street Was Mostly Cleanup

Fixing all four houses at Pecan Street took me almost a full year. The total job cost close to $14,000. However, much of that money was credited toward my own labor. Obviously, you can't pay yourself. But since you're not writing payroll checks to anyone else either, *you're actually saving the money*. Roughly $3,000 was spent on paint, several new windows and doors, miscellaneous lumber, and exterior siding. I spent $2,500 for grading and paving the dirt driveway, and I paid $750 to a local contractor for installing a new chain link fence between the houses.

Working part-time, I estimated my compensation to be less than $8 per hour (20 hours each week, and approximately 1,000 hours total). In contrast, my later fix-up jobs would earn me $50 to $300 per hour. As you can see, I did improve as time went by, and my fix-up skills got better. I've often heard seminar gurus tell their listeners, "You should never perform your own labor because you'll be reducing yourself to a common, ordinary wage earner when you do!" And my question to that assertion has always been, "Who will do the work if I don't have the money to pay someone else?" Surprisingly, that simple question baffles many seminar givers.

Follow the Proper Sequence for House Fixing

What I'm about to tell you next is one of my most valued fix-up tips. You should remember this well because if you'll do what I'm suggesting here, you'll save yourself tons of grief, plus you'll make allies of all your tenants as opposed to uncooperative idiots!

Do not even begin to think about rent increases until you've done something that benefits each of your new tenants. "What do you mean?" you ask. Fix the leaky faucets, repair the window locks, and replace those two burners on the stove top the former owner promised to fix many months ago. You might even toss in a paint job or a new bedroom carpet (cheap carpet, of course). The point is, make 'em smile—and win them over. **You'll win a whole lot more tenant battles with love than you will with lots of rules.** I've seen the most obnoxious tenant you can imagine melt like butter after I repaired his countertop and installed a toilet that flushed properly.

Forget about introducing yourself on the first day on the job at your newly acquired fixer property. The tenants couldn't care less about who you are or where you came from. In fact, most would be tickled to death if you dropped dead! You need to understand that junky properties and unruly types of occupants go together. *They know you're there to change things*, and most people instinctively resent change, even though you think it's for the better. Your best introduction is to leap out of your pickup and begin cleaning up the mess! That's the only introduction you need.

Fixing up Pecan Street took me far too long. I spent countless hours just standing around looking for extra stuff I could do. *Falling in love* with your property is a habit you cannot afford to keep if you intend to be profitable in the house fixin' business. Pecan Street was my first multiple-unit property, and it was definitely *a love affair*.

Sometimes I would work all day at the property, run home for a quick bite to eat, then return to think up new things I could start working on. This is called *seat-of-the-pants fix-up*. What it means is that *I hadn't taken enough time to plan the job: how much work was really needed*, or even *how much money the job would cost*. Obviously, this is not the way to fix houses if you plan to profit. This is the method used by most homeowners for their pet projects around the house. It's also the reason I earned less than $8 per hour fixin' up the Pecan houses. Remember, *fixin' houses should not be treated like a hobby*.

You Can't Hit a Target You Don't Have

Without a fix-up plan or even a budget, it's hard to know whether you're on target or not. You can't hit something you're not even aiming at! Fortunately for me, Pecan Street was what I now call a *light fixer* as far as fix-up costs were concerned. There were lots of projects that were mostly cosmetic and cleanup oriented which kept my expenses down. I classify fixer jobs as *light fixers* and *heavy fixers*. Light fixers will cost me about 10 percent of the purchase price for fix-up. Heavy fixers run approximately 20 percent of the purchase price, sometimes slightly more. These estimates do not include capital improvements like roofs or completely new plumbing systems.

As I mentioned earlier, Pecan Street cost approximately $14,000 for the fix-up job, which as I look back, I now consider an overrun. Even with the hired contractor expense for grading the driveway, I still spent several thousand dollars' worth of labor (mostly mine) that wasn't needed. **Overspending** is perhaps the most common sin that afflicts nearly every fixer-upper investor. I simply cannot overstate the value of having **a well-thought-out financial plan** before you begin any project. I've never met a house fixer yet who has stayed 100 percent on budget. Nevertheless, there is real value in having a budget to start with! You must have a target to shoot at so you keep getting better.

You can't make money any faster as a house fixer than you can from working in the front yard. For some odd reason, most start-out investors have difficulty understanding this. They insist on working inside the house first. This goes double for most licensed contractor types! Fix-up investors must wear many hats, but none will ever be more important financially than your *marketing hat. Fixing up houses is about making money*, and those who give little thought to marketing will lose out to the competition.

Now back to the front yard where our marketing begins.

Adding Value Quickly Starts Outside

First, you need to understand that *both buyers and renters make their decisions to do business with you, or not to do business, when they are driving by your property at about 30 miles per hour in their automobiles.* If they are not impressed, *or worse yet*, they don't like what they see, all the money you've spent inside the house ain't worth a hill of beans! *The battle to win their business will be won or lost outside the house before they ever set foot inside.*

I have sold many properties for $10,000 to $20,000 more than I might otherwise have simply because I watered the front yard weeds, planted a few cheap evergreen shrubs (Pyracanthas), and installed a three-foot-high *old-fashioned white picket fence* around the front yard. If there are no trees in the front, I suggest you plant a couple of medium-sized purple plum trees to add a bit of color. In my state where the sun shines almost every day, you can water the front yard weeds and begin mowing them once a week, *and presto*, you've magically turned your weeds into lawn (*at least close enough*). Nothing sells a house or rents one any faster than a front yard **oozing old-fashioned charm.**

Several well-written fix-up books suggest that a $2 return for each $1 spent is enough to earn you a substantial profit. I will certainly agree; however, **front yard fix-up** can boost your earnings by many times more. Creating an attractive looking front yard is a very high payback

activity—$10 *return for every rehab dollar spent is what we're talkin'
here*. Make no mistake about it, the front yard appearance counts for
everything; plus, it's the kind of **high-profit work** that nearly all novice
investors can do by themselves.

By spring, my front yard at Pecan Street looked greener than our
hometown park. It's hard to believe the incredible change a front lawn
(manicured weeds) can make. *Same thing goes for a quick coat of paint.*
Often at my Fixer Camps, I'll show the class my *before and after pictures
(slides)*. They are always completely amazed when they see the striking
changes. Sometimes they accuse me of substituting the fixed-up pictures
from someone else's property. Still, they're always quite impressed by
how quickly looks can be changed!

Fix What Pays You a Profit

Always work on the kind of stuff that pays you back quickly! Obviously,
not all fix-up work will do this. For example, installing a new roof won't
earn you a nickel more rent each month, but obviously, it's necessary
because you must keep the property in habitable condition. Leaky roofs
don't meet habitability requirements, and besides, you don't want yucky
mold spores to incubate on the rent money.

Window coverings are an excellent example of fix-up work that will
pay you back quickly! I install draperies, miniblinds, and colorful curtains
in all my houses. Window coverings add a great deal of charm to any
house *but especially to older houses*. During house showings, they also
tend to block out sunlight, which streams through naked windows showing every little paint blemish or imperfection. Most of all, they give any
house *the completed look*. Window coverings create a softer, homier feeling. The resulting effect is much like that achieved by home builders
when they have furnished their model homes for showing.

In terms of profit making, I can install window coverings in my average rental houses (nine windows) for approximately $400 (today's prices).
That includes a shower curtain tossed in when needed. Houses with curtains will generally rent for about $30 more per month than houses with-
out them! That means that I can recoup my total *window covering costs*
in about 13 months. This is the kind of fix-up return I'm talking about

when I recommend working on stuff that pays you back quickly with higher rents or sales prices. Any improvement that will pay its entire installation cost back in 36 months or less deserves to be on your high-priority fix-up list!

You Can Manage Tenant Turnover without a Big Fuss

Tenant Kevin, in the back house, could no longer stand up under the strain of rapid change at Pecan Street. Chain saws roaring at 10 a.m. aggravated Kevin's sleeping pattern until he finally reached his breaking point. Suddenly one night, he shuffled off in the darkness (owing 25 days' rent), never to be heard from again.

Kevin's unscheduled departure allowed us to clean up his two-bedroom house and rerent it for $125 more per month. Over the years, I've found that working outside in the yard to begin with gives me a great opportunity to evaluate the tenants I've inherited. Seldom do I ever need to forcefully evict anyone. When I'm dealing with tenants who don't pay their rent, I can generally talk them into leaving on their own. Sometimes it might take a little *sweetner* like two or three hundred bucks. Or sometimes, I might even volunteer my truck or trailer to move their stuff—*free of charge*, of course.

The whole idea behind my fix-up strategy is to keep the cash flow coming in as long as I possibly can from the renters I inherit. Many investors seem to feel it's necessary to evict everyone living on the property in order to perform the fix-up work. My suggestion is to keep the rents coming in to supplement your fix-up budget. After all, you can't work on all the houses at the same time anyway! In my experience, almost every tenant I inherit when I acquire a property will be gone and all but forgotten within 18 months from the day I take over. The reason is that tenants who are paying low rents when I purchase the property are most likely paying as much rent as they can afford. Obviously, *a 50 percent rent increase* within 24 months is beyond their means.

My fix-up goals are *to increase the income (rents) by 50 percent and double the property value within a period of 24 months or less*. To accomplish this task, I will need a whole new group of customers who can pay my higher rents. You must always remember that it's the property that draws the tenant. When you transform a junky rundown property into clean attractive housing, you'll find that most of the tenants you started with will be long gone by the time your fix-up job is done.

Beginners Have All the Luck

Increasing rents by 50 percent and doubling the property value might sound like a "piece of cake" if you've never attempted to do it before. However, I can assure you, there are lots of ways you can mess up. *Overpaying for the property to begin with, spending too much money for fix-up, and mismanaging the tenants are at the top of the list.* Pay very close attention to all three of these if you expect to earn your journeyman house fixer badge.

During my early years, I purchased several properties that worked my tail off, *but produced very little profit for my efforts.* I've since written those early deals off as part of "learning the business," which sounds better than some of the other excuses I've used! With Pecan Street, I had much better luck, *beginner's luck perhaps* but regardless, it was better luck. In just 14 months after I purchased the property, my rents increased from $650 to $1,125 per month. **Wow—that's over 70 percent!** If you don't count my overspending (mostly my own labor) and my overloaded Visa card, I was in a positive cash flow position.

With the fix-up work completed and all four houses bringing in increased rents, I was really quite proud of my accomplishment. I was also itchin' to find my next fixer-upper property. Like most new investors just starting out, the only thing standing in my way was, *"Where can I find my next down payment?"* The answer came to me rather quickly: *I would borrow the money from my newly fixed up Pecan Street houses.* After all, my houses now looked terrific! My rents had almost doubled, and I was sure my houses were worth lots more than when I started!

The appraiser showed up bright and early Monday morning. I had already notified my tenants that we'd need to see inside. As you might have guessed, they weren't nearly as excited to see the appraiser as I was. In fact, in both the back houses, we had to wake up the tenants first before we could get inside. Another thing I must tell you, is that the tenants' housekeeping would have never won my mother's homemaker seal of approval. Luckily, the appraiser didn't seem to mind tripping over their stuff. About an hour and a half later, it was over. Now I began to worry and wonder if I had passed!

A Most Pleasant Surprise Had Arrived

At first I couldn't believe my eyes, but the numbers were **boldly typed** on the loan form. I'll never forget that day! "As soon as you can come down and sign the papers," they told me, *"you can pick up your check for $51,220.* Your Pecan Street appraised for $169,000."

Here's a property I should have bought for $70,000, although I paid $80,000. I spent $14,000 worth of *time and labor* doing the fix-up job, and now they're telling me it's worth $169,000. I must confess right here and now, that I was totally flabbergasted! Had I paid the right price to begin with, *I would have made a cool $100,000 fixing up Pecan Street.*

That was more money than *three years' worth of wages* working full-time for the phone company back then, *and yet*, Pecan Street was only my part-time moonlighting job. Needless to say, I knew I was on to something big! I now had $51,000 cash in my pocket. Plus, I still had $50,000 of unused equity left in my houses. **Not a bad return for my $7,500 down payment**, wouldn't you agree?

When you borrow $51,000 on a property, it's like a dream come true—*but only for the first 30 days*. Then your first loan payment comes due! Line 7 on my loan documents took away the cash flow status I had worked so hard to achieve. In fact, *I was upside down*, as they say in the used-car business, *and by a whole bunch too*! I now had two monthly mortgage payments of $600 each with only $1,125 rent to pay them with. No matter how creative my math might be, it's clearly obvious that *I had a serious cash flow problem*! The only answer I could think of was to sell, *so that's exactly what I did.*

Take the Money and Run

Five months' worth of negative cash flow taught me a valuable lesson: *all that glitters ain't necessarily gold*! Obviously, I had found the money for my next down payment, *but at what cost*? If there's one truism in the house rental business, it's that you can't make up for negative cash flow with volume. If you plan on keeping your houses, *which I highly recommend that you do*, you must arrange your affairs so that you don't borrow one nickel more than you need to move forward. *Moving forward* doesn't mean vacations to Tahiti. It means finding money for your next deal, **and that's all it means!**

Real estate investing, *my way*, is a very forgiving business. You can make a number of mistakes or bad judgments and still come out a long ways ahead. Pecan Street might fall into this category because *I borrowed way too much, and I paid an excessive interest rate to boot.* I decided to sell the property and take out my earnings quickly rather than dumping too much of my borrowed money back in the property. I also wanted to eliminate the god-awful interest rate I was paying the "Godfather" mortgage company.

Right out of the blue, an all-cash buyer showed up. I sold Pecan Street quickly for $149,950. The sale put another $32,000 cash in my bank account. If these dollar numbers sound a bit piddly to you (like in California), don't forget that gas was only 34 cents a gallon back then!

What did I do with all my borrowed money? *Here's where I got everything right and earned my gold-plated investor's badge.* With all that new money in my pocket, I went totally bezerk and I bought four more properties even uglier than my Pecan Street houses. If you get an opportunity to attend my Fixer Camp sometime, I'll be more than happy to show you what they look like now! Naturally when you come, I'll share my fix-up magic! I've become quite an expert at turning ugly weeds into lawn and hanging curtains so you can't see bubbles in my sheetrock.

11

Fixer Jay's Winning Formula

In his autobiography *Grinding It Out* (Contemporary Books, 1977), Ray Kroc, founder of the McDonald's Corporation, tells his readers, "I didn't invent the hamburger; I just take it more seriously than other people." Who could doubt the man behind the world's largest restaurant chain? If you should read this fascinating story about the highly competitive fast-food industry, what immediately jumps out from the pages is Kroc's uncompromising focus on simplicity and his uncanny intuition about people. He understood that selling hamburgers began with selling people.

Like most entrepreneurs, Ray Kroc struggled at first, but he quickly developed his winning formula, with the help of some very talented people. He then began repeating his success across the country in rapid order. The lesson learned here is that *once you've tested a winning strategy and it works, it's time to roll it out and conquer the world—or at least achieve your personal ambitions.*

I can't over emphasize the value of keeping your investment plan simple. Lord knows, it will complicate itself as you go along without much help from anyone. Real estate is a people business, and in order to do well, you must learn to deal with people in many different ways. You will have great difficulty explaining complicated deals to ordinary people. And if you can't explain the deals, most likely, they'll walk away from your proposals.

A Plan That Works Forever

Although I do many different things in my real estate business to extract the benefits, my basic strategy, or *template*, for acquiring properties has remained about the same over the years. I stick with my basic plan because it keeps working over and over for me. Borrowing on the words of Mr. Kroc, I didn't invent fixing houses and adding value, but I do take the job more seriously than most people I know. Fixing up rundown houses may sound simple enough, but there are a number of different ways to profit from these houses that most investors have never heard about.

My buying formula sounds fairly simple. I'm looking for multiple-unit properties of from 6 to 15 units, preferably detached houses or duplexes on a single lot at one location. House-apartment combinations will work, and quite often an old hotel or motor lodge will stir my interest, depending on the configuration and where it's located. I'm searching for ugly, rundown looking properties, most likely with tenant problems, that I can acquire for a **substantial discount**. To me that means 20 to 50 percent less than what I believe the fixed-up value will be.

There are several accepted methods to calculate the value of income-producing properties. However, the **gross rent multiplier (GRM) formula** has always worked best for me. The calculation simply expresses the amount buyers are willing to pay for a property based on the amount of income it generates. The purchase price can also vary a great deal based on the location, age, and condition of the property.

Take, for example, my fixed-up 52-year-old, six-unit property located in an average neighborhood. The property shows well, and each unit brings in $725 rent. In my town, investors are willing to shell out about

11 times the gross annual rents to purchase this property. Here's how the numbers look:

$$6 \text{ units at } \$725 \text{ each} = \$4,350 \text{ per month}$$
$$12 \times \$4,350 = \$52,200 \text{ gross annual income}$$
$$11 \times \$52,200 = \$574,200$$

Remember, these numbers are **my numbers** for **my investment area.** They may be too high or too low for your town. Also, these numbers are continually changing, so you will need to update your numbers from time to time. When I first began keeping close track of selling prices in my town, hardly any investor would ever pay more than 9 or 10 times the gross rents for the very best units.

Knowing Values Is Your Responsibility

Investors must develop this information for their own investment areas. It takes some time and effort, but it's critical for determining how much you should pay and *ultimately*, whether or not you'll end up with cash flow and profits. Tons of worthless information concerning income properties is handed out by selling agents, and it's information that doesn't mean diddly-squat about bottom-line results.

In the business of profit making, you must focus on **two important numbers.** First, what will your customers pay for your product? Second, what purchase price can you afford to pay to provide your product and still make a profit for yourself? You should not move forward without the answers.

Figure 11-1 shows you the current rents and values for a typical six-unit property in my investment area. You'll notice the rents vary from a low of $375 for what I call a "falling-down property" to $900 per month for Snob Hill. This chart is based on my most popular size rental unit: two bedrooms, one bath, with approximately 750 square feet. It's also my most profitable rental unit.

Determining the rents and values in order to build your **gross rent multiplier chart** comes from doing all the grunt work. To learn rent values, pretend you're a renter in search of housing. Call telephone numbers in the classified ads for different locations within your investment area.

GRM	Description	Rent, $	Rents (6), $	Annual, $	Value, $
15X	Snob Hill	900	5,400	64,800	972,000
14X	Premo	875	5,250	63,000	882,000
13X	Deluxe	835	5,010	60,120	781,560
12X	Desirable	795	4,770	57,240	686,880
11X	Average plus	725	4,350	52,200	574,200
10X	Average	675	4,050	48,600	486,000
9X	Rough	595	3,570	42,840	385,560
8X	Rundown	525	3,150	37,800	302,400
7X	Pigsty	450	2,700	32,400	226,800
6X	Falling down	375	2,250	27,000	162,000

Typical Small Income (Six-Unit) Properties: Two Bedrooms, 750 Square Feet, in Jay's Investment Area

Figure 11-1. Gross rent multiplier (GRM) chart: income/value

Drive out to see what $700 per month will buy you in a two-bedroom house or apartment. Do the same for $500, and so on. Once you become familiar with different parts of your town, you'll be able to read the prices in newspaper ads and have a pretty good idea about what the property will look like and how well it has been maintained.

Another important benefit that comes from actually checking out rentals and talking to people, is that you'll begin to learn about locations and where tenants at various rent levels choose to live. You'll learn about the "hood" areas and where the dopers hang out. Don't let the age or condition of a property fool you here! Dopers will sometimes live in newer buildings, and trashy properties can often be found in excellent rental locations. Sometimes out-of-town owners will milk a good property until it completely runs down and looks like a pigsty!

It's important to know how much rent the majority of renters can afford to pay in your investment area. For example, in my town I rent two-bedroom, single-bath houses to young couples with a small child or two.

I also rent to seniors. Both these customers can afford to pay about $750 rent. Knowing what my customers can afford helps me determine what properties I'd like to own. Smart investors will study the marketplace in order to deliver the right product (affordable houses) to their customers. It's important to remember that *if my tenants can't afford to pay for my houses, I can't afford them either*! It would be very unwise and risky to own a stable of houses renting for $900 per month if you lived in a town full of $750 renters. If the majority of renters in your area can easily afford your houses, it's much easier to keep them occupied and profitable.

Property Values Are Your Business

Learning about property values in your investment area can be accomplished much easier with the help of a knowledgeable agent or broker. Obviously, they don't have time for teaching wannabes and looky-loos. They need to earn commissions to buy groceries and beer for themselves. If you're not quite ready to buy a property just yet, you'll need to polish up your acting skills and pretend you are if you expect much help from agents.

Most real estate agents have files full of information about what properties actually sell for. They can even tell you how they're priced to begin with and what sections of town investors like best. When you know what properties are selling for within your buying area *along with the rents they generate*, it becomes fairly easy to develop a gross rent multiplier chart just like mine.

As you talk with buyers and sellers, *making offers and negotiating deals*, you'll soon discover that it doesn't take very long to develop a good working knowledge of rents and property values. Folks will sometimes ask me, "Isn't that what appraisers are supposed to do?" Of course it is, but you need to know values for yourself so you can respond immediately when you need to make an offer. As I've already told you, investment property values are primarily based on the amount of income they produce. If you'll take the time to learn rents and values, you'll be able to act very quickly when a good property becomes available. While your competition is still running around gathering stacks of information, you'll have the deal in escrow *and closed*.

Although there are other considerations when acquiring income properties, they're far less important than determining whether you'll end up with cash flow and profits. Investment properties can suffer many different problems, but most of them can be fixed if the property makes money. One warning is worth repeating here: **do not buy income property in slum areas.** You'll have great difficulty recovering your fix-up costs. Also, your maintenance and repair expenses will run about double in slums. The second reason, *equally as important*, is that you're not going to like the rental applicants who come calling to rent. Even if the purchase price is cheap, it's extremely difficult to increase the value no matter how much fix-up you do. Just remember, the biggest single reason for failure in this business is lack of cash flow. It's for this reason, that **cash flow has always been my number 1 priority.** Everything else begins in second place!

When I first began fixing up properties, I made the same two mistakes almost every fix-up investor makes before he or she can receive a diploma. First, I shied away from **true fixer-uppers.** I bought properties that didn't need a whole lot of fix-up done. The only reason I painted one property was because I didn't like the color. I also spent too much time and money adding *special customized features* like tiled entryways simply because I liked them myself. Second, I paid more than I should have to acquire several properties. Needless to say, these early mistakes kept me from graduating with honors! But worst of all, they kept me from making any profits.

Improving the GRM Guarantees Profits

To say that I could do this in my sleep might sound a bit boastful, but it's not a terrible stretch from the truth. It's a fact that people will pay a lot more money to acquire attractive real estate. Tenants will pay higher rents when they perceive more value—**looks** and **value** are my stock and trade. It's where the money's at in the fix-up business.

I purchase lower-end fixer-upper properties. Referring to my gross rent multiplier chart, I'm always looking to acquire *six- or seven-times-gross properties*. The reason is that these lower-end properties can be quickly cleaned up and fixed almost immediately, creating substantial equity. For example (using my GRM chart), if I'm able to fix up a six-times-gross multiplier property so that it becomes an eight-times-gross multiplier, my chart shows I've added over $140,000 value to the six-unit property. How long should this take? My goal is to complete the task in 24 months or less. In terms of cash flow, I've increased my rents from $375 to $525, or a total of $900 per month.

This cleaning and fix-up activity is called **forcing the value up**, and it works almost anywhere, at any time, as long as you follow a few ground rules. For starters, don't purchase properties in the slums or near airports. Both investors and renters alike are afraid of troubled areas where they can see problems. Consider locations where neighboring properties will not affect the operation of your property. For example, many investors will acquire a single four-unit building in a project with many other four-unit buildings, all in the same group. I don't recommend this type of investment because you give up too much control. If the other owners rent to deadbeats or druggies, you can't fix the problem. I much prefer houses or apartments on a corner lot location that are somewhat separated from potential troublemakers. I call this the *isolation factor*. Buying a property next to a crack house for 50 percent of the asking price could easily be a nightmare instead of a bargain.

The Risk Factor with Fixers

Avoid the greatest danger of all: **running out of money!** I have yet to meet a start-out investor whose finances are not stretched tighter than a banjo string. Investing for the average person is always a real strain on the pocketbook. It's for this reason that students who attend my House Fixer Camps always pay extra close attention during our discussions about finding money.

Assuming for a moment that you've acquired the six-unit property we discussed above. You bought it for *six times the gross income*. Now you're cleaning and fixing, hoping to improve the value to eight times the GRM. You've spent all your personal funds; plus you've even raided the kids' piggybanks *and your Visa card*. What you need is some breathing room now *or even faster*! If you paid 20 percent down for an average (nonfixer) tract house investment, you can forget about looking for any help! You still owe an 80 percent mortgage, and there's no additional equity you can tap.

Your fixer-upper property is different. Assuming you've completed your fix-up job on the six rental units, you've created borrowing equity. Your *loan-to-value ratio* could easily be less than 50 percent, which means that relief is only a lender away! Naturally, I'm not suggesting that you concentrate on borrowing money. But when you find yourself with no wiggle room left, you must resort to more drastic measures, like a small equity loan. I'm sure you agree that it's a lot more comforting to know that because you bought the right kind of real estate, it can now come to your rescue! You've been saved by sweat equity, and it doesn't matter whose sweat. What matters is the value added to the property, which gives you an automatic safety value.

12

Sniffing Out Profits Takes Vision

Standing on the second-story balcony of the old Ripley Hotel, you get a bird's-eye view of Redding's older downtown district. You can watch the tipsy customers coming to and leaving the popular Sportsman Bar & Grill, one of the half dozen or so 6 a.m. drinking establishments in the area. Looking south, you'll be treated to a commanding view of Taco Bell and the local alcohol rehabilitation center. As you've probably guessed already, the Ripley Hotel is not listed as the featured attraction on the city's popular sunset walking tour.

The Best Locations Are Where the Money's At

"What's the single most important consideration when you're looking to purchase income properties?" Nine out of ten real estate agents will answer that question by saying, "Location, location, location." It's the old adage I've been hearing since I began investing many years ago. Certainly, I'll be the first to agree that *location is very important*. But in my opinion, it is **not the most important**! For me, **cash flow** is king of the hill. I'm talking about properties that will earn crisp green foldin' money for their owners every month without waiting too long for some unpredictable event to happen in the future.

Some properties can have the *best locations* in the world, but they will quickly become anchors around the owners' neck if they must perform all the work and manage the property without having any paydays. Even the most beautiful real estate begins to look ugly when you risk all your money, work your tail off, and have nothing left over at the end of the month to reward yourself *or boost your confidence.*

The Ripley Hotel was located in what I call *a marginal location* in my town. *Marginal* means you're not likely to see joggers in microfleece shorts running down the streets, and you certainly won't see many garage doors that open and close by themselves without anyone touching them. But on a more positive note, there's no history of any axe murders or Hillside stranglers either! An older "blue-collar" commercial district would pretty much describe the location I'm talking about.

Wider Vision Creates Bold New Opportunities

Buying houses and duplexes becomes almost second nature to investors like me, but it's easy to get stuck in a rut! This happens when you develop what I call *tunnel vision*. Don't get me wrong here: "specializing" is good. Once you get good at something, it will pay big dividends to expand your vision and conquer new territory. That's exactly what I did when I purchased the Ripley Hotel. The Ripley was still an operating hotel, although the operation was very loose! *So loose*, in fact, that the owner was losing money every month. Obviously, that's the reason he was quite motivated to sell the place.

I had already earned substantial profits converting an old motel into monthly rental cottages for single seniors, but this would be my first attempt at fixing up a combination *residential-commercial building*. The Ripley was a large two-story structure with 11 double-room apartments, two vacant retail stores, and three oversized storage rooms filled to the ceiling with junky furniture and auto parts. Only 6 of the apartments were rented, and neither commercial space—a key shop and used-clothing outlet—had been occupied for over three years. Even worse for the owner, the 6 occupied apartments (two hotel rooms joined together) were only bringing in about half the rents they should be earning. This fact (*low rents*) did not escape my attention.

Find a Better Mousetrap

There are two ways to make a ton of money in the real estate business. *The first way* is to find an owner who wishes to sell and be sittin' on his doorstep first in line! In other words, try to deal directly with the seller, one-on-one, before anyone else has a clue about what's going on. With this method, you have no competitors bidding up the price. *If your offer is structured in a way that gives the seller the benefits he needs*, or thinks he needs, there's very good odds you'll close the deal, leaving any would-be buyers around you *wondering what happened*! Writing cold-call letters, the kind I describe in my book *Investing in Fixer-Uppers* (McGraw-Hill, 2003), Chapter 5, is an excellent way to put yourself in contact with potential sellers like we're talking about here.

The second way to make tons of money with income-producing real estate is to *design a better mousetrap*. That's exactly what I did at the Ripley Hotel. *Designing or building a better mousetrap* means doing things **differently or better** than what the current owner or operator has been doing. The very minute I looked inside the Ripley, one fact jumped straight out at me: *there was a whole bunch of rentable space that wasn't earning the current owner one thin dime*! Much of the space was wasted, not being used for its highest or best use. Retail stores in the Ripley Hotel would be deader than last year's love affair—*most definitely a fish in the wrong pond*. On the other hand, affordable apartments for low-income single men or women were as scarce as hen's teeth in my town.

The only reason the apartments at the Ripley were vacant was that they were filthy and desperately in need of repairs. *Also, there was hardly any effort to rent them.* The live-in manager in apartment 7 had a cardboard sign hangin' on his door that said, "Back in 10 minutes." However, his early-to-rise routine, *along with the half dozen local saloons within walking distance*, took a serious toll on his regular business hours. Taking a closer look at the tenants in the Ripley, one might easily conclude that *being somewhat like the manager* would probably be the most important criterion for qualifying as a resident! *The real lifesaver for the seller* was that he owned the Ripley free and clear. So he wasn't under the extra burden of coming up with a mortgage payment every month, *which could have easily put him under.*

Don't Let Others Control Your Money

Attempting to operate an old residential hotel from 60 miles away was more than the owner could handle. *Besides losing money,* he was forced to depend on his tipsy manager to handle the maintenance and repairs, deposit whatever rents he was able to collect, and interview prospective tenants. Buildings like the Ripley can be big cash flow generators but only under the watchful eye of an owner who hangs around to make it happen. I learned later on that the owner had once lived in the building himself. And while he was there, the building stayed fully occupied.

As I do with most properties I've acquired, I began driving by the Ripley at various times during the day not only to observe what goes on but also to *think and plan* about what I might do with the building if I became the new owner.

Almost immediately, I realized the unproductive space—*two empty stores and three storage rooms*—could easily be converted to more apartments. All I would need to do is relocate a couple of interior wall partitions and build a few new nonbearing walls (creating rooms) inside the building—*all inside, behind closed doors.* No one would even observe that I was adding walls or building additional rooms because my new construction would be inside the existing building. The electrical panel was large enough for the conversion because it had plenty of blank spaces available for additional electrical circuits to each new apartment. Common bathrooms with multiple showers were located on both floors and were large enough to accommodate additional residents. Two apartments had their own private bathrooms. Incidentally, they were rented at $125, the same as rooms without baths—Wow!

I estimated my costs would be about $3,000 for each new room I added, but since I would be the builder, *approximately 65 percent* of the total expense would be savings to me for doing the work myself. In other words, my actual *out-of-pocket costs* would be about $1,000 for each new apartment. Another thought that kept whirling around in my head, besides *adding apartments* for additional income (my better mousetrap technique), was the fact that all the existing apartments were *substantially underrented at $125 per month*. Obviously, the five vacant units would add substantial income *with minor fixing and cleaning*. The unused space for adding additional rooms, plus increasing the below market rents, seemed to me to be a "dead-bang" guaranteed plan for creating respectable cash flow, *and rather quickly too*!

Shop for Benefits

You must train yourself to "dig out" the benefits, *much like a gold miner* panning for specks of gold hiding in the rocks and sand. It's the benefits that will make you rich, *not the buildings*. Buildings are merely the vehicles that take you there. Looking at the Ripley Hotel *and thinking about becoming rich* would be a real stretch for most folks.

That's why I had no buying competition. The Ripley was a disgustingly ugly building made even uglier by the putrid bluish green paint. The hotel was a 90-year-old brick structure covered with a thin layer of dirty brown colored stucco, *painted over* with horrible light green paint! I can certainly understand, *looking back*, why no one had the courage or the vision to make an offer. The looks alone had turned every potential buyer away, *except one*! By now, I think you can guess who that dummy might be.

The seller was asking $199,000 for the property, but he had indicated that he was willing to negotiate a little and also offer seller financing, according to the local real estate agent. A "For Sale" sign had been hanging in a lower-level apartment window for several months before I became aware of the sale. Obviously, the $199,000 price, *in my opinion*, was designed to snag out-of-town dummies who often have lots more money than brains. Who knows, a new paint job with a more pleasing color might have been enough to snag an out-of-town investor!

The real estate agent explained it this way: "The Ripley is a wonderful opportunity for a do-it-yourself investor who can handle the repairs and maintenance, keep the stores and apartments rented, *and, of course,* be available to take care of business." He went on to explain that when the current owner lived in town, he always made at least $1,000 spending money every single month.

I don't know about you, but I have always marveled at the optimistic picture most real estate agents paint for their clients when they discuss (pitch) **wonderful opportunities** and **income potential**. For the most part, I've learned to hold my tongue, but my thoughts are always the same: *If it's such a wonderful investment with gobs of income, how come you don't buy the property for yourself?* On those occasions when I actually ask the question, I just love to watch 'em squirm, tryin' to come up with some reasonable answer.

The agent's listing sheet—**Property Income and Expenses Data**— showed the following scheduled income for the Ripley:

11 apartments rented at $125 per month each	$1,375
"New to You" clothing store, 800 square feet, lower level, front	$ 325
ABC Key Shop, 425 square feet, lower level, side	$ 250
Total income	**$1,950**

Formulating My Plan to Make an Offer

For the same reason sick folks are often advised to seek out a *second opinion* concerning their medical treatment and/or decisions, I decided to do the same thing with my rehab plan for the Ripley. Obviously, I was quite certain that adding more apartments made good financial sense, but it never hurts to hear someone else's opinion. My room construction plan was to cover all the lower, street-level windows with plywood or cardboard so that anyone walking by the building could not see what was going on inside.

The job itself was not too complicated for a *handyperson* because it merely involved constructing smaller rooms inside a larger room and building a short section of new hallway for the entrance. Adding new electrical wiring inside plastic conduits to each new apartment would be easy enough. And since no plumbing work was involved, I felt quite capable of doing most all the work myself, *with my helper of course*!

My trusted handy worker and I took a good hard look at the job together. He then quickly gave me his *second opinion*: "It's a walk in the park," *he said*. "Let's jump in and get it done! Working together, we could both do the job in two months easy, *including our coffee breaks*."

After our visit, I was completely sold and rarin' to go! It was now time to see just how motivated the seller might be. Obviously, no one, in my opinion, should expect to sell a junky rundown hotel building for $199,000 with only $750 monthly income. There would need to be a great deal of compromise.

Back then, *nine times the current gross income* was more than a fair price, in my judgment, so that's exactly what I offered in my written proposal. Needless to say, the owner felt differently! My offer of $80,000, or nearly $120,000 less than his asking price, did not impress him one iota! After his flat-out refusal, which included a short lecture, we began having serious discussions back and forth (via his agent) about the future potential of the Ripley versus what was actually going on right then with the building. It was quite obvious to me that if the owner kept his current live-in (tipsy) manager, his income would never get much higher. In fact, it might even get worse. Although the owner never directly admitted it, I'm certain he agreed with me. Even his real estate agent, *acting as the Ripley overseer*, was taking home more money from the hotel than the owner was.

It took two and a half more months *with a long 30-day silent period in between* to reach an **acceptable compromise**. Had anyone else ever showed up with an offer, I'm almost certain it would have knocked mine out of the running. But mine stood because it was the only offer he had. I agreed to pay **$99,500** for the Ripley with a **10 percent cash down payment**. The owner agreed to carry back the balance of $90,000, secured by the building.

After a little more haggling, I reluctantly agreed to monthly payments of $800 or more, including 8 percent interest until the entire balance was paid. When I pointed out that the $800 payments were more than the current *income from rents*, I received little sympathy from the seller. He would agree to $700 payments—but only if I increased the sale price to $149,000 and gave him $49,000 cash down. *I respectfully declined that proposal!*

About a month after we closed escrow, I boarded up the lower windows so no one could look inside, and I began building the walls for our new apartments. To further discourage any *inquisitive passers-by*, especially anyone from the *city building department*, we hung big bold "For Sale" signs on the building, *just as if the building were still vacant* and still for sale.

Covering all the street-level windows with plywood so no one could see inside was my plan to stay hidden so that I could complete the framing work before *anyone realized what happened!* The strategy worked very well. *Not a single soul ever dropped by or even knocked on the door to ask any questions*. My guess is that anyone who might have heard the strange pounding noises, then immediately spotted the oversized "For Sale" signs in the windows, probably chalked the noises up to ghosts or perhaps even the colorful group of tenants who called the Ripley Hotel their home.

Avoid the Big Mistake Most Dummies Make

Pay close attention here, 'cause what I'm about to tell you next will make you a ton of money. *It will also keep you out of trouble with your tenants and the law*. Do not even dream about raising rents when you first take over a property. *Yes, I know you're the new owner*, and so does everyone else. And, yes, I'm aware that your rental income sucks, and you're upside down in the property. *But who's fault is that?* You bought it, didn't you, so don't start punishing your tenants so soon!

Let's agree on this: **lousy rents are not the tenants' fault!** Rents at the Ripley were *lousy* (meaning low). But when you looked at the rooms, you could quickly see why. *The rooms were lousy too*, and several of them would have been judged **uninhabitable** if put to a test. *If this were not the situation, there's no way on earth I could have ever purchased the Ripley for only half the asking price*. Raising rents at this point to increase the income enough to pay my expenses and mortgage payments would be taking a major risk, and it would *also be asking for trouble!* The city building department, local HUD housing office, legal aid attorneys, and even the county health authorities could have shut the whole building down without batting an eye. *Believe me, the timing was not right for a rent increase!*

Think about this for a second: if you were a low-income tenant living in the Ripley *and you were just barely making ends meet*, how would you like to receive a big fat rent increase for no other reason than *tycoon Fixer Jay* has come along to make a killing in real estate? Stirring up a beehive with a short stick might be a whole lot safer!

Income Properties Should Generate Income

My rent increase strategy is akin to the thinking behind buying a young child a *small inexpensive gift* for Christmas. Naturally, she would like to have more. Still, she feels somewhat grateful and even thankful toward me. Most likely, she feels a bit obligated to give me something back in return even though my gift was just a small one! **That's human nature.** When you give something *first*, you immediately change the other person's attitude. This in turn allows you to be compensated (as in raising the rents) without the threat of stirring up hostilities. *See how easy this is when you think it through!*

For at least the first month or so, I always concentrate on improving the tenants' living conditions and making the outside (exterior) of a property more attractive. Obviously, when you acquire fixer-upper properties for greatly reduced prices, **there is always a reason why!** The biggest reason, I've found, is because the property is a mess— *completely rundown inside and out*. The Ripley was no exception. Tenants complained that no one ever fixed anything. As the new owner, I immediately began visiting each apartment to make repairs as my tenants requested. Most repairs were minor and the cost to me was mostly my own labor! Carpets were threadbare, so we replaced them in all the occupied rooms. In less than a month's time, all six of our tenants became quite friendly with us. *They were very thankful to us for fixing their apartments*.

Looks Can Earn a $50,000 Bonus Overnight

Outside, the Ripley was different from most other properties I've acquired. Sidewalks were the only yard, except for 20 feet of bare ground and a clump of shaggy trees in the back. Obviously, **an attractive paint job** was my first priority—even though my plan called for new windows sometime down the road. At that moment, my budget was running on empty.

Exactly 41 days after becoming a new owner of the Ripley Hotel, *soon to be renamed* the Ripley Apartments, the two-story building sported a brand new paint job. All it took to cover up the pukie green color was 24 gallons of exterior paint. I can truthfully tell you that painting the Ripley changed the entire look of a whole city block. Had the seller done the painting before listing the property for sale, I'm absolutely certain $149,000 would have been a very achievable sales price!

Exterior painting is a high-priority profit maker. I spent $520 for 24 gallons of top quality exterior paint and about $2,500 to have it sprayed on. The $50,000 likely price markup for the new paint job, *mean that the ex-owner left a cool $47,000 value sitting on the table for me*. It's real easy to run out of *thank you cards* when you can find sellers willing to give you gifts like that!

Moving Onward and Upward

My two investment goals are **double the value within 24 months** and **increase the rental income 50 percent**. The Ripley was already on the fast track—and only four months had past since I had become the owner. Remember those empty storage spaces filled with junk? They were now *apartments 3, 13, 14, and 15*. My biggest apartment, which I named "the deluxe model," became my new downtown rental office. It turned out to be an ideal location for many of my tenants who pay their rents in cash. Cash flow at the Ripley had already improved enough to cover my mortgage payment ($800 per month), plus all my operating expenses, *and rent increases* were now on the way. Remember those two tenants with their own private bathrooms? I gave them a choice: either move to a newly painted apartment for $150 or stay where you're at for $175 per month. They both stayed and paid an extra $50 for private bathrooms.

A small "For Rent" sign was all it took to end my problem with vacant apartments. Suddenly, I was flooded with people dropping in to inquire. Obviously, not everyone would qualify. Some asked if we were planning to open a bar too! One thing was obvious from the start: there would be no need to advertise rooms in the local classifieds. As I had already guessed, there were plenty of customers for all the rooms I had.

Making Big Bucks on My 1040 Tax Form

Back in the days when I acquired the Ripley Hotel, taxpayers were allowed to arbitrarily pick the **remaining economic life** of their real estate assets. That meant answering the question for depreciation purposes, *"how long do you expect the building to last?"* When I first looked at the Ripley, my guess would have been *not much longer*, but the tax folks at the IRS are looking for a better answer. So, I set up books for the Ripley Apartments using a *10-year depreciation schedule*. My rationale was that since *the Ripley was 91 years old at that time,* and sand was falling out from between the bricks every time a train went by, there was probably about 10 years' worth of sand left. *I never heard one small peep from the IRS in response to my depreciation schedule.* Naturally, a short-term depreciation schedule creates a bigger tax loss—meaning more **net income for the taxpayer.** Obviously, the tax code is always changing, so don't try this today.

In less than a year of ownership, every room in the Ripley was rented. The least expensive apartment was now $150 (*gas was 39 cents*). *Phase 2* of my fix-up plan was now in progress, which included replacing carpets in the hallways and stairs. We added an extra stall shower in the common bathrooms, both upstairs and down. We also upgraded each shower stall, adding a new plastic surround for better waterproofing and durability. Since every apartment was furnished with a saggy iron bed and broken-down wooden dresser when we started, I gradually began to replace these items with higher-grade *yard sale furnishings*.

Fix-Up Money Needn't Be Spent All at One Time

Doing fix-up *never ends*. Naturally, the most significant economic benefit for doing the fixing is that *you won't need a ton of money saved up to begin with!* If you start out **working on safety problems inside and improving the looks outside,** you'll find, as I have, that the less urgent fix-up stuff can be scheduled over a longer period of time. This method allows you to at least partially fund your improvements with additional cash flow coming in from *increased rents and vacancy fill-ups*. Many fix-up investors mistakenly believe you must fix up everything in one big expensive swoop. **That's not so!** When you do it my way, *one phase at a time*, you can reduce the heavy strain on your Visa card.

With all the apartments rented, I was now collecting three times more income than when I started. My income had reached $2,300 per month for 15 apartments, *not counting number 16,* which had become my full-time rental office. Wow! Talk about increasing rents 50 percent in 24 months—what about 300 percent in just 12 months! Figure 12-1 shows an income property analysis form for the Ripley 12 months after I acquired the building. Figure 12-2 explains why my *actual cash flow* was much higher than the $395 shown on line 14 of property analysis form.

How did the cash flow increase so fast? There were three primary factors involved here. **First,** market rents for the one-person apartments were substantially under market ($125) on the day I bought the building. **Second,** lousy management had accelerated the seller's motivation to sell, which, of course, allowed me to steal the building. *"Steal" is my characterization; most folks thought I got screwed!* And **third,** I had the vision to see how all the unused space could be turned into four additional income-generating apartments (the better mousetrap). Together, these three *important factors* allowed me to turn the Ripley Hotel into the Ripley Apartments and *my personal money machine.* As you can see, my **actual cash flow** was approximately three times greater than the property analysis form indicates.

Quite often at seminars, people will ask me if there is very much work to all this stuff I talk about. Yes, of course there is! I have never yet figured any way to get around it. Work is never mentioned on those late-night TV infomercials. They just show you the big checks—*you gotta love 'em for their creativity!* My personal feeling about the work is kind of old fashioned: **you gotta do it in order to build your money machine.** If your money machine happens to be income property like mine, *the more work you do early on* (setting it up), the less work you'll need to do later on when it's kickback time.

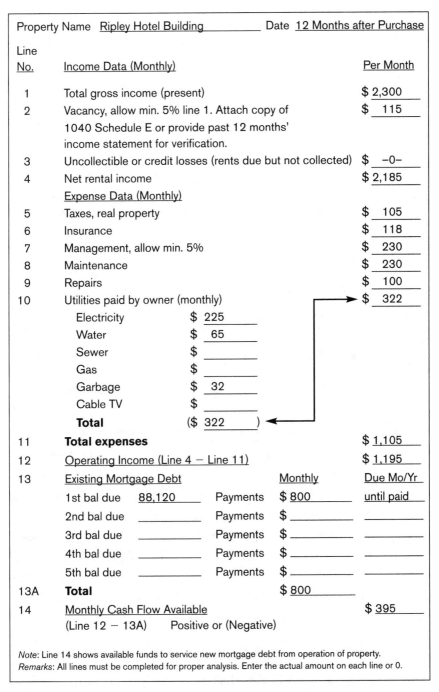

Property Name Ripley Hotel Building	Date 12 Months after Purchase	

Line No.	Income Data (Monthly)	Per Month
1	Total gross income (present)	$ 2,300
2	Vacancy, allow min. 5% line 1. Attach copy of 1040 Schedule E or provide past 12 months' income statement for verification.	$ 115
3	Uncollectible or credit losses (rents due but not collected)	$ –0–
4	Net rental income	$ 2,185
	Expense Data (Monthly)	
5	Taxes, real property	$ 105
6	Insurance	$ 118
7	Management, allow min. 5%	$ 230
8	Maintenance	$ 230
9	Repairs	$ 100
10	Utilities paid by owner (monthly)	$ 322

Electricity	$ 225	
Water	$ 65	
Sewer	$	
Gas	$	
Garbage	$ 32	
Cable TV	$	
Total	($ 322)	

11	**Total expenses**	$ 1,105
12	Operating Income (Line 4 − Line 11)	$ 1,195

13	Existing Mortgage Debt		Monthly	Due Mo/Yr
	1st bal due	88,120	Payments $ 800	until paid
	2nd bal due		Payments $	
	3rd bal due		Payments $	
	4th bal due		Payments $	
	5th bal due		Payments $	
13A	**Total**		$ 800	
14	Monthly Cash Flow Available (Line 12 − 13A) Positive or (Negative)		$ 395	

Note: Line 14 shows available funds to service new mortgage debt from operation of property.
Remarks: All lines must be completed for proper analysis. Enter the actual amount on each line or 0.

Figure 12-1. Income property analysis form, Ripley Hotel

General Notes

Analysis form shows **$395 positive cash flow**; however, when you add back expenses for work I did myself plus fill vacant apartments, cash flow is improved dramatically.

Adjustments

Line 2	Vacancy allowance: We now had a waiting list of tenants wanting to move in. No vacancies anticipated.	Add back $115
Line 7	Management	Add back $230
Line 8	Maintenance	Add back $230
Line 9	Repairs	Add back $100

Credit

Apt. 16: Move my rental office from another rented location to my own building (savings = $200)	Add back $200
Total Add back cash flow	$875

Property Analysis Form (Figure 12-1) Line 14 =	$395
Add Back Cash Flow	$875
Line 14 (Revised), Actual Cash Flow	**$1,270**

Figure 12-2. Property analysis form explanation, 12 months after purchase

Combining Businesses at the Ripley

Moving my rental office to the Ripley cost me $200 a month I otherwise would have received from renting apartment 16, but the move more than paid for itself. Buildings like the Ripley can generate tremendous cash flow. On the flip side, however, they do require more maintenance, upkeep, and tender loving care than houses and duplexes. Keeping one of my workers (employees) on site at the Ripley allowed me to process rental applications, handle repair calls, and collect rents from my other properties. In between these duties, there was always plenty of time left to handle the cleaning and maintenance at the apartment.

Worthwhile or Not: You Be the Judge

Brick buildings, like the Ripley, filled with low-income occupants don't appreciate like houses facing San Francisco Bay, *but they don't need to!*

Real estate benefits come in many forms, and as I've already said, **cash flow is my all-time favorite.** During my 10 years of ownership, other than the first several months, my spendable income averaged between $1,500 and $2,000 every month, or approximately $21,000 annually. When you figure $21,000 times 10 years equals **$210,000,** you can quickly see that my net income was more than enough to pay for the old brick building twice!

Selling the Ripley came unexpectedly. I had just purchased the largest hotel in my town. It was in a perfect downtown location for conversion to senior apartments. The building came with nine commercial store fronts, including a noisy bar, which played loud punk-rock music 'til 2 a.m. *That's only three hours before most seniors get up,* which was not at all compatible with my master plan for the building.

Trying to rid myself of the popular night spot turned out to be a bigger task than I had visualized. My legal action was met with a formidable challenge—enough so that I backed off and decided to use my charm instead. The bar owner and I kissed and made up over my hasty eviction attempt, and then I took him for a ride to visit the Ripley.

I told him that this *lovely old building had just become available.* I also pointed out that the Ripley was perfectly suited for his type of business with only a few minor modifications. Almost immediately he saw the potential, but then he explained his limited financial situation to me. At this point, I hadn't even mentioned a price, but I had talked about a possible "good deal." I told him that there was no need for any bank financing because *he was lookin' at the bank—it's me!* We settled on a price of $295,000, or roughly three times the amount I had paid *just 10 years earlier.* His $45,000 was an acceptable down payment, and he agreed to turn off the punk-rock music within 30 days if we completed the paperwork.

Strange how the numbers work, but my sale ended up just under seven times the gross rents. You'll recall, I had purchased the Ripley for approximately nine times the gross rents. Yet, with my $250,000 carryback mortgage at 7 percent interest for 25 years, I would eventually rake in $530,000. When you add that to the rents I had already collected, $210,000, you begin to see exactly how powerful a small **$10,000 down payment** can be when you mix it with those *three important factors* I told you about earlier.

13

Unique
Opportunities

Not every property that looks rundown, ugly, and distressed is a gold mine in disguise. In fact, if you were to purchase some of the properties described by sellers and real estate agents as "fixer-uppers" chances are that you'd end up without the gold! Don't misunderstand me here: I'm not trying to slow down your efforts to buy diamonds in the rough. What I am trying to do is help you understand that everything that glitters ain't necessarily gold. Like the radio broadcaster Paul Harvey says, *"Now, for the rest of the story,"* because there is more if you intend to make any serious money with fixer properties.

In my efforts to find the right properties that fit my investment criteria, I'm constantly looking for specific **problems** or **situations**. I want properties I can turn into positive money makers. This transformation can involve changing the property's physical appearance, sometimes restructuring the financing, or dealing with problem tenants who are causing the owners to drink more than they should! Many times, I'll find properties that have all three of these problems going on at the same time!

Have a Money-Making Plan

You must always remember that you don't get bigger paydays simply because you own the property. Big paydays come from doing something that increases the value of the real estate. A value increase can come from solving problems, even without any normal appreciation. For example, if a property doesn't go up one nickel in value but it is made to produce more *net income* because the expenses have been controlled, you've certainly created a lot more value for yourself.

Try to think about things to increase the value as you search for properties. Many investors pass up golden opportunities because they lack the knowledge to take advantage of a situation that's a bit out of the ordinary. Often, asking for a little help from someone with more experience can snag you a real bargain that most investors would simply pass over.

One of the most common examples is the argument against buying houses that don't have full perimeter foundations. Conventional wisdom suggests you should never buy houses without standard concrete foundations. That's good sound advice as *a general rule*; however, there are always exceptions. In my case, I happen to own a number of them, and it just so happens they produce the highest cash flow of all my houses. The reason is quite simple: I paid only about 50 percent of what the equivalent-sized houses with perimeter foundations would cost. As a result, my mortgage payments are roughly half as much. Rental income is not affected by pier foundations as long as my floors are solid and safe. In fact, years ago, pier foundations were considered the normal type of construction. The only negative issue I've found is that banks won't loan money on properties without full perimeter foundations. However, that's easily remedied with seller financing.

Location Counts—But Not for Everything

When I look at potential investment houses, I am always concerned about location. I need a decent location for the specific plan I have in mind for the property. Bear in mind that all my plans are not the same, but they all have the same objective, **which is to make a profit**. The way I will do it varies a little with each new property I acquire.

Some houses make excellent long-term investments. At least, that's the way I judge them. You must be very cautious when trying to out-guess the future. Don't bet the family ranch and all your prize laying hens on long-term predictions. *Anything over five years is simply a guess*. With nonfixer properties in top locations, you can expect to pay more to acquire them. Sellers can demand *and get* higher prices when the property looks horrible because the competition will bid up the price since it's a top location. It you pay extra for a top location and if your pre-diction about the future is correct, you might end up a big winner some day. Still, there's a lot of ifs while you're waiting!

On the down side, higher acquisition costs and bigger mortgage pay-ments will cost you lots more money. It could take considerably longer for you to ever realize any profits or cash flow. Don't forget that guessing can be the difference between surviving or going broke! Start-up investors **need cash flow first** and long-term profits later on. If you get these two mixed up, you may never get to "later on."

I like to think about locations as A, B, and C. Naturally, *A locations* are the best. We'll call B the local average, and C would be a stone's throw away from the county dump. With a little study and some driving time, you can easily determine these locations in your own investment area. Investing in A locations is fine, but it generally takes a lot more cash to buy properties. *I've already told you the reasons why*. My choice is B loca-tions, but I always look at the Cs to make sure I don't miss anything exciting. I stay away from large HUD projects, high crime areas, and places where I don't feel safe being there! Regardless of how cheap the prices might be, neither renters nor buyers want to wear bulletproof vests and metal flack jackets over their underwear.

Isolation Equals Better Control

I'm always interested in properties that are isolated or somewhat sepa-rated from the neighboring houses around them. Isolation offers much better investment control. I call this the *isolation factor*, and to me it's very important. For example, when I purchased Yale Court, I acquired five trashed real estate owned (REO) houses from the bank that had fore-closed them. They were all located together on a short dead-end street.

With only six houses on the street, I knew that once mine were fixed up, I'd have almost total control of anything that happened on the street. My plan was to keep the houses as rentals, so I wanted to have complete control over such things as junky cars, yard upkeep, exterior house paint, and of course, *the type of renters* who would live on the block.

Contrast this strategy with buying a rundown property and then fixing it up, only to learn that the next door neighbors are raising pigs in their yard. Worse yet, out-of-town owners are renting the house to druggies who sleep all day, play Meatloaf records, and work on junk cars all night. It's extremely difficult to attract decent renters *or buyers* no matter how much you fix your property if the next-door neighbor's house looks like a pigsty.

One of the main reasons I like to purchase small groups of houses that are *located* together *on a single lot* is because I have much better overall control. These properties are like a small campus, and quite often they are isolated from surrounding neighbors. Fences, trees, and mature shrubs will often provide adequate barriers from adjacent properties. End-of-the-street locations are generally better, and houses located next to small stores and office buildings will often make excellent rental properties. Most renters are looking for convenience in safe, clean surroundings. Buyers, on the other hand, are more often looking to purchase houses in the newer subdivisions. Renters don't care about zoning or the future potential of the neighborhood. Many actually seek out downtown commercial locations where they can walk to work and enjoy the many services within strolling distance.

Average tract houses found in sprawling subdivisions can make excellent long-term investments, but you mustn't be fooled when you calculate the cash flow. You should never count on making a killing any time soon because these kinds of investments mostly rely on appreciation for any sizable profit taking. Tract houses are also very sensitive to normal real estate up and down price cycles. Buying and selling quickly for profits is mostly about speculation, *as opposed to investing*. Flipping houses can be profitable if the timing is right, but allowing tenants to gradually pay off your real estate over time will make you a lot richer in the long run. I have found that it's very difficult to purchase rundown tract houses cheaply enough to fix up and still turn a decent profit quickly. On the other hand, these houses are great **properties to hold for the long term,** as long as you have **adequate cash flow coming in.**

Buy Properties Outside the Box

Older, nontract houses, or *leper properties,* as I often call them, offer a much better profit potential because these properties are unique and different from each other. Since they don't build houses the same way anymore, these older properties are almost like original paintings. Once I complete the fix-up work and establish my selling price, it's quite difficult for anyone to argue about my pricing using the normal comparable sales approach. That's because there ain't no comparable sales information to be found. Most appraisers can guess *or estimate* within $10,000 or so, judging the value of a $300,000 tract house. But with *older nonconforming houses,* it's different. I've had offers of $650,000 and $795,000 on the very same seven-unit rental property. Both offers were made within a four-month time frame.

There are many profit opportunities available for investors who specialize in buying the older fix-up properties. First, when you find them in a rundown condition (which is often caused by poor management and neglect by the owners), you are in an excellent position to negotiate a substantial reduction in the purchase price, *far below the properties' fixed-up value.* Once these older nonconforming houses are fixed up, *especially multiple units or small groups of houses,* it's extremely difficult to accurately determine their true value. The comparable sales method is not normally used because there are no comparisons to be found. What this means is that you have a great deal of latitude when you establish your selling price. It's not too likely you'll get many offers $145,000 apart like I did, but I will tell you that it's extremely difficult for most folks to judge whether *nonconforming properties* are worth $700,000 or $795,000. As you might well imagine, I've always been inclined to use the higher numbers when I'm selling.

The **rental income return** in relationship to what you pay for older rundown houses will blow the socks off the earnings from newer houses—that's even after you spend another 10 to 20 percent for fix-up!

The reason is that renters are willing to pay about the same rents per square footage whether they decide to live in a newer house or in a 60-year-old fixed-up property. In fact, in some locations, tenants are willing to pay even more for older houses in part because such houses are so rare. Obviously, when you can acquire older houses for about half the cost of newer ones and finance them for 50 percent less while keeping the rents about the same, you shouldn't need a calculator to determine which is better.

People Problems Are Worth Big Bucks

One problem *or condition* I'm always on the lookout for is destructive, deadbeat renters. *People problems* create more profitable investment opportunities than you might ever imagine. Just one bad tenant experience is sometimes enough to cause an inexperienced owner to bail out cheap. One owner of a four-unit apartment in my town sold his building cheap because he was afraid to go near his property. Bikers and druggie types had literally taken over the apartment building. The owner was too scared to even ask for his rent money. He lost total interest in the property and just wanted out. A friend of mine gave him an old ski boat and two color TVs for his equity. The only cash he spent was on two delinquent mortgage payments and a past-due bill to replace three windows. The deal was almost a no-money-down transaction, except for closing costs and court fees for evicting the tenants. After all the dust had settled, my friend owned a good solid four-unit building with $56,000 equity, *acquired for peanuts!* If my friend had sold his boat and TV sets at the local auction, he wouldn't have got a dime over $6,500 for the works. There are plenty more of these deals out there for investors who learn what to look for and have the skills to handle the tenants.

Most buyers are completely turned off when they see a property with flaky looking tenants hangin' out the windows! The buyers don't want the hassle or the problems, but I'll let you in on a little secret: *My friend has yet to see any of the tenants he evicted.* He never went near the place 'til they were all tossed out! Our local marshal did all the dirty work. The key to this opportunity was Jim's landlording skills. There's not much hassle when you know what you're doing. As I said earlier, fixing people problems can make you a ton of money, without a lot of effort, if you'll learn good landlording skills. In fact, I've always considered my landlording skills to be one of the big reasons for my house fixin' success!

Building Wealth Doesn't Happen by Accident

Every so often I hear about some speculator who makes a killer deal and needs a wheelbarrow to haul his money home. But there's one thing I've observed about most speculators: **they seldom stay rich very long.** They tend to speculate on risky deals that don't pan out, and they're right back starting with nothing again.

When you study wealthy people as I like to do, you'll soon discover that *killer deals rarely lead to long-term riches.* By far the best strategy is a simple plan that takes you from one successful deal to the next, without your assuming unnecessary risks. The plan must be easy to understand because complicated schemes rarely work. A good plan should be one that does not depend on appreciation or new bank loans to make it work.

14

Finding Gold at Miller Street

"**Y**ou don't know how hard it is to find a good deal where I live. The competition is beyond fierce, and prices are totally insane. You won't find anything that comes even close to cash flow in my town! I've read your books, Jay, and you make it sound like there's a good deal waiting around every bend. Either you're reminiscing about the 1950s or you're smokin' those funny cigarettes. I've talked to every Realtor in my town, and I religiously search out every program for distressed properties, and I'm still batting zero!"

Nonbelievers Will Not Share in My Kingdom

If I were paid a single dollar for every time I've heard that pitiful story, I'd be plenty rich enough without ever messin' with real estate! Besides, listening to sob stories is a whole lot easier than doing all the work it takes to create good real estate deals. *Did you hear what I just said?* **I said, Create good deals!** I've never yet found a good deal just sittin' there waiting for me, and I began my search more than 45 years ago.

You find the property first; then you must turn it into a good deal. Can you see the big step you may have missed here?

The truth is that real estate investment opportunities can be found almost anywhere by the trained eye. When I say **trained**, I mean trained to find the kind of properties you are qualified to invest in and, of course, properties that have the potential to earn you profits. For example, if you work a day job down at the box factory, it's likely you'll have very limited funds to invest and there will be strict limits on your available time. Buying a decent property that requires a sizable cash down payment along with hefty mortgage payments is probably out of the question. You simply can't afford it!

On the other end, *a total pigsty property* falling down with biker types of tenants might well be cheap enough, but this kind of property will require tons of extra time. That's assuming you know enough to handle all the problems! The first question all serious-minded investors must ask themselves is, "Will my *skills*, my *available time* for investing, and my *bank account* be adequate for the kind of property I'm looking for?" Naturally, this thinking process will help define the type of investment property best suited for you.

Money Doesn't Level the Playing Field

A fool and his money are soon parted in the real estate investment business. This has been going on long before the Sierra mountainsides were carved up and peddled as romantic retirement home sites, even before the northern Yankees were snookered into buying underwater lots in the sunny Florida swamplands. Seems like there's always been room for *imagination* and *unlimited creativity* when it comes to selling real estate to someone. A value perceived is often sold for the same price or more than the true value. Paying extra money for a property, however, will not buy you any more value.

I often hear from folks who have read my books, and they know I had very little cash for down payments when I started. What many of my readers would like to know is this: "Is it a lot easier to purchase properties when you have a little extra cash available?" It might be, but buying easier is not the goal. **The goal is to buy properties wisely**, and that means paying the right price so that you end up with a profit. It's very important that you know what the property's value is to you. Notice I said **to you!** It will likely be different for me.

Let's suppose for a moment that I'm an unscrupulous seller! Also, let's imagine that you enjoy yapping a bit too much, and you let it slip out that you'd be willing to pay up to $100,000 cash down for my seven rental houses. That's if I'm willing to give you **good leverage** and provide **seller financing.** Since you've told me what you can pay (that's a big no-no), I immediately view you as a tenderfoot *or as a newbie.* **How about 9 to 1 leverage, I say!** I'll sell you my houses for $900,000, and you'll still have money left over after paying the mortgage payments. *How do you feel about that?* "Wow, I'm having great beginner's luck," you say. "Just show me where to sign!"

Not too far down the road you discover that *10 times the annual gross rents of $80,000* was the right price for my seven rental houses. Now you realize that I simply converted your $100,000 nest egg into extra profits for me. You asked me for good leverage, and *I gave it to you!* You wanted seller financing (terms). *I gave you that too!* What you didn't ask for or bother to find out was the right price to acquire seven rental units generating $80,000 per year income in my town. As you can see from this example, your $100,000 cash down payment gave you no special advantage whatsoever. It did allow you to pay me more than my property was worth!

Buying Right Is Only Part of Building Wealth

First, allow me to tell you what not to do. Stay away from those *flash-n-dash* seminar gurus who recommend buying properties light years away from where you live. How in the world can you possibly know the market when you've never been there? The simple notion that because a property is five times cheaper in Mississippi than in California doesn't mean a hill of beans. It's brain-dead information! I'm not interested in the cost. I need to know if the property will produce **cash flow and profits for me.** Obviously, the price must be in line with the income and expense numbers, or I don't want the property no matter what it costs.

When you decide to invest away from where you live, you must put your faith in other people—*beginning with the person you select to manage your property*. This can quickly become a disaster. Small-time, investors generally don't have enough knowledge to know what goes on, nor do they have the extra money for vacancies or operating shortages. It's very common for professional property managers to squander most of the income for overpriced plumbers, painting crews, and hand-picked cleaning teams, using up any possible cash flow from rents. Naturally when this happens, the owners don't get diddly-squat!

What's a poor owner to do when he or she lives 1,000 miles away from his or her investments? Let me tell you exactly what two such owners did in my town. *They sold their properties to me*. They were 100 percent motivated and *completely fed up with real estate* when I made both offers. *Always buy your first several investment properties where you can take a short drive to see them—and even touch them!* If you follow this advice, you'll soon have enough experience so that the issue will never come up again. You'll also increase your odds for success by at least 10 times or more, *believe me!*

Tenants with Dangling Chains

I've become very fond of renters who wear dangling chains and belly-button rings. *No, I'm not looking for a date*. I'm looking for a deal. Styles of dress mean nothing to so-called professional property managers, but they do to me. The reason is because a mode of dress represents a particular lifestyle. For example, in my state, most biker gangs always dress about the same way. They're easy to pick out in a crowd. Don't read me wrong here, bikers may have hearts of gold, but I'm not in the business of *"It's what's on the inside that counts."* That's better left up to their pastor. My only concern is from a landlord's point of view. As a landlord, I know that biker looking tenants don't mix with my "straight-arrow" renters. Mixing these two types can make a landlord's life almost unbearable and at the very least cause uncontrollable drinking!

Dangling chains, sparkling belly buttons, and bold tattoos were the official dress attire at Miller Street. *Seven units in all*, the property was located on a west city street in a neighborhood mixed with older homes and smaller-sized apartments. I liked Miller Street because it had mature landscaping—nicely shaped trees, small lawns, and assorted evergreen plants. Evergreen without water in Redding's summer heat quickly turns *"ever-brown,"* and that's exactly how Miller Street caught my eye in the first place.

Driving by on the way to my own property, it was hard not to notice the rapid decline of Miller Street. The grass had died. Junk was piling up, and bicycles were being ridden in and out of the front doors. It appeared as if the tenants had simply abandoned their junky cars around the property in favor of gas-free transportation. The property had changed from seven attractive looking rental houses to an ugly pigsty in just slightly over a year! This was when I started to develop an interest. **I decided to investigate.**

Lieutenant Columbo Bob Visits the Laundry Room

It's been my experience that when you need to check out a property quickly, you won't find out what's happening any faster than by making a personal visit. I call this my *laundry room detective technique*. I usually show up between 7 and 8 a.m. with a clipboard in hand and my "Bob's Cut-Rate Electric Service" decal pinned on my shirt.

Usually, I'll find an "early bird" tenant washing clothes before the neighbors are up. If not, I'll fumble around and hang out a while. When Beth finally showed up, I asked her if she had seen Mike yet.

Beth: Who the hell is Mike?
Jay: He's my boss, but it looks like I got here first!

That's normally how I make my introduction and present myself. *After that, my detective work begins.*

Jay: These apartments look like fairly decent places to live.
Beth: I'll say. Sure, if you don't mind living around jerks that party all night.
Jay: I guess they keep the rents pretty affordable around here.
Beth: Yes, if you think $500 a month is affordable for these dumps! *Personally*, I think they're gougin' me a bit, *especially since management never fixes anything*. They've been promising to repair my air conditioner since last summer, but it's still blowin' hot air like the manager.

Jay: These apartments look like they are pretty large inside. I imagine you've got quite a bit of space to cool down!

Beth: Big? *Are you nuts!* I can just barely walk around my queen-sized bed, *and* there's hardly any closet space. The only decent-sized room in the place is my kitchen, and I don't even cook!

Jay: I've sorta been lookin' around for an apartment myself. Do you know if there are any vacancies here? Maybe you can tell me where I might find the owner?

Beth: I know there are two empty units right now, but I seriously doubt if they've even been cleaned up yet! You'll have to call Five Star Management Co. over on Hill Street. The owners live down near San Diego somewhere.

Jay: Would you happen to know if they have extra parking spaces around here because I've got a small fishing boat.

Beth: You can park up next to your apartment. As you can see for yourself, everyone here has their stupid cars parked everywhere! Most of them don't even run. If you ask me, the place looks like a total junk yard!

Jay: Well, thanks for all your help, Beth. *I really appreciate it.* Looks like my boss (Mike) musta gotten lost somewhere. If he shows up, would you please tell him Bob went on to the next job? Thanks again!

My informal interview only took about 15 to 20 minutes, *but I got more information this way than I ever could from the Five Star Management Co.* Besides, I'm sure it's more truthful too. More importantly, it's exactly the kind of information I need to know in order to *write up an educated offer* that will hopefully *appeal to the owners*. Naturally when I contact them, I'll ask for some of the same information again so I can verify it.

Over the years, I have found that most people love to talk. *If you create a friendly atmosphere*, folks will tell you things you'd be afraid to tell your mother! The real beauty of this technique is that there's always at least one or two tenants who are willing to tell me everything I need to know about what's going on at the property. By the way, this gal even invited me in to see her apartment. I thanked her but said that my boss, Mike, would have a fit if I went inside.

My Secret Offer to Purchase Miller Street

Keep in mind here, that Miller Street was not for sale, and it was not listed with any realty company. But it was professionally managed by Five Star Management Co. My offer to purchase would be *under the radar*, so to speak, because no agents or anyone else would have even the slightest idea that I had written it! Secrecy was very important here because I didn't want competition if I could avoid it. After all, I did all the hard work and research. *I was the actor who played the electrician in the laundry room.* I didn't want some copycat competitor learning my secrets and overbidding me.

One of the two best ways to acquire investment real estate is to put yourself in a position so that you and the potential seller are the only two people who know about the deal. *One-on-one with the seller*, I call this! Okay, I know you're itchin' to know the other way so I'll spit it out: **It's adding value to a property** by using strategies that will quickly produce more income. We'll tackle that technique at a later time. For now, let's break the ice with the San Diego owners. My laundry room chat with Beth had given me about all the information I needed to make my proposal.

"Whoa, Jay, hold on just a minute here. Pardon the interruption, but you haven't mentioned anything about what the expenses were at Miller Street. Aren't you getting a little hasty with an offer here?" Friends, if you're not up on what it costs to operate rental units, please keep up with your studies. For heaven's sake, don't buy anything until you do. *Meantime*, in the interest of moving along, here's the expense number you can use. *Write it down and underline it.* You may use this number for estimating the cost of operating any older apartments (30 years or older). It includes a small vacancy allowance as well as 5 percent for uncollectible rents, *as in stiffed.* The answer is 50 percent of the scheduled rents. Miller Street had seven apartments with scheduled rents of $500 each. Therefore, 7 times $500 equals $3,500 income. The cost of operating Miller Street was $1,750. Remember, *mortgage payments* are not expenses. They just feel like it when you write the check.

My letter to San Diego was direct *and purposely informal!* I closed with my desire (low key) to acquire the property if it should ever become available for sale. I also enclosed **six glossy full-color photos** clearly depicting "life at the Miller Street property." Although I make no claim to be an experienced paparazzi, I must admit that *these six pictures were quite revealing!* It's often said that a picture is worth a thousand words. However, pictures like the ones I take can be worth thousands of dollars when it comes to long-distance negotiating. My plan was to mail pictures of Miller Street to the owners who lived a thousand miles away, *along with my proposal of course!*

Negotiating pictures are not like regular pictures! Pictures like the ones I take for negotiating are staged—something like making a Hollywood movie where timing is most important. All the actors (the tenants) must be in their proper places, dressed in their native attire. Needless to say, the pictures I take will not be the least bit flattering. The pictures I took of Miller Street were solely to assist me in obtaining a favorable selling price should Miller Street eventually become available for sale.

All the actors (tenants) at Miller Street were pretty much available for picture taking most any time because seldom did they ever leave the property much before noon. My picture taking began about midmorning, and it took me almost a full hour to snap one roll of film. Unlike making regular movies, my pictures needed to be taken without the actors' looking at my camera. I stayed out of sight, hidden behind the bushy shrubs between two old storage buildings across the street.

From Investor to Paparazzi

The two young men living in the light tan house in the rear would definitely win my vote for the Academy Award on this day! Apparently, they were raising baby pitbulls inside their house. Both men were shirtless, and both had colorful tattoos almost everywhere. My pictures clearly showed them playing with three different midsized puppies on the living room carpet. *They had the front door propped wide open.* The mommy and daddy pitbulls were chained to a small oak tree in the narrow side yard, and their chains had almost cut through the tree from the dogs circling around it. Five pitbulls living in one small house—Wow! Insurance companies will often cancel an owner's liability policy with just one of these cute little dope dealer playmates!

Filming the way I do takes a little time and patience since it's best not to be observed. I shot 24 pictures to make sure I had all the bases covered, even though I usually only need 5 or 6 good ones for negotiating. Almost every picture clearly showed the lack of supervision and how ugly and rundown Miller Street had become. I had pictures of dead grass, shrubs turning brown from lack of water, and a dozen or more nonrunning autos jacked up on concrete blocks or sittin' on stacks of old tires. There were so many broken-down cars at Miller Street that I decided not to come back in the evening the way I normally would do when after-hours festivities draw additional people and even more cars to the property.

One of my *most creative shots* was a picture of black mold growing up the stucco wall on the larger pink house in front where a leaking air conditioner line was spraying water on the house. Just guessing but I would judge the leak had been squirting water for at least a year or so because the whole bottom half of the wall was oozing a dark colored slime. Apparently, no one but me had even noticed. Although it's easy enough to clean off, color photos somehow make a wet moldy wall look much worse than it is. Of course, most landlord–apartment owners or their managers already know that just the mere mention of mold conjures up visions of health department citations, sniffer tests, and lawsuits—*everyone, that is,* except the Five Star Management Co.

The Letter to the Miller Street Owners

You'll notice that my letter is *nonconfrontational.* I don't blame the owners in any way for the property's terrible condition. I don't even mention Five Star Management Co. by name! I place the blame solely on the tenants so as not to offend any of the parties I might have to work with should I strike up a deal later on. As you can see, my letter offers an inexpensive way out for the owners if they are even slightly leaning toward selling. You'll notice I don't mention selling until the fourth paragraph. *First, I offer my fix-up or rehab services.* Once in a while, folks will ask me for a cost estimate to fix up their property. Once they hear my estimate of costs, that normally brings them back to a discussion about selling instead.

Dear Mr. and Mrs. Sullivan:

My name is Jay. I'm a property owner–investor in Redding, California. During the past few years, I've been acquiring small rundown rental properties that need fix-up and rehabilitation work. I have a small crew that does the work, and I've kept most of these properties as rental units. Occasionally, my crew does fix-up work for other local property owners when they are not working on my projects.

The reason I'm writing this letter is because I drive past your houses on Miller Street several times every week on my way to my property only three blocks north of yours. During the past year or so, I can't help but notice how junky and rundown the houses have become. I remember just two years ago that they were the nicest looking houses on the block. It's my guess that whoever manages your property has allowed the wrong kind of tenants to live there. This is exactly what happened to me! I can tell you from experience that the wrong kind of tenants will tear up a property faster than I can fix it. I tried four different managers when I had my Sacramento property, and things only got worse. Never again will I own property where I don't live. It cost me over $100,000 to learn the hard way.

The big problem was the tenants. Since all property managers were competing with each other, they seemed to take almost anyone who showed up with rent money and a deposit. Of course, once the house was rented, that was it—the manager never seemed to have the time to check out how they lived! Believe me, the wrong tenants will totally destroy any property. They leave their junk all over and accumulate nonrunning cars. And naturally, almost everyone has pets—*usually destructive pets*. In Redding, I've never found a property manager I've been happy with. I've tried hard, believe me, but I have always ended up taking over again. I can tell you that owners are the only ones who seem to care about property upkeep.

If you should ever need help with any fix-up or rehab, I've enclosed my business card and telephone number. When you're in town, take a quick drive by my six houses at 8001 Miller, just north of yours. Also check out my eight units a couple blocks east at 1112 Tenth Avenue. You'll get an idea of how I rehabilitate and maintain my properties. Also, if you should ever think about selling, please allow me to make you an offer. Naturally, there would be no commission to pay, and quite frankly, when seller financing can be used, I've found that owners can sometimes net-out twice as much income from monthly mortgage payments as they were receiveing previously from expensive property managers.

I've enclosed several recent pictures of your property to show you exactly what I mean about the tenants. They can really mess up a nice property in no time at all when managers allow them to do as they please. As I already mentioned, I had my expensive lesson in Sacramento, 160 miles away where I couldn't keep an eye on what was happening. I'll never make that mistake again. Please call me any time if I can be of assistance.

Sincerely,
Jay
Enclosed: Six photos

Over the years, cold-call letters, like this one, have been exceptionally profitable for me. It takes only three or four deals like Miller Street to make you a millionaire, *or very close*. I write these letters only when I sense that something is drastically wrong. Naturally, I'll do my homework (investigate) before I grab my pen. With Miller Street, it was obvious from just driving by that something was seriously out of whack. My *letter-to-the-owner technique* is one of the best ways I know of to position yourself so you end up dealing directly, one-on-one, with the property owner who has reason for concern. In all probability, he or she has no idea what's happening at his or her property because it's *a thousand miles away*.

Real Estate Cycles Are Worth Big Bucks

Real estate activity is greatly affected by **up and down selling cycles**. Buying and selling in the right cycle is extremely important, as well as very profitable. For example, in my town there's generally about a 20 percent price swing between the cycles. In a buyers' cycle, there's a good supply of properties available but only a few buyers looking. The buyers are on top, and they can pick and choose, and, in my experience, they are able to buy properties about 20 percent cheaper. That means a $500,000 property could likely be purchased for about $400,000. I think you would agree that $100,000 is a big wad of dough for simply buying at the right time (in the right cycle).

Naturally, it's exactly opposite in a sellers' cycle. Lots of ready and willing buyers are available, but there are only a few properties to choose from. If I should choose to sell in this period, I can probably sell my $500,000 property for around $600,000 simply because I picked the right cycle for selling *and for no other reason*. Over the years I have made a lot of *bonus profits*, as I call them, merely by doing my deals in the correct cycles. Correct cycle for me, that is! Miller Street was no exception. No one seemed very interested in seven junky houses when I began to negotiate for Miller Street.

My letter got an immediate response from San Diego. I'm certain the owners were somewhat shocked looking at my pictures, but they didn't let on a great deal during our conversation—only that they knew there were management problems and that they had been exploring a change. Unfortunately, Five Star is not a whole lot different from most local management companies, but I kept that opinion to myself. Our telephone conversation didn't last more than four or five minutes. It was friendly, but not much else. It would be more than a month before we would talk again.

As with most California real estate, the prices always seem too high to most folks, even during a recession. *Buying and selling cycles come and go*, but the retail prices never seem to go down very much no matter what. It's almost as if real estate prices are tied to the same pricing formula as gasoline. When prices go up, it's by great big chunks. Coming down, the numbers are smaller than a bikini! Where I live, the values have soared, but the rents have lagged behind. Investors today are paying a great deal more for rental units (price per door) than I would have ever imagined when I began buying years ago. *To be successful*, you must know true values inside and out and how much income (rents) the property will generate. You must know these values *both before and after fix-up* if you intend to profit using adding-value techniques.

Out-of-Town Buyers Often Pay Too Much

Almost 95 percent of all small-time start-out investors overpay for income properties. It gets worse when they buy properties away from home where they seldom spend the time to learn true values and the rental market. The Miller Street owners were no exception. However, lucky for me, they had paid a substantial down payment (about 35 percent); otherwise, they would have been upside down in the property. Auto sales people use the term *upside down* to explain that you owe more on your car than it's worth! Because Miller Street was allowed to run down and become unattractive, the rents were lagging behind. I figured they were at least $100 less than they should have been, maybe more.

I will never know for sure, but I had heard rumors that several potential buyers had been looking at Miller Street, *but looking was all that ever happened*. Eventually my phone rang, and the owners seemed willing to negotiate. They told me that Five Star Management Co. had asked them for a listing to sell the property, but of course by this time, the owners were totally fed up with Five Star! Miller Street still had the same two vacancies, just as it did when I visited Beth in the laundry room. By now, the owners had quit talking to Five Star altogether. They felt totally betrayed, and, obviously, signing their listing agreement was completely out of the question.

My First Offer Met with Rejection

It's extremely difficult to purchase properties when sellers have very little equity. For example, let's say a motivated seller is asking $500,000 for her dumpy rundown property but has a $400,000 mortgage on it. Let's say that I'm willing to pay $375,000, which, of course, is less than the mortgage debt. To accept my offer, the seller would have to pay me $25,000 to take her property. It's a very emotional roadblock for most people, even though it might benefit them financially.

On the other hand, with a bit more equity, the seller might very well do the deal. With a mortgage of $350,000, my offer would still net the seller a little spending money rather than insult her. It's for this reason that I won't waste my time pursuing deals with marginal equity. I've found that sellers who paid too much to begin with will seldom agree to take a loss without a fight. Fortunately for me, the owners' large down payment (approximately 35 percent) at Miller Street created enough equity so my offer would not insult them.

My initial offer was $300,000. I knew it was a bit low, but it was about the same amount the owners had paid. Also, the market had suddenly turned sluggish. *We were entering a buyers' market cycle.* There was a time in bygone years when $43,000 per door would be a top-selling price in my town for seven junky houses on a large single lot. It didn't take more than 60 seconds for the sellers to inform me that *bygones are bygones* and they were gonna stay that way. The sellers even jabbed me a little about the "sky-high" prices in San Diego. "A shack on the beach," one of the sellers said, "*goes for a million-two.*" I reminded him that prices are much cheaper a thousand miles away when you don't have a beach. *Also*, a large percentage of our tenants work at places like Wal-Mart and Burger King. *I could have mentioned that half of his renters didn't even work at all,* but I didn't. You must never insult the sellers when you're tryin' to "steal" their property.

Investors Must Know Rents and Values

Sales in my town indicated that most investors would be willing to pay about *nine times the gross rents* for a property generating $42,000 annual income. Had all seven houses been rented for $500 each, that's what the income would be. Vacancies are generally not counted during early negotiations. Obviously, *nine times the gross rents* made my $300,000 offer seem a bit low. Still, the property was badly rundown and looked awful. I knew that most investors in my area would not offer much more. Most would not even be interested at all once they saw who lived there.

Out-of-town owners who rely on property managers for information on *property values* and *rental rates* are at a big disadvantage when it comes to the property's potential. Managers will charge whatever rents the market will bear. However, value is primarily based on location and how desirable the units are. Miller Street was well located, but its rundown condition severely limited the amount of rent most tenants would pay to live there. In fact, when a property looks as ugly as Miller Street, most decent tenants won't live there. I'm absolutely certain the owners had no idea how low rents were at Miller Street compared to average units. In my judgment, $650 to $700 would have been about right *if the property were cleaned up and looked presentable*. The average selling price for decent looking properties in good locations would have been somewhere around *11 or 12 times gross rents*—Wow!

Seller Financing: The Secret Is Good Credit

The owners countered my offer with their own version of the value: $400,000. I remember thinking, "maybe I should send more pictures." But about then, they agreed to carry part of the financing, which immediately softened me up. They did agree to a $15,000 credit for cleanup (the first one I'd ever received), so we ceased negotiations and settled on a price of $385,000. The price was fair in my view—*not an absolute steal* but certainly good for both sides. As it turned out, they required a down payment of only $25,000 after running me through a thorough financial check.

Students continually ask me how I get sellers to agree to carry back financing for me. What's my big secret? The real secret, my friends, is having good credit and keeping it that way. The very first thing most knowledgeable sellers will do is to run a credit check on potential buyers, *as they should*.

I always provide sellers with a current **profit and loss statement**. I also provide my **financial statement** showing my assets and liabilities Last, and perhaps most important, I provide a **complete list of all my rental properties**: addresses, mortgage amounts and payments, and the people I send the checks to with their names, addresses, and telephone numbers. With this information, sellers can get a very clear picture of how I run my business. That's the **big secret to how I convince sellers** to carry my mortgage.

Transactions like the Miller Street deal are basically hidden from the public. It's just me and the seller, one-on-one! This transaction was set up by my cold-call letter so no one else even knew the property was available. You can effectively eliminate all your competition using this method. And although cold-call letters have accounted for only about 15 percent of my total buying, these deals offer *more opportunities* for creativity. Obviously, a major selling benefit to the sellers is that they can avoid paying any selling commission when dealing directly with a buyer like me.

The Guts of the Miller Street Transaction

As I said earlier, I didn't steal Miller Street. Still, it was a good transaction for both sides. In fact, doing this type of transaction (fair for everyone) is how you get sellers to finance their properties for you. You treat them fairly so they like doing business with you. The sellers agreed to my small down payment of $25,000 and an interest rate of approximately 6 percent, and I agreed to take over (or assume) the existing first mortgage with an unpaid balance of $183,400. The sellers would then carry back a promissory note and deed of trust for the balance of the sale price (the sellers' equity). Here's how the deal looked:

Selling price agreed to	$385,000
Cash down payment	25,000
Jay will assume mortgage debt (subject to) or take over payments	183,400
Seller will carry back balance, second mortgage (terms of sale)	176,600

At an average cost per house of $55,000, my rent-to-value ratio was 0.09 percent (rent divided by the asset value). I try very hard to achieve a minimum rent-to-value ratio of 1 percent, which equals a 12 percent annual rent return. However, as I mentioned earlier, the $500 rents at Miller Street were extremely low in my opinion. The biggest problem I would have would be covering my expenses and mortgage payments with the current income. Paying the existing first mortgage would be easy enough to do, *but the new seller carryback mortgage* would put me in the red. I would need a little extra help from the sellers to make my dollars stretch.

Looking at the property analysis form in Figure 14-1, you can see my problem. After covering my expenses and the existing first mortgage payments, I would have only $367.86 left to pay the sellers' carryback mortgage. There was simply not nearly enough income generated by the houses to pay the sellers a reasonable amount for their equity. Offering to pay just $368 per month for the sellers' equity of $176,600 would be an insult, in my opinion. You must not insult the sellers if you expect their cooperation! In this case, the sellers had agreed to accept my small down payment and carry back a major part of the financing. The $368 cash flow shown on line 14 of my property analysis form was not a reasonable amount to pay for the sellers' equity, *nor was it a fair amount*!

The first thing I always do is prepare a *property analysis form* to determine how a property looks financially. This form will save you lots of future heartaches if you use it for every property you acquire. It makes you thoroughly analyze how you'll be able to pay for property. Many times you can't, and of course, **that's the point**! It's also an excellent negotiating tool when you and the sellers are sitting side by side discussing the income and expenses.

As you can plainly see on the property analysis form, my operating income (line 12)—what would be left after expenses—was $1,632. The payments I had agreed to take over—that is, the payments on the existing first mortgage—would be $1,264.14 per month. That would leave me only $367.86 to pay the sellers' carryback mortgage of $176,600. As I just told you, offering the sellers a whimpy 2.5 percent interest payment on their generous carryback mortgage would put me in the same category as Five Star Management Co. in the sellers' minds. Besides, I wouldn't accept such a ridiculous offer if I were the sellers! It was simply not a fair rate. The first mortgage interest rate was 6.5 percent.

Certainly, the sellers were motivated, *but they were not stupid*. I decided to ask for terms that would allow me to pay smaller payments initially and then pay increasing amounts as I began fixing up the property and raising my rents. Interest rates of 6 to 7 percent were about right for the times, so I decided to ask for what I call **my variable-rate 6 percent mortgage**.

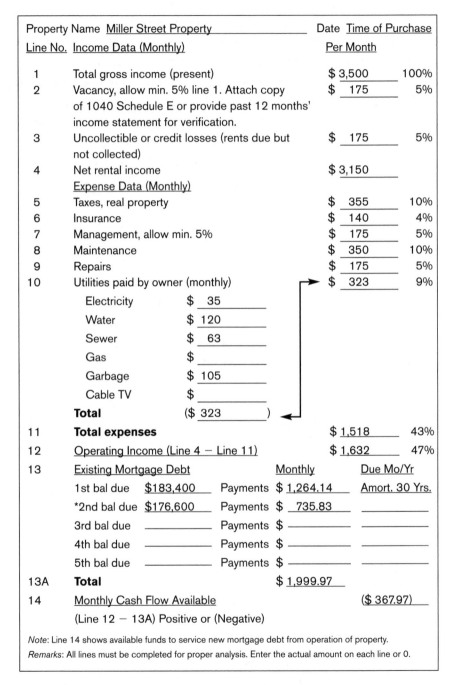

Property Name Miller Street Property		Date Time of Purchase	
Line No. Income Data (Monthly)		Per Month	
1	Total gross income (present)	$ 3,500	100%
2	Vacancy, allow min. 5% line 1. Attach copy of 1040 Schedule E or provide past 12 months' income statement for verification.	$ 175	5%
3	Uncollectible or credit losses (rents due but not collected)	$ 175	5%
4	Net rental income	$ 3,150	
	Expense Data (Monthly)		
5	Taxes, real property	$ 355	10%
6	Insurance	$ 140	4%
7	Management, allow min. 5%	$ 175	5%
8	Maintenance	$ 350	10%
9	Repairs	$ 175	5%
10	Utilities paid by owner (monthly)	$ 323	9%

Electricity	$ 35	
Water	$ 120	
Sewer	$ 63	
Gas	$	
Garbage	$ 105	
Cable TV	$	
Total	($ 323)	

11	**Total expenses**	$ 1,518	43%
12	Operating Income (Line 4 − Line 11)	$ 1,632	47%

13	Existing Mortgage Debt		Monthly	Due Mo/Yr
	1st bal due	$183,400	Payments $ 1,264.14	Amort. 30 Yrs.
	*2nd bal due	$176,600	Payments $ 735.83	
	3rd bal due		Payments $	
	4th bal due		Payments $	
	5th bal due		Payments $	
13A	**Total**		$ 1,999.97	
14	Monthly Cash Flow Available			($ 367.97)
	(Line 12 − 13A) Positive or (Negative)			

Note: Line 14 shows available funds to service new mortgage debt from operation of property.

Remarks: All lines must be completed for proper analysis. Enter the actual amount on each line or 0.

Figure 14-1. Income property analysis form, Miller Street Property

Simply stated, my variable-rate mortgage means that I pay less interest in the first several years but more interest later on. I've found that sellers like this arrangement much better than accepting a fixed but lesser interest rate for their carrybacks. The variable-rate mortgage means that they get market rates, eventually but they agree to accept softer payments initially to make the deal work.

Jay's 6 percent variable-rate note

Year 1 (mos. 1–12)	Pymts. shall be $735.83	Int. only 5.0%
Year 2 (mos. 13–24)	Pymts. shall be $809.41	Int. only 5.5%
Year 3 (mos. 25–36)	Pymts. shall be $883.00	Int. only 6.0%
Year 4 (mos. 37–48)	Pymts. shall be $956.58	Int. only 6.5%
Year 5 (mos. 49–60)	Pymts. shall be $1,030.16	Int. only 7.0%
Year 6 (mos. 61–180)	Pymts. shall be $1,058.82	P&I 6.0%

Beginning in year 6, payments shall include both principal and interest at 6 percent using a 30-year amortization payment schedule with the entire mortgage (principal and interest) due and payable at the end of 15 years.

In this case, I did not ask for the full 30-year payback term because the sellers had already mentioned that they didn't mind carrying the paper for 10 or 15 years, and I stayed with their suggestion. However, the payment schedule can be whatever you and the sellers agree to. In acquiring Miller Street, I felt that starting at the 5 percent rate would net the sellers more income than the amount they were receiving from Five Star Management (the monthly owners' draw), especially since there were still two vacant houses when I took over.

The obvious question you're probably asking yourself as you compare my proposed note payment schedule and the property analysis form is this: "With only $367.86 cash flow, how can Jay come up with a payment of $735.83? Does he have to pony up the shortage of $367.97, or what? It looks like a negative cash flow to me!"

It's true that my property analysis form showed a negative cash flow. However, the form has some built-in safety valves for us do-it-yourself investors. For example, who would get the $175 management fee? If you guessed Jay, give yourself a gold star! Also, approximately 70 percent of the maintenance and repair expenses would be labor costs (lines 8 and 9: $350 plus $175 equals $525 times 70 percent equal $367). Since Jay would be doing the labor, he would get that too. So, although the chart shows $367.97 negative, that amount would be offset by the amounts I would earn from the management fee and my personal labor for the maintenance and repairs expenses.

My Terms Were Acceptable

Quite often I'm asked, "Where do you find sellers who will carry the financing and accept small down payments like Miller Street?" My general answer is, "**You must look for the right situations!**" Situations are created by both the property and the sellers. The Miller Street owners were older sellers who did not wish to trade their equity for another property (as in a 1031 exchange). They were obviously concerned with the tax consequences of their sale, so my small down payment worked well for them. Installment selling is the next best method to postpone taxes if you don't wish to trade.

The key to this installment sale was my good credit and proof that I was financially responsible. Providing my personal financial statement, my profit and loss statement, and my current list of properties that I own that also showed the names and addresses of folks I send mortgage payments to (beneficiaries) did the trick! One of the routine provisions in my offers when I'm asking sellers to carry back financing for me is to offer them my financial documents so that they can determine my creditworthiness. I offer them this information through the escrow company *right after the sellers accept my offer*. Naturally the offer is contingent upon the sellers' approval of my financial documents. This approach works nearly every time, and it's one of the important buying techniques I teach every student at my Fixer Camps.

Creating Beauty Was Cheaper Than I Thought

My average costs for fixing up rundown properties like Miller Street normally run about 20 percent of the purchase price for heavy fixers and 10 percent for light fixers. Looking at the nasty pictures I took, you'd swear that 20 percent would never get the job done! For the Miller street property, 20 percent of my purchase price would be $77,000. As it turned out, the entire job cost under $46,000—*the labor accounting for 75 percent ($35,000).* That's a bit higher than my average labor cost, but the job involved a lot more trips to the dump and extra cleanup. I spent less on actual fix-up work. Fourteen months after I started, Miller Street was a beautiful sight to see! It was now the nicest looking property on the block. Only one tenant stayed with me throughout the fix-up. *You probably already guessed:* It was Beth! Remember Beth from the laundry room? She finally got things figured out. She knows now that I'm not really an electrician and that I'm no longer waiting for my boss!

Are We Millionaires Yet?

About three years after acquiring the Miller Street property, my average rents had soared to $750 per month. Just for practice, grab your red pen and plot the new income and expense numbers on the property analysis form. You'll quickly discover that this is the type of property you need to own to have any chance whatsoever of making the next Forbes millionaires list!

Medium-priced rental units in decent locations in my town were selling for at least **11 times the gross rents**. This means that the seven houses renting for $750 each (7 times $750) would result in $5,250 per month. The annual income of $63,000 times 11 equals $693,000. My equity now would be about half the new value. If I were to suddenly sell out and decide to never again look into the smiling faces of my Miller Street tenants, I could pretty much figure on a $700,000 sale without much effort. By offering good terms like 10 percent down ($70,000) and seller financing for the balance ($630,000), I could use a wraparound mortgage or contract *for 7 percent interest with reasonable payments of $3,695 per month.* This would create a net income for me of $1,372 per month for years to come—*even more after the underlying mortgage debt was paid off.* How many properties like Miller Street would you need to own before you became financially independent? I'll let you decide for yourself!

15

Making Big Bucks with Private Mortgages

Standing back about 200 yards didn't help much! If anything, the old apartment building looked even uglier than it did standing up close. Years of neglect, lack of management, and out-of-town owners were clearly showing on the old converted two-story building. Over the years, the once stately Victorian had become a junky looking apartment building with 10 units. The "For Sale By Owner" (FSBO) sign was no longer visible to passers-by, having long since been trampled in the weeds and deteriorated by time.

Almost every local real estate agent had tried to sell the property, but the looks, plus the fact that it had been a large house converted to apartments, frightened away all the looky-loos. All but one, that is—my student Paul. Paul was somewhat inexperienced, even though he had acquired a duplex and one single-family house since attending my Fixer Camp. Inexperienced, yes, but his new knowledge about fixer houses had turned on the light. "Maybe," he thought, *"just maybe*, this is the type of property Jay teaches about!" Before Paul called me, he had been out to visit the property at least 20 times, he said, and each time he looked, he came away a little bit more confused. Still, the old building kept drawing him back.

I couldn't possibly count the number of times I've gone back to revisit different properties *over and over again*, trying to figure out some plan that might work. It's almost as if I can feel some mysterious urge deep inside telling me, "There's truly an opportunity here. *What must I do to sieze it?*" That's exactly the dilemma Paul faced each time he drove back for another look. Twenty different trips to visit one property might sound like the all-time record, but I assured Paul that it wasn't enough to win the gold medal. There's no question that I made at least that many trips before I finally acquired the Hillcrest Cottages, and I'm guessing I made even more before I was able to muster up enough courage to purchase the old Ripley Hotel.

Planning and Thinking Are More Important Than Speed

Victoria Gardens stood out like a sore thumb, mostly because it was such an ugly building. The paint job looked like the final stages of leprosy, and the obscene color was totally out of sync with the neighborhood. *And as far as any gardens on the property*, the only plants that were still alive was a giant cactus in the front yard and several ugly bamboo stalks along the driveway. Surprisingly enough, there were only three vacant apartments, but that was only because the rents were so cheap. However, there was a great deal of confusion about who was actually paying, and when!

It wasn't until we started snoopin' around, *doing some Lieutenant Columbo–type detective work*, that we discovered that the property had been listed yet again with another local real estate agent. When Paul called the new agent, he was told that the owner was an out-of-town real estate agent who was extremely motivated to sell the property. The local agent told Paul that 10 percent cash down would likely be acceptable and that his client would be perfectly willing to carry the financing. The only problem, he said, was that there were four existing private-party mortgages on the property, and three of them were several payments behind.

Of course, new financing would fix all this, he said, so there shouldn't be much of a problem.

According to the local agent, if the building were painted and all three vacancies were rented, it should easily appraise for $400,000. Armed with this information, Paul trotted straight down to see the local bank manager to get his opinion and, hopefully, a new mortgage. This was Paul's first bank visit and his introduction into the world of commercial financing. He was about to find out what most bankers think of older, nonconforming junky real estate. It was a painful lesson that Paul wouldn't soon forget.

Bankers Consider Junk Property a Waste of Time

As it turned out, the bank manager was already somewhat familiar with Victoria Gardens. He also knew about the delinquent mortgages on the property. He promptly advised Paul that the property was **far too risky** and most certainly the bank would not be interested in making any new loans. "In fact," he explained, "it's the first time I've even heard of four separate mortgages on a single property." He said that the bank was allowed to make only first lien mortgages. "Occasionally," he said, "we might offer a second, but that would certainly be our limit! As things stand right now, any one of the four mortgage holders has the right to foreclose on the property any time because of the property's rundown condition. That's even if all the payments are current! The reason is because the owner has allowed the security for the mortgages to deteriorate. You'll find that it's one of the terms written in most mortgages or trust deeds."

Confused would be an understatement when Paul called to discuss this deal with me. Needless to say, his introduction into the world of banking had left him with some serious doubts about the whole stinkin' mess. "It's no wonder they haven't sold this building," he said. "*What a can of worms this is!*" Before I let Paul hang up the phone, I said to him, "Bankers will never understand us creative types of investors. But regardless of what the banker says, I still believe we have a good shot at making something happen here." Suddenly there was a pause and dead silence on my phone. Then finally, I heard a barely audible, "*Okay, Jay!*"

Benefits Are Just Like Gold: They Take Some Digging

By now, I wasn't the only one talking to Paul on the phone. The broker was calling him too. He said his client would sell the apartment for $280,000 and that his client had agreed to credit the buyer for all the delinquent mortgage payments from the cash down payment money. In other words, Paul would still be responsible to make up the missed mortgage payments, but whatever that amount was, he could deduct it from his $20,000 down payment. I advised Paul to do it: "Write the offer, and let's get it signed! I think we're on to something here!" I'm only guessing, but I'm almost certain that Paul thought I had lost all my marbles.

An electrician by trade, Paul saw no problem fixing up the old building, but he would need additional guidance working with the delinquent mortgages. As Paul had learned at Fixer Camp, any time you can find a property like Victoria Gardens with four privately held mortgages and a seller willing to carry part of the financing, you've got the ingredients for a very profitable deal! Now it was up to Paul to test his newly acquired knowledge.

Income properties like Victoria Gardens with multiple private mortgages get that way from *churning*. That means the property keeps getting sold over and over again. With each subsequent sale, the new buyer typically pays a small down payment, then agrees to take over, or assume, the payments on the existing mortgages. An additional mortgage will be created for the balance of the seller's equity; *hence, with each new sale*, another private mortgage gets added to the property.

One of my favorite profit opportunities over the years has come from buying mortgage debt. Buying debt can be extremely profitable when it's done in connection with acquiring distressed properties like Victoria Gardens. I'm always searching for income properties with **multiple private mortgages**. When I'm lucky enough to find one with four mortgages, like Victoria Gardens, I will sometimes pay a little extra to acquire it. Quite often, real estate agents will steer their clients away from properties like Victoria Gardens with its multiple private mortgages, claiming that *they're simply too much hassle*. At the very least, they'll suggest their client should obtain a brand new mortgage to clean up the mess, as they often call it. If you buy rundown properties as I do, you should never allow this to happen! If your agent keeps insisting, fire him or her immediately. Let me show you why.

Buying Debt Can Be Extremely Profitable

Buying debt means that I contact the beneficiaries or mortgage holders, offering them a chance to receive immediate cash payoffs rather than continue to receive monthly payments. Naturally, my immediate cash payoffs would be discounted, which means that the mortgage holders would get less than what's owed on their mortgage balances. Perhaps you might be thinking, "Why in the world would people take less money than what they're owed?" There are many different reasons, but it often boils down to the risk. In the Victoria Gardens case, the security for the mortgage debt was an ugly rundown apartment building suffering from serious neglect and constant churning.

Let's assume for a moment that you had once owned Victoria Gardens. You sold the property to an investor and carried back a mortgage for the larger share of your equity. You've since retired and moved 2,000 miles away from the area. In the beginning, you received your payments like clockwork. But lately, they've been showing up way past the due date, and several payments have been skipped altogether! You've talked to the owner on the telephone, and he admits that he's struggling but hopes he can do better. *The big question for you is*, what can you do to protect your financial interest in the property?

Aside from crossing your fingers and hoping for the best, your choices are rather slim. The only legal recourse you have is to foreclose the property for nonpayment or a default under the terms of your mortgage. For most mortgage holders, the idea of taking back a junky property like Victoria Gardens, filled with deadbeat tenants, is not very appealing. The next question you must ask yourself, assuming you don't want the property back, is, how much would you be willing to take to be free of the problem? *Remember*, if a mortgage holder senior to yours decides to foreclose and you do nothing to protect your interest, *such as make up the payments and pay the foreclosure expenses*, you'll lose everything. Your mortgage will get totally wiped out, and you'll end up with nothing except memories.

Victoria Gardens had four existing mortgages (promissory notes) accumulated from past sales, or *churning*. Each mortgage was assumable, and three had long-term payoffs, with attractive under-market interest rates. All had monthly payments, and, as Paul discovered, three of the four mortgages were behind in their payments.

Contacting the Mortgage Holders

Always ask for copies of the mortgages or promissory notes immediately after you open escrow so that you can personally verify exactly what's owed, delinquent payments, and the balances. You also need to know the payoff dates. Paul and I determined that the existing mortgage balances were $61,000, $52,500, $40,260, and $75,400. The seller agreed to carry back a new fifth mortgage for the balance of his equity with payments for 10 years. The mortgage would have a subordination clause that would allow Paul to refinance as long his new loan did not exceed the total amount of the senior mortgage debt—meaning *the four mortgages ahead of the seller's carryback mortgage.*

Paul and I obtained the addresses of all four beneficiaries (mortgage holders) and quietly began to negotiate with each of them. I say "quietly," because you don't want your discounted offers known to anyone else except the party you're dealing with until all negotiations with each of the beneficiaries have been completed. As things turned out, three of the four mortgage holders were more than happy to "bail out," as I call it.

Our very first contact, the $61,000 mortgage holder, agreed to take Paul's $38,000 worth of telephone company stock in exchange for his mortgage. That trade eliminated a $575 monthly payment. The holder of the second mortgage with a balance of $52,500 did not wish to discount at all; *he told Paul he'd rather continue receiving monthly payments.* The holder of the $40,260 mortgage quickly exchanged his mortgage debt for a small mountain cabin and fishing boat that Paul had inherited from his father. Paul said it was a good deal for him because he never had much time to use it. That trade eliminated another $400 monthly payment.

Paul's next move was to secure a new loan on the property for the purpose of rehabbing the building and, hopefully, buying out the remaining mortgage ($75,400) at a reasonable discount. All by himself, with very little help from his teacher, Paul negotiated a $45,000 all-cash payoff, contingent upon his obtaining a new $100,000 loan. The mortgage holder did insist on a 30-day loan escrow, but when it took 65 days to fund, the mortgage holder decided that he'd grab the $45,000 before, anyone had a change of heart. He took the money and disappeared! We were hoping only for a reasonable discount, but Paul got a whopping 40 percent reduction; furthermore, that payoff eliminated another $700 mortgage payment. The balance of Paul's new loan ($55,000) would be more than enough to fix up Victoria Gardens.

The Result: Cash Flow Plus $216,660 Equity for the Effort

Paul had truly discovered a gold mine where at first glance most investors would have visualized only the shaft! After all the dust finally settled, my good friend was now the proud owner of a newly rehabbed apartment building worth at least $400,000. Only three mortgages remained, totaling $183,340, meaning that Paul's equity was $216,660. The old mortgage payments Paul had eliminated ($1,675) were more than enough to make the payments on his new $100,000 loan. In addition, the new loan gave Paul most of his down payment money back, *plus all his fix-up costs*. In less than a year, rents were increased an average of $45 per unit, turning the old victorian into Paul's private "money machine." Looking at the newly rehabbed Victoria Gardens with its white picket fences, shiny new paint job, and "born-again" lawns, it kinda makes you wonder why it took Paul so many visits before the lights came on!

Deals like this are not uncommon when you **look for situations** and **opportunities**, not just properties. I must point out here that Paul did not find a good deal; **he found an opportunity with potential to create a good deal**. Negotiating with the people involved is what turned Victoria Gardens into a winner. Quite often, investors like Paul will arrange for a new loan first, then attempt to secure discounted payoff commitments from all the mortgage holders before closing escrow and becoming the new owner. *I much prefer to close escrow first*, then present myself to the mortgage holders as just another struggling investor *without much money*, who can promise the beneficiaries only that I'll try my very best to keep the apartment building up and running. Painting this kind of image creates a great deal of uncertainty, and obviously it translates to a much higher risk if you're a mortgage holder living 2,000 miles away.

For do-it-yourself investors like Paul, there's no better game in town, when it comes to creating quick cash flow, than buying junky looking properties with multiple private mortgages and *then working with beneficiaries to buy down the mortgage debt*. Paul's efforts reduced $63,000 from the purchase price before he ever painted a single board or fixed a toilet! Remember, look for the benefits first. The property is the vehicle to take you to them.

Summary of the Victoria Gardens Transaction

Figure 15-1 shows the Victoria Gardens transaction: part 1 was the close of escrow; part 2 was how the mortgages were revised; and part 3 shows the mortgages after revisions.

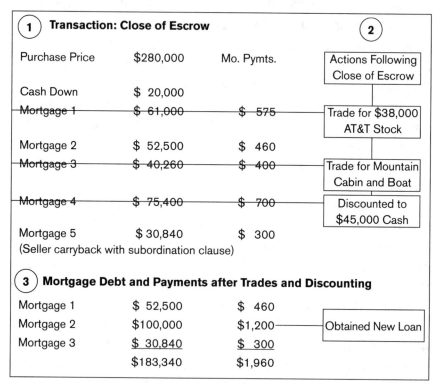

Figure 15-1. Victoria Gardens transaction

Figure 15-2 shows the property analysis form before fix-up. Figure 15-3 shows the property analysis form after fix-up. Figure 15-4 provides an explanation of Figure 15-3—that is, who gets the money.

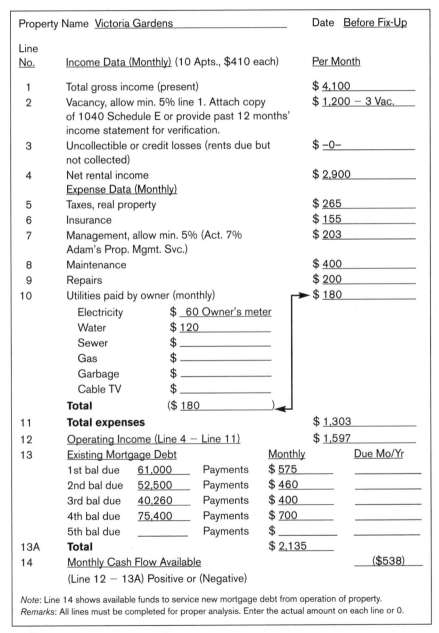

Line No.		Per Month
Property Name Victoria Gardens		Date Before Fix-Up
	Income Data (Monthly) (10 Apts., $410 each)	Per Month
1	Total gross income (present)	$ 4,100
2	Vacancy, allow min. 5% line 1. Attach copy of 1040 Schedule E or provide past 12 months' income statement for verification.	$ 1,200 − 3 Vac.
3	Uncollectible or credit losses (rents due but not collected)	$ −0−
4	Net rental income	$ 2,900
	Expense Data (Monthly)	
5	Taxes, real property	$ 265
6	Insurance	$ 155
7	Management, allow min. 5% (Act. 7% Adam's Prop. Mgmt. Svc.)	$ 203
8	Maintenance	$ 400
9	Repairs	$ 200
10	Utilities paid by owner (monthly)	$ 180

Line 10 detail:

Electricity	$ 60 Owner's meter
Water	$ 120
Sewer	$
Gas	$
Garbage	$
Cable TV	$
Total	($ 180)

11	**Total expenses**	$ 1,303	
12	Operating Income (Line 4 − Line 11)	$ 1,597	
13	Existing Mortgage Debt	Monthly	Due Mo/Yr

13				Monthly	Due Mo/Yr
	1st bal due	61,000	Payments	$ 575	
	2nd bal due	52,500	Payments	$ 460	
	3rd bal due	40,260	Payments	$ 400	
	4th bal due	75,400	Payments	$ 700	
	5th bal due		Payments	$	
13A	**Total**			$ 2,135	
14	Monthly Cash Flow Available				($538)
	(Line 12 − 13A) Positive or (Negative)				

Note: Line 14 shows available funds to service new mortgage debt from operation of property.
Remarks: All lines must be completed for proper analysis. Enter the actual amount on each line or 0.

Figure 15-2. Income property analysis form, Victoria Gardens before fix-up

Investing in Gold Mine Houses

Property Name Victoria Gardens   Date   After Fix-Up

Line No.	Income Data (Monthly)		Per Month
1	Total gross income (present)		$ 4,550
2	Vacancy, allow min. 5% line 1. Attach copy of 1040 Schedule E or provide past 12 months' income statement for verification.		$ 230
3	Uncollectible or credit losses (rents due but not collected)		$ 230
4	Net rental income		
	Expense Data (Monthly)		$ 4,090
5	Taxes, real property		$ 235
6	Insurance		$ 160
7	Management, allow min. 5%		$ 455
8	Maintenance		$ 455
9	Repairs		$ 227
10	Utilities paid by owner (monthly)		$ 205
	Electricity	$ 60 Owner's meter	
	Water	$ 145	
	Sewer	$	
	Gas	$	
	Garbage	$	
	Cable TV	$	
	Total	($ 205)	
11	**Total expenses**		$ 1,737
12	Operating Income (Line 4 − Line 11)		$ 2,353

13	Existing Mortgage Debt		Monthly	Due Mo/Yr
	1st bal due	52,500	Payments $ 460	Amort.
	2nd bal due	30,840	Payments $ 300	Until paid
	3rd bal due	100,000	Payments $ 1,200	10 years
	4th bal due		Payments $	
	5th bal due		Payments $	
13A	**Total**		$ 1,960	
14	Monthly Cash Flow Available (Line 12 − 13A) Positive or (Negative)		$393	

Note: Line 14 shows available funds to service new mortgage debt from operation of property.
Remarks: All lines must be completed for proper analysis. Enter the actual amount on each line or 0.

Figure 15-3. Income Property analysis form, Victoria Gardens after fix-up

Line 1	Rents increased $45 each: 10 × $455 = $4,550.
Line 2	Apartments all rented: Allow 5% vacancy.
Line 3	Uncollectible rents: Allow 5%.
Line 4	Net rental income.
Line 5	Taxes—real property: California Proposition 13 adjusts taxes to approximately 1.1% of selling price.
Line 6	Insurance: Liability and property damage.
Line 7	Management: Allow 10%—Owner will do.
Line 8	Maintenance: Allow 10%—Owner will do.
Line 9	Repairs: Allow 5%—Owner will do.
Line 10	Utilities paid by property owner.
Line 11	Total expenses = 42% of net rental income: With vac. allowance + uncollectible added on, the costs to operate the property = 48% of total income.
Line 13	Only 3 mortgages remain—total = $183,340.
Line 13A	Total mortgage payments.

Line 14	Cash flow from operations	$ 393
	Since owner will manage, he also keeps	$ 455
	Owner will perform labor for maintenance and repairs	
	Labor = 70% of $455 (line 8) and $227 (line 9) =	$ 477
Owner-operator's total income =		**$ 1,325**

Bonus Income

Although I haven't included the vacancy allowance (line 2) or uncollectible rent (line 3) as potential income, it's possible in a perfect world for the owner-operator to pocket an extra $460 if he or she is lucky—and a good manager.

Figure 15-4. Explanation of Figure 15-3, income property analysis form after fix-up

16

Bankruptcy Ruins Perfect Day

I've always enjoyed looking back at my many real estate accomplishments over the years. I suppose I'm not much different from a painter standing near the exhibit wall admiring his or her work. Looking back, it's rather easy to forget all the hard work and struggles and even a few missteps I made before arriving at this point. That's what happens to me every time I start reminiscing about Creekside Estates. "But," you ask, "wasn't Creekside a big success?" Yes, but it was not without hard work and struggles *and a good bit of pain tossed in!*

Ben's Management Problems Came to Visit

Creekside Estates was where Murphy's law made a big believer out of me. You'll recall it was Murphy who said: "If something can go wrong, it will!" Two years after my sale to Uncle Ben, my serious concern or *intuition* about Ben's management skills suddenly came home to roost! It took almost two years, but the mystery was over. Ben, it turned out, was a lousy manager. Everyone could see it, especially his tenants. Under

Ben's tyrannical management style, the good tenants moved out and the deadbeats stopped paying rents. Even the local HUD manager was up in arms about Ben's treatment of tenants, and he showed his displeasure by withholding the rent subsidy checks.

Right about now you might be thinking, "Just why on earth does Jay give a rat's hoot about Ben's stupid management problems?" The answer, my friends, is the **mortgage payments!** That's how I discovered Ben's problems to begin with. Do you remember the fifteenth *of each month*? That's when I boogie on down to my mailbox to fetch Ben's $2,400 payment. This time, I was in for a big surprise: Instead of a $2,400 check, I received only half a payment along with a personal note. Ben was requesting that we meet at a local coffee shop to discuss what he called "**our problem.**" Can you see how seller financing works like a boomerang when something goes haywire? Ben was right, it was *our* problem. But with only half my payment in hand, it felt a lot more like mine!

Nonpaying Tenants Cause Financial Disaster

Nothing was overly complicated about Ben's financial situation. He was running out of money to pay his bills, which, of course, included *my $2,400 note payment!* Furthermore, his financial problems were not just limited to Creekside. Ben managed all his properties terribly. Consequently, his cash flow had dried up everywhere. In simple terms, Ben was in very deep doo-doo! Most of his good paying tenants had left, leaving only the deadbeats and a file full of nonpay evictions to work through.

Meeting with Ben turned out to be a real genuine shocker. Just three sips into my first cup of coffee, Ben turned the conversation into a bankruptcy discussion. He even had the gall to ask me what I thought about bankruptcy! I'm rarely at a loss for words, but this meeting turned into one of those times. With all the money Ben had started with, how in the world could he have ended up broke so fast? *Was he pulling my leg?*

Unfortunately for me, he was telling the truth. As he continued to explain, most of his troubles were about getting along with his renters. His no-compromise management style had taken him from being in a very profitable cash flow position to talking about bankruptcy in the short period of two years' time. I had always felt from the beginning that *acquiring too many properties too fast* might eventually be Ben's undoing. And it turned out that I was right.

No Advice Is Often Better Than Bad Advice

The month following our meeting, my $2,400 payment showed up in my mailbox right on time. However, Ben's future was about to become anything but normal. One more half payment showed up, and then several weeks later, I was served with Ben's Chapter 11 bankruptcy papers. They weighed almost two pounds as I recall, and, naturally, most of the wording read like gobbledygook to me.

A Chapter 11 bankruptcy is very different from the more commonly used *Chapter 7 bankruptcy*, which is a total liquidation. Chapter 7 is where today's "rock 'n' roll" spenders dump their hospital bills and credit card debt when collection agencies start calling the house every evening at dinner time. Chapter 11 is a business type of bankruptcy with a workout plan for the *reorganization of debts*.

As I would soon learn, however, that's only the *stated purpose*. It's seldom what happens to small players like Ben. United Airlines and Pacific Gas & Electric can usually wade through the mess and continue on with their businesses. Ben told me that his attorney had advised him that he could do exactly the same thing. He could even stay on as manager and collect a management fee for doing so. Ben's attorney did not come cheap: $35,000 up front just for the filing. Wow! That's a whole fistful of my $2,400 mortgage payments gobbled up in one big swoop!

After Bankruptcy, There's No Check in the Mail

My monthly mortgage payments stopped dead in their tracks after the filing. In bankruptcy jargon, this stoppage is called the *automatic stay*. Letters by the dozens began pouring in from the bankruptcy court and Ben's attorney. They mostly talked about future meetings, court hearings, and the inventory of all Ben's properties. From the bankruptcy papers, I was able to learn the names and addresses of other property owners involved in the bankruptcy. That's how I found Ron and Irene who held the first mortgage on the Harmon Street houses. You'll recall that the Harmon Street houses were additional collateral for my promissory note and deed securing the

Creekside Estates property. Together, Ron, Irene, and I decided we had best hire a bankruptcy attorney to protect our interests. We had all stopped receiving any mortgage payments by this time.

I had always been under the impression that because my payments were secured by deeds on both properties, I would either start receiving my payments from the rental income or I had the option to foreclose and take over both Creekside Estates and the Harmon Street houses. **How totally wrong I was!** I couldn't get my payments, and I couldn't foreclose the properties either!

Welcome to the world of bankruptcy. **What a total rip-off!** Bankruptcy has its very own system, and **it's the U.S. federal court.** This might partly explain why foreclosure laws, which are *state statutes*, don't mean diddly-squat to a federal bankruptcy judge. Any thoughts I might have had about foreclosing or receiving my mortgage payments were pretty much a laughing matter to the bankruptcy trustee.

The *trustee* was the person approved by the court to take control of all Ben's assets (properties and bank accounts). Whatever a trustee says or decides to do is almost the law. Ben's trustee immediately hired his very own special handpicked hardball attorney. This lawyer made Hannibal Lecter look like a high school chaplain. Together, the trustee and the attorney were a very powerful team with complete and absolute control over my $2,400 mortgage payments and, of course, *the properties*. All bankruptcy hearings would be heard in the federal courthouse, conveniently located just 175 miles from where I live. What a total bummer that was!

Originally, basic bankruptcy rules were written to give people *a second chance*. The idea was to stop beating on them once they were down and yelled uncle. Let 'em try again. That's fair, it's the American way. Chapter 11, or reorganization bankruptcy as it's often called, provides some extra time for business folks to pay their bills. The courts will often allow up to five years for debt reorganization. Real estate rental operators don't normally qualify as a business under most rules; however, Ben qualified because of *the high dollar value* of all his assets. In other words, he was much too wealthy for the plain old liquidation type of bankruptcy known as "Chapter 7."

Bankruptcy Strips Wealth in Many Ways

At my seminars, folks are always asking me, "What's the scariest part about being a real estate investor? Is it partnership investing, being sued by the tenants, or hiring handyperson workers?" My answer is, bankruptcies! Not mine, of course, but the kind we're discussing here. My reason is that you can't do anything to help yourself. You can't quit, run away, or hide. You're just plain stuck until it's over. It's a whole lot like dancing with a gorilla because the dance is never over 'til the gorilla says so!

My bankruptcy experiences before this fiasco had involved just a couple of my tenants who had filed Chapter 7s to keep from paying rents for several months. This tactic is very irritating, of course, but it's nothing like losing $2,400 payments every month. That, my friends, crosses over the line from irritating to just plain sickening! Worse yet, Chapter 11 bankruptcies leave you totally helpless to do anything on your own without hiring an attorney. Even with an attorney, you won't get relief much quicker. Every time I made any suggestion or attempted to help the cause, my own attorney would write a letter confirming exactly what I told her. Each of these letters would cost about a full month's rent, so I quit making suggestions!

Ben continued to collect rents and manage the properties just as his attorney had promised he would. What the attorney hadn't told Ben was how long that arrangement would last. At the very first meeting of creditors, everyone complained bitterly about the *fox's guarding the chicken house*. Without hesitation, the trustee immediately removed Ben from the job and hired a local management company. I'm quite certain that Ben's attorney knew this would happen. As for Ben, of course, *he didn't!* Now he was completely cut off from all fees for managing, and any other rent deposits he might manage to pocket. Needless to say, he was one very sorry camper. Later on, I learned this *bait and switch technique* is pretty much the standard operating procedure for Chapter 11 cases like Ben's. A big part of the initial attraction for Ben had been the promise that he could still *collect the rent money and earn management fees after filing*. Now, all that was gone!

The Elusive Formation of a Plan

The stated goal in Chapter 11 bankruptcy procedures is the reorganization plan, otherwise known as the *court-approved restructuring of debt*. In reality, this seldom happens in cases like Ben's. What happens instead is that the assets (real estate equities) are gradually sold off to pay for the bankruptcy expenses, which are many. Meetings, *courtroom hearings*, and letter writing will continue as long as there is equity *or money in the pot* to pay the bills. Most meetings and discussions will generally center around the proposed plan. Meanwhile, the assets are being converted to cash *and drained off* to pay expenses mostly for the star players.

Much like a high-priced sports franchise, most of the money goes out to pay the star players. Not a single soul ever showed the slightest concern about my delinquent mortgage payments. And like most sports teams, the top players always get the lion's share of the money. Ben's bankruptcy team had one standout superstar—namely, *the trustee's counsel*. Since every action, or *motion*, made in bankruptcy cases must be approved (rubber-stamped) by the court *with notices* sent to everyone involved with the case, it's easy to track the payouts (the amounts of money being squandered). The trustee's attorney was by far the highest-paid player on Ben's bankruptcy team. As time passed, it became increasingly clear to me that I would never see another mortgage payment from this court-approved ripoff.

Once the trustee had Ben's properties appraised, the free and clear properties were sold off quickly. "Where did the money go?" you ask. If your guess was *attorney expenses*, you've got it! No one ever informed me how much Creekside appraised for. But with my $350,000 mortgage on the property, a sale would not likely produce one thin dime after paying the selling expenses. Essentially, Creekside had zero value to the bankruptcy as far as I could see. The Harmon Street property (my additional collateral) was pretty much the same. It was encumbered with a 65 percent first mortgage *in addition to my second mortgage*. The trustee would obviously not net even one nickel from the sale of Harmon.

The way it looked to me was that both Creekside and Harmon had absolutely no value to the bankruptcy because neither would sell for more than the mortgage debt owed against them. Even though my own attorney completely agreed with my assessment, she did absolutely nothing to help our situation. *She did inform me* that we could petition the court to have both properties **released from the bankrutpcy**! We could, but she didn't; she always told me she was waiting for the trustee's concurrence! You guessed it: nothing ever happened!

Watching My Money Fly Away

Have you ever watched the geese fly down from Canada? If so, perhaps you've observed how they all stick together and how they always fly in a very tight formation. This is exactly what attorneys do in a Chapter 11. **They fly united!** My attorney would tell me only what she thought I should hear, but she never once strayed from the tight bankruptcy formation. As long as there was still a few dollars left in the trustee's bank account or *until that was spent,* my cries for help would simply fall on deaf ears. Thirteen months passed without even a whiff of any mortgage payments. At the same time, my attorney fees were mounting up rapidly without any signs of relief in sight.

I can't remember exactly how many times Ron, Irene, and I drove the 175 miles, *one way,* to the federal court or to meet with our attorney, but I'm sure it was a dozen times or so. It's much easier for me to remember the results *because there weren't any!* That is, unless you count the education we received, along with our fleecing! It became increasingly clear to us that until Ben's remaining assets were sold off (completely liquidated) and paid out (squandered) for bankruptcy expenses, there would never be any **debt restructuring plan.** Of course, once all the money is spent, *what good would any plan do?*

Finally our group decided it was time for a different strategy if we intended to come out of this bankruptcy alive. We were totally fed up with all the formal bankruptcy nonsense. Starting now, we would pursue a different strategy and try to cut our losses. *Our first step was to fire our attorney!* She was costing way too much money for absolutely no results. Instead, we would brush up on a few bankruptcy procedures and do battle on our own.

Going Where Creditors Aren't Welcome

Bankruptcy courts, and the judges who run them, operate much differently from other courts I'm more familiar with—namely, the superior and small claims courts in California. The first thing that's obvious when you arrive in the courtroom is that laypersons are not welcome at Chapter 11 hearings. *It's my guess* that they just assume that Chapter 11 creditors should still have enough resources (cash) to afford their own attorneys. When I showed up to represent our three member team (Ron, Irene, and me), there was already a large group of bankruptcy attorneys present and waiting in line like Volkswagen buses at a Grateful Dead concert. The sight alone (so many attorneys) was quite intimidating. Finally when the judge appeared, they all snapped to attention like Marines in a dress parade! Indeed, this courtroom was a far cry from eviction hearings where everyone is allowed to scream at the same time.

Although I wore my dark blue power suit and tried to look cool, it was obvious to every person in the federal courtroom—*including me!*—that I didn't belong there. Still, I was determined to have my say in spite of the fact that I was the only nonattorney there except for the court clerk. That aside, I took my place in the long winding line of *look-alike lawyers*, just as if I were one. Looking back, I still remember how my unexpected visit stirred up more than a few chuckles in that otherwise dreary looking courtroom.

Bankruptcy Court: The Untouchables

The first thing you'll always notice in a bankruptcy court is that hardly anything ever gets settled. The long line of attorneys would all be finished with their business before lunchtime because most of them simply made a new motion of some kind. A few just extended their cases 'til the next hearing. One big advantage of being in the middle of the line is that you get to hear a few cases before it's your turn to speak. This way, you can determine if the judge is *user friendly* or not! Will he or she help the conversation along or just sit there listening, *saying nothing*, perhaps uttering an occasional grunt? This time the line moved quickly, and, finally, it was my turn to face the judge.

I'll always remember the very first words the judge spoke to me: *"Sir, where is your attorney today?"* I explained that our group had hired an attorney with whom we had worked the past 15 months or so, but we had now run out of money to pay her. *"Furthermore, your honor*, we're not one stinkin' inch closer to a solution than the day we started!" For just a moment or two, the judge appeared to be totally befuddled. He just stared straight at me and said nothing. Gathering his thoughts, he told me, **"Creditors don't normally represent themselves in a bankruptcy court."** I said, "That's fine, your honor, but what else can I do without any money to pay my attorney?" Then he asked me, "what is it that you want this court to do?"

I explained that our properties had absolutely no equity and therefore were of no value to the bankruptcy. I told him that our hired attorney had failed to ask for their release from the bankruptcy, even though we had repeatedly asked (almost begged) her to do so.

The judge then asked me if the trustee agreed with my opinion about the property values. I told him, *"Yes, sir, he does!"* Showing obvious signs of irritation, the judge barked at me again: **"What is it that you want from this court?"** I answered, *"Your honor*, I would like our properties released from the automatic stay so that we can foreclose and start recovering all the mortgage payments we've lost." He just glared down at me and said, "Okay, they're released! Are you happy now?"

Suddenly, applause broke out in the courtroom! Every single attorney was laughing and clapping at the same time. I stood there rigid as a buck private facing a commanding general! I could plainly see that the judge was not the least bit amused!

No Equity Is Basis for Release

I told the judge, *"Thank you, your honor*, I am satisfied, but I'll need your signature on my paperwork, I believe." He simply nodded, "Okay, fine, bring me your paperwork and I'll sign it!" I had already typed up and brought with me an official looking release form for both properties (the Creekside Estates and the Harmon Street houses). However, the clerk advised me that these would be inadequate and that I needed the correct release forms. I also needed the proper forms to submit our formal *motion for relief*. When this fiasco was finally over, *my one and only* bankruptcy court appearance, although a bit unconventional and not politically correct, essentially ended our bankruptcy stalemate. However, it took another couple of months for me to get the official paperwork routed back through the court system. When I did so, the judge signed all my forms as he had said he would. We were then free to foreclose and take back both properties from my ex-Uncle Ben!

After being stiffed on mortgage payments for more than a year and then finally getting our properties released from bankruptcy, you might think that we'd be all set to take over our properties and begin collecting rents. If you thought that, you can forget it! Ben still owned the property the same as he did on the day he filed bankruptcy. We were then faced with taking it away from him. This would have to be done through the foreclosure process, and Ben was not likely to give us his full cooperation and undying support!

Bankruptcy is federal court action while foreclosure is governed by state statutes. When a bankruptcy trustee dumps a property (meaning it's no longer of any value to the proceeding), it automatically reverts back to its legal owners. What I'm about to tell you next is mighty important. If you are a beneficiary on a mortgage and become a secured creditor in a bankruptcy and suddenly you find yourself caught up in a mess like this, you best pay very close attention to *my next paragraph*.

Bankruptcy Court Ends, but the Pain Continues

As soon as the automatic stay is lifted, as fast as you can run, you need to immediately find an attorney experienced in foreclosures and proceed to have him or her petition the court to **appoint a receiver for the property.**

The *receiver* is generally a licensed real estate broker or someone familiar with keeping accurate records, *which must be approved by the court*. The receiver's job is to manage the property until such time as legal title can be transferred back to you. This will obviously cost you a few more dollars, but it's still cheaper than allowing someone like ex-Uncle Ben to pocket the rents and *then pillage and plunder the property*.

In this case with both the Creekside property and the Harmon houses, I dillydallied around for several weeks longer than I should have, and it cost me several thousand dollars' worth of rents and deposits *plus* 10 evaporative coolers worth $400 each. If the bankrupt owner is allowed to take control of his property, I can guarantee you that he will most always rent out the vacant units quickly to deadbeats and then keep the deposits, plus every dime of rent money he collects. *Unscrupulous operators*, like ex-Uncle Ben, will strip away everything they can tear loose, frantically trying to recoup their losses as they're forced out by foreclosure. **You must act quickly and appoint a receiver** because several months will pass (depending on state foreclosure laws) before you become the legal owner again. Speed is your best hope to ensure that there's still a few boards left to recover when you finally get your property back.

Losing $36,000 in mortgage payments pretty much used up my original down payment from ex-Uncle Ben. As you'll recall, the down payment was $45,000. Also, I still had to pay out nearly $10,000 for my share in hiring our hotshot bankruptcy attorney. **WOW!** *Creekside was supposed to be my retirement nest egg*. Taking a quick inventory, not only was my nest gone but Uncle Ben had snatched all my eggs too! Looking back, this was definitely a very low point in my investment career.

Although it seemed like forever, it was only a few months before I once again became the owner of Creekside Estates. This time, however, I got a little more for my money. I had told Uncle Ben at the closing table nearly two years before, "I'm more than willing to sell you my Creekside property with *a low down payment and easy payback terms*, as you request. However, if you don't *pay as you say* you will, you will lose more than just the Creekside property. I'll also be taking your Harmon Street houses, which you've now pledged as **additional collateral**. If you recall, we called this 'Jay's 2-fer sale.' I'm selling you one property now, but if you don't pay as you promise, **I'll be taking two properties back**." Well, that's exactly what happened! Besides owning Creekside Estates once again, I also owned Uncle Ben's Harmon Street houses to boot. Can you see the beauty of additional collateral? *Ben can, I'm sure!*

Ugliness Is Only Skin Deep

Half empty apartments, junky cars, and tattooed tenants are enough to make most investors run the other way. To be truthful, both properties looked a whole lot uglier on the outside than they actually were inside. Neither property was as rundown as most of the properties I look for to make offers on. The work needed was mostly cleanup, hauling junk, and painting. When I got inside, there were hardly any holes kicked in the sheetrock. Seems like tenants don't kick in the walls as much when they're living *rent free*. Naturally, that was about to change!

In terms of actual *fix-up expenses*, I estimated it would cost about the same as I typically spend on my **light fixer projects**—*approximately 10 percent of the purchase price*. The value I used for this estimate was my original selling price for Creekside ($395,000) plus the additional collateral value I estimated for the Harmon Street houses ($140,000). Therefore, my **total fix-up estimate** for both properties was $53,500. For 22 rental units, that equaled about $2,400 per house, which I considered quite good in this business, *especially* when most of the expenses involved cleanup, hauling, and painting. That was *in-house work*, meaning that I could do it myself, along with my lesser paid *nonskilled* helpers.

The importance of *nonskilled work* is that 70 percent or more of the total job cost would be credited to me or spent for my lesser paid helpers. My *rule-of-thumb cost* for average fix-up jobs is split **70 percent labor and 30 percent materials**. This meant that my helpers and I would share about $37,000—that is, the 70 percent allocated to labor. As an owner, I could not legally pay myself, but I would benefit by saving the same amount I would have earned as an employee. **More importantly to me**, it meant that my *out-of-pocket fix-up costs* would likely run much less than my $53,500 job estimate suggested.

Riding Out the Storm

I don't wish to leave you with even the slightest impression that there's any joy in being caught up in a bankruptcy. For the record, let me simply say **that it's definitely not much fun.** However, looking back, I will also tell you that it was a very valuable experience that taught me a great deal about people and forced me to learn several things I now use to protect myself—especially things like hiring an attorney quickly and having the court appoint a receiver, as we discussed above.

The long journey from the time Uncle Ben filed bankruptcy to the time that I was fully rented up again took a big slice out of three years. During my tribulations, I also learned a little something about *accounting* when you take properties back in a foreclosure action. Although I now understand how things work, my initial thinking was a whole lot different! Since I hadn't received any mortgage payments for over a year *and* because the property was badly torn up, half vacant, and looked like a pigsty, I just assumed I would end up with a huge tax loss. **Not quite so, according to the IRS.** The IRS asks, *"Where's your loss, Jay?* You got your property back, *didn't you?* Now you're whole again!"* Oh well, nothing ever turns out the way you think it should. Your accountant can explain this rare phenomenon to you. If he or she can't, get a new one.

After Every Storm There's Always a Rainbow

Wow! Taking properties back from a bankruptcy: could there be a hidden profit strategy here? I'll guarantee that you won't think so when you're smack-dab in the middle of one. But down the road a piece, *things start lookin' up!*

When Ben and I first negotiated our additional collateral agreement (the Harmon Street houses), the rents for Creekside and Harmon Street combined were $6,410 per month. It's hard to believe that they were almost $9,000 when I finally got the properties back. The biggest increase was Creekside (over $2,000 per month). Back then, all rents in my town had suddenly shot up! Using a modest **gross rent multiplier (GRM)** of seven times gross rents, Creekside then had a potential market value of more than $500,000. Although I would eventually sell Creekside a few years later, at the time, holding seemed like my best option.

The Harmon houses—*which in hindsight I should have kept*—would be my next sale. Obviously, I was looking for a cash infusion to recoup my bankruptcy and foreclosure costs. Looking back, I could have squeaked by without selling, but since Harmon Street was serviced by septic tanks instead of the city sewer system, I conned myself into thinking that selling then would avoid costly sewer hook-up expenses in the future. *In hindsight* that was all poppycock! In almost 20 years of flushing, I've never once heard of any sewer problems. Today, I can honestly tell you that it's always better to error on the side of keeping properties than selling them. The problem with the Harmon Street houses was never about septic tanks. The only problem was between my ears. Today, the income at Harmon Street has doubled, and the seven-unit complex is worth at least three times what I sold it for. On a positive note, it's always best to make these stupid mistakes early in your career and get them out of your system!

Selling Harmon Street (seven small houses on a large city lot) for $179,000 didn't take me very long. I sold it to a local contractor and his brother who already owned several similar properties. Selling expenses were minimal, and the terms were just what the doctor ordered for my anemic bank account: cash to the existing loan. The first mortgage (loan) balance *owing* was approximately $92,600, so, as you can see for yourself, *the additional collateral property* is what saved my bacon in terms of recouping my bankruptcy and foreclosure expenses.

In round numbers, my losses at Creekside were as follows: $36,000 in missed mortgage payments; $10,000 for my share of our bankruptcy attorney fees; $27,000 for *out-of-pocket cash* and Visa card fix-up costs; and finally, $4,600 for the Harmon selling expenses. Combined, these expenses totaled nearly $78,000. My accountant explained it to me this way: "From a taxpayer standpoint, taking back your Creekside property has made you whole again!" Although I nodded as if I agreed, *I've always felt it was Harmon Street with $86,000 worth of equity that kept me from losing my shirt!* I'm thoroughly convinced that Harmon Street made me whole again, because without Harmon, I'd be in a hole instead!

Taking Back Properties Is Not My Goal

Taking properties back in a foreclosure action has never been a very attractive proposition to me, even though I've come out financially okay. The best *defense,* or *guarantee,* to avoid this is to structure your carry-back financing, or *terms of the sale,* so that your buyers can actually make a few dollars every month as opposed to dipping into their wallet to make up for an income shortage. Operating negative cash flow properties discourages new buyers quicker than anything I know of! Discouraged buyers will often default, *giving their properties back!* When I sell out, it's my plan to do something else. *I don't want my rental houses back.* I've already made my profits from *rents and selling.* It's now time to begin living on *the mortgage interest payments.*

Often at my seminars, students will ask me, "Is it better to sell for all cash or to take monthly payments?" The answer is not a *simple clear-cut* yes or no. It depends on your personal financial situation. However, there's a ton of money to be made when you finance your own sales, *believe me.* I will refer you to my popular book *Start Small, Profit Big in Real Estate* (McGraw-Hill, 2004)—in particular, to the Riley Street houses, Chapter 11. You'll find this book at your nearest bookstore in the real estate section. I advise you to read it!

17

Escrow, Writing Offers, and Closing Deals

Many wannabe investors, especially those who have yet to write their first offer, incorrectly believe the key to a successful purchase offer has something to do with using the right forms. *The magic is in the forms*. Allow me to shoot that idea down by telling you that it **just ain't so**. If there is any magic to writing offers, it's in convincing wannabe investors to do it themselves.

You don't need a real estate agent to write offers; you can do it all by yourself. There is no right or wrong way. Nothing about an offer to purchase real estate has to be in any particular sequence or order. You won't be graded as if you were taking an eighth grade algebra exam. Best of all, no one has ever flunked Offer Writing 101. All you need to do is clearly write down the terms and conditions so that the sellers can understand exactly what you'll agree to.

Magic Purchase Forms: Baloney

Hardly a week goes by that I don't get a call from some starry-eyed investor requesting my standard purchase offer forms. Friends, *I don't have any standard purchase offer forms*! To my way of thinking, there should never be a standard purchase form that fits all offers. Every offer I've written has always been a little different from the others. Perhaps not much, but different just the same. What are the odds that every property you might make an offer on would be identical to all the rest? That would be like saying that every investor wears a size 42 shirt!

The different clauses and contingencies in each of my offers are written specifically for one particular deal. They are precisely the terms and conditions I'm willing to accept for the purchase of *that one property only*. I would caution any buyer about using any so-called standard purchase offer forms. Once again, what are the odds that standard purchase forms would just happen to contain the very same terms and conditions that you're using in one particular transaction? A million to one I'd say, unless of course, the seller just happens to wear a size 42 shirt!

"Apparently, Jay, you've been sleeping for the past several years: otherwise you'd know that my real estate agent won't even present my offer unless it's written on her special purchase forms approved by her division of the local real estate association. In California, they're called a residential purchase agreement, joint escrow instruction and receipt for deposit."

Thank you for your *sleeping comment*, but I only appear to be sleeping (my more compassionate friends often call it "old-age dozing"). Yes, I agree, your real estate agent has every right to present your offer on her approved purchase offer forms. In fact, she's obligated to do it. Notice I said, she's obligated, *not you!* You can write your offer on toilet paper if you choose. Your agent can then take your toilet paper scribbling and rewrite your offer on her *Realtor-approved* purchase offer forms. Now she's in total compliance with the local association rules for licensed real estate agents. Once she transfers your written offer to her boilerplate forms, you can then sign the offer, and you're both good to go with only one small, but very important request: ask her to staple your *toilet paper offer* to her "politically correct" offer so that they can both be presented together. Now everyone's happy!

Avoid One-Size-Fits-All Offers

Printed forms are the real estate industry's answer to a size 42 shirt for everyone. All offers consist of 14 pages (my state), and they all have the same *boilerplate language*! They are designed to cover every imaginable situation or contingency that could possibly come up when writing an offer. And for average home buying transactions, they do a fairly decent job. They're like *check-the-box divorce forms*, and they do provide some uniformity, as opposed to offers written on napkins, toilet paper, and crinkled grocery bags! Creative offers, like the ones I write, are much easier to understand and much more likely to be read because I include only those terms and conditions that apply to the particular transaction I'm working on. Unlike my real estate agent, as a nonlicensed person, I'm under no obligation to use printed forms. In Appendix D you can take a look at an actual offer that I made and see how it differs from standard form offers commonly used by real estate agents.

A frequent question pops up at my seminars about the response my *toilet paper offers* get from title companies and escrow officers. Students ask me whether they are acceptable. The answer is, yes, as long as they have all the information required to close. Escrow officers could not care less about the particular format. However, signed offers are also used for escrow instructions so it's very important for escrow officers to clearly understand the wishes of both parties (buyers and sellers). Many new investors incorrectly believe that title companies and escrow officers are off limits to them and that only licensed real estate agents are permitted to use their services. *You can forget that idea.* Any person who is of sound mind and decent character may hire the services of an escrow company. And judging by some of the folks I've met in escrow office conference rooms, having a sound mind might be a real stretch!

Escrow companies, like all for-profit businesses, are interested in fees and, of course, peddling their title policies. Their primary responsibility is to see that something called *concurrent performance* takes place. That means that all the stuff that constitutes a legal property transfer happens at the same time—that is, the sellers get their money and the buyers get their deeds and so forth.

Experience Is Well Worth the Effort

As a hands-on sorta guy, I believe every investor needs to experience what goes down at an actual closing. You should start by taking your toilet paper offer right through the front door of a local title company, meeting an escrow officer, and opening your first escrow account. Most title officers are very good about explaining what goes on to new folks who are interested in learning. The officer will assign you your first *escrow file number* before you leave.

As I write about this subject, I'm fully aware that in many states where mortgages are used instead of grant deeds, it's customary for real estate attorneys to handle the closings. If that's your situation, keep on reading so that you understand what your attorney is billing you for. Besides, many investors I know acquire properties in several different states, so you might end up dealing with both escrow companies and attorneys.

My toilet paper offers, typed on plain 8$\frac{1}{2}$-by 11-inch sheets, perform another valuable function for me. They allow me to specify things about a property that could have a strong influence on the sellers' decision to respond with a counteroffer. For example, one of my terms might state,

> BUYER IS AWARE THAT ROOF IS IN BAD CONDITION AND REQUIRES REPLACEMENT. THEREFORE, STANDARD ROOF INSPECTION IS WAIVED, AND BUYER WILL HOLD SELLER HARMLESS FOR ALL LEAKS.

That particular clause might sound like so much B.S., but it has the effect of reducing value in the sellers' minds. Another typical term, or clause, I use is this:

> BUYER HAS OBSERVED ASBESTOS IN UNITS 3, 5, 7, AND 10 AND AGREES TO WAIVE STATE INSPECTION REPORT AND HOLD SELLER HARMLESS FOR REMOVAL.

Several of these *customized terms,* or *conditions*, in my purchase offers will often put sellers in a defensive mode. Defensive sellers are often afraid to counter my offers or make any changes for fear that I might have second thoughts *and withdraw my liberal terms*.

Naturally, the primary purpose of my offers is to acquire properties and obtain the kind of terms that will allow me to operate on a profitable basis. Writing my kind of offers also helps me to determine exactly what the sellers will take to make a deal happen. It works something like discovery in a court trial. I'm trying to find out what's really important to the seller. Is it top price they are after? Do they really need cash? **Will they bend on the terms and agree to seller financing?** These are things you can learn (or discover) fairly easily once your offer is presented to the sellers.

Let me caution you here about thinking for the sellers: don't do it! There's no way you can possibly know what the sellers are thinking. Many investors I've counseled get stopped in their tracks trying to guess *or figure out* what sellers might be thinking or what they will agree to. That's wasted effort. Just write up your best offer, present it to the sellers, and let them tell you what it's gonna take to reach the Promised Land!

I attempt to avoid complicated and expensive contingencies that might cause sellers to toss my offer in the trash bucket and never even consider making a counteroffer. That defeats everything I'm trying to accomplish. If the sellers won't respond to my offer, all the research and the detective work I've done are down the drain. Before I ever write my offer, I've thoroughly researched the property, and I have already decided that if my offer gets accepted, I've got a winner. I'm always prepared to jiggle the terms a little, as long as I still get what I need the most. That, my friends, is a transaction that will have **cash flow** after I acquire it.

A Price Increase Is Okay If the Payments Stay the Same

One of the most common adjustments, or jiggling, of the terms occurs when the sellers are sensitive to their price. They feel their property is worth more money than I'm offering. Let's say, for example, my offer says I'll pay $500,000 with $50,000 cash down, and I'm asking for seller financing—*20 years with payments of $2,500 or more per month, including 6 percent interest*. The sellers' counteroffer indicates that they are a bit more proud of their property than I had hoped! Their counteroffer has raised the sales price to $575,000 (15 percent increase).

Chances are that I'll go along with this selling price adjustment, as long as the monthly payments remain at $2,500. I've already determined that the property has adequate income (or soon will have) to pay the $2,500 mortgage payment, but I'm not willing to increase the payments. You might be wondering, "How can the price go up and the down payment stay the same without the mortgage payment being higher? Won't that require a larger amount for the sellers to finance?" The answer is yes, but it still must be done with payments of $2,500 per month because I won't change the payment amount. Interest-only payments are okay with me, but negative amortization is not acceptable. The sellers must be satisfied with a higher sales price, and I insist they keep my monthly payments the same. To repeat what I said above, **cash flow is sacred territory to me.** I'm willing to make almost any other adjustment to the sellers' counteroffer as long my cash flow is not jeopardized.

On-the-Job Training Works Best

Learning the basic functions of a title company is best accomplished by following the process through from start to finish. Obviously, for closings done by attorneys, watching how they do it might be a bit awkward. Many closing attorneys don't want you to see how easy it is to learn this stuff. Some would rather have you believe they are performing some kind of magic! Magic commands higher fees than simply doing boring paperwork, which most escrow officers would call "routine."

The first thing that happens when you take your *signed offer* (meaning that both buyer and seller are in agreement) to the title company, is that an escrow officer will sit you down and look over the written offer. The officer will then ask you a few questions about closing dates, fire insurance (*who will provide*), whether the funds to close are available now, rent and deposit schedules for rental properties, and whether bank funding will be required. If so, when will the check arrive at the title company?

As you can see, this is not really rocket science or brain surgery. Working your way along *or just stumbling through* a couple of real estate closings will drastically improve your confidence level and put you far ahead of most real estate agents who initiate most property transfers.

Besides, having an escrow officer as a friend will be a valuable source of information for future deals. The escrow companies are in an excellent position to do you a lot of favors if you'll remain loyal to them.

Once you've met a real live escrow officer and managed to open your first escrow, you've now set in motion a chain of events that will end with the property being legally transferred. The first document you'll see from the title company will be what is called in California a *prelim*—that is, a *preliminary title report*. In some states, this document is called an *encumbrance report* or a *commitment of title*. But whatever it's called, it reflects the conditions under which the title company is willing to issue its standard title insurance policy. This report will show the legal history of the property, passing from one owner to the next, along with recorded liens, mortgages, deeds, easements, status of county taxes, and anything else that affects the title to the property. It will also provide the legal description of the property and a copy of the tax assessor's map showing the parcel being described. Most title companies have their own record department called the *title plant*. The best way to learn what's important on the prelim is to have the escrow officer introduce you to someone working in the title plant. A 15-minute visit with the title officer will make you an expert—or at least just as smart as most real estate agents who pretend to read them!

One question I'm asked on a regular basis is, "Jay, do you think title insurance is necessary?" As I'm sure you know, title insurance is an expensive part of any escrow. When I answer the question, I'm always reminded of an old TV commercial sponsored by a group of local dentists. The patient asks, "Do I really need to have all my teeth cleaned every year?" "Only the ones you intend to keep!" is the reply. I feel the same way about protecting my investment properties. They are very important to me because they pay my bills. They're also the reason I can eat more than I should! I sleep much better at night knowing a complete title search was done and that I own a policy that guarantees I'll have a marketable title when it's time to sell or trade my property. Only a title insurance policy written *for the new owner* will insure the title that is being sold and will protect the buyer if there should be any defects that do not show up in the records.

When Escrow Goes Haywire

Although I rarely open escrows that fall out (fail to close), it can and does happen! If the sellers decide for some reason to back out, I simply consider it part of doing business, and I try to get my earnest money deposit back. I have no intentions of suing for breach of contract or otherwise making a big issue over it. I'm usually a little peeved because when this happens, I'm almost certain that another offer (better than mine) has suddenly appeared surreptitiously (that means in a rat fink sorta way). Obviously, I'm not very happy to lose a good deal that I've spent time researching, but it's much better to move on and avoid becoming negative over one deal that goes haywire. Believe me, there is no shortage of my kind of properties!

Since this issue is not usually addressed in my hasty toilet paper offers, you may wish to write in a default clause in your offers if you're doing an escrow without a real estate agent. You have two choices when your deal falls apart. You can *sue for specific performance* or *set a dollar limit for liquidated damages—such as your $1,000 earnest money deposit*. If the sellers back out, they will most likely refund your deposits held in escrow. This is especially true if they have another offer better than yours! There are penalties for sellers who sandbag on deposits. If you use a real estate agent and the standard purchase offer forms, there's a default clause with *check-the-box choices*. I always put my "X" in the liquidated damages box. I'd suggest you do the same.

In my opinion, **offers to purchase income property** should be easy for the sellers to accept and sign. That means that the terms you specify should not cost them big bucks to get their approval. Your offer should be made for a purchase price that reflects the condition of the property. Most sellers, particularly owners of older rundown properties, do not like contingencies that require them to spend money fixing things up in order to sell. They simply want out—"fast in easy." It should be obvious that when buying dirty rundown properties, the sellers are less than perfect operators. Why insult them with a contingency clause that might say, "Seller warrants that all units will be sparkling clean at close of escrow." Simply deduct $5,000 or $10,000 from your offer and clean the units yourself. I like to write offers that don't require the sellers to spend money or think too hard. I'm looking for their signatures with the least amount of jawboning back and forth!

I mentioned earlier that developing a good friendship with a local escrow officer can be a valuable benefit to you as an investor. Obviously, if you're buying and selling properties, you'll be needing the services of a title company, and of course that works both ways. The title company, escrow company, or closing attorney needs your patronage as well. I have made it my business to use the same title company whenever either Fred, my agent, or I open an escrow. Because of my loyalty, the title company and, more importantly, its title plant will do almost anything I ask to help me research the properties I'm interested in. I suggest you do the same because with loyalty comes many benefits I've found.

Many title and escrow companies offer free parcel maps, along with copies of recorded deeds to regular customers. Where I live, they call this information a *property profile*, and naturally it's very helpful to investors. You can calculate the last purchase price and also find out who holds the debt on a property—whether it's a bank or privately held financing. You can find out the beneficiary's name and mailing address in case you wish to learn more about a promissory note or the balance owed. If you've ever asked a real estate listing agent whether there's one, two, or three mortgages on a property *and how much is owed on each*, you'll understand why getting this information yourself is a whole lot faster. You can also avoid that strange, *deer in the headlights* look you get from most of them just for asking.

Information Needed for Closing

In order to prepare the closing papers for income properties, your escrow officer will need a schedule of rents, *rent due dates*, who pays them, and the security deposits held by the sellers. Make sure that any last month's rents collected in advance when the tenants moved in are also accounted for. The rents will need to be prorated, along with property taxes—*and, sometimes, insurance*—to the day set for closing. You can think of prorations *as debits or credits*. For example, if your closing date was set for November 15, the sellers would get to keep 15 days' worth of current rents and you would receive a credit on the closing statement for the

15 days following the closing: November 16 through 30, *assuming* all the rents were due November 1.

This discussion about prorations would be incomplete if you haven't yet figured out the best time to close when you're acquiring income properties, especially properties with quite a few rents involved! *You can turn a cash down payment transaction into a no-money-down deal by manipulating the closing date to your advantage.*

For example, let's say you're acquiring a 10-unit property with rents of $750 per unit and security deposits of $800 per unit. This means that a full month of rents will total $7,500, and security deposits for all 10 units will equal $8,000. If you close escrow on October 31, the sellers keep all the rents, and you receive only a credit for the deposits ($8,000). If you close escrow on November 2 instead, you receive credit for 29 days' worth of rents ($7,250) in addition to the security deposits of $8,000. Let's say your cash down payment is $15,000. Now you've got all your money back in the form of a $15,250 credit at closing. If the sellers are wise to this maneuver and want to close escrow on the last day of the month, start coughing immediately, point to your throat, and quickly jump in bed 'til November 2. You should feel well enough by then to sign the closing papers!

What's an Escrow Anyway?

I'm constantly amazed at the number of folks who open escrows who have very little knowledge about what goes down at the closing, or *settlement* as it's sometimes called. These folks take all the paperwork to the title company, dump it off on the escrow officer's desk, and then wait for a phone call when their checks are ready. What happens in between seems to be a great mystery to many of these participants.

Escrow is a means for enabling the transfer of real property ownership using an impartial third party to make sure the wishes of both the buyers and sellers are carried out in accordance with the terms they've already negotiated and agreed to. Escrow enables the buyers and sellers to conduct business with the least amount of risk because the responsibility for handling all the money, and the required documents, is placed in the hands of a neutral party who is not the least bit affected by the outcome. The escrow holder, which can be a title company or a real estate attorney, has a legal obligation to safeguard the interest of all parties affected by the transfer of ownership. Can you see how simple this stuff really is?

Like always, my recommendation for learning what goes on at the closing is to jump right in feet first and experience the action firsthand. That means get in there and do it! Attend a few closings in person. I'll begin by introducing you to the cast of escrow players and the roles they will each perform at closing.

It's possible that anywhere from three to a half dozen people might show up, but the basic closing crew will generally consist of the buyer, seller, escrow officer, and now and then a loan officer if a bank mortgage is involved. Every so often an attorney wanders in to represent a buyer or seller but not too often where I live in a trust deed state. In mortgage states, attorneys perform the closings like escrow officers do in California. For the most part, the people who show up at closings are pretty much strangers to each other, brought together to sign papers and make sure they receive what they've already agreed to. The escrow officer will oversee the paper flow, obtaining signatures and notarizing documents that will be sent out for recording.

Most Closings Are Not Formal Events

Have you ever watched people who don't know each other very well try really hard to impress each other? I've attended closings where several participants could have won Academy Awards trying to B.S. the others—*acting as if they knew everything*. At one such closing, I recall five or six people were in attendance, including a couple of loud-mouth friends of the seller. They kept asking the escrow officer stupid questions, but when she finally inquired as to why they were there, neither one would answer. Instead of blabbing any more, they sat back in their chairs like they'd been highly insulted.

At the same closing, there was one smartly dressed chap from the loan company, and he kept flashing a $300,000 certified check. He made absolutely certain everyone in the room could see the dollar amount on the check. Then he boldly announced several times that he was there only to make sure everyone knew the loan would be funded. It was the only time I've ever seen funds delivered personally to a closing. Normally, they're wired directly from the bank to the escrow officer. The seller's goofy friends kept asking if they would be able to cash the check that day. They seemed quite perturbed when the escrow officer informed them, "We're only here to sign papers today." I found out later on that these friends had loaned the seller money and the reason they were there was to keep a close eye on the sale—or at least on the money.

Signing All the Paperwork

Most closings are not formal meetings where everyone shows up at the same time. For escrows where a new loan or mortgage is required, there's basically only three people who want something from the closing. Obviously, the buyer wants a new property, the seller wants money, and the lender is looking for a good investment. In order to make all this happen, there's a truckload of documents to be signed by the parties, and some will need to be recorded. Where I live in California, the escrow officer will prepare all the documents and then most likely notify each party separately to come in and sign. The officer is careful to maintain the privacy of each party by keeping separate files for the buyer, seller, and lender. Different documents are needed for each party to close the escrow.

When I'm the buyer in California, property is conveyed to me by a *grant deed*. In many other states, a *warranty deed* is used to convey title. Obviously, the seller gets the money (down payment) and, in most cases, a promissory note, which is the buyer's personal promise to pay the balance of the purchase price in accordance with the terms already agreed on. Obviously, these terms are spelled out in the note. The seller will also receive a recorded trust deed showing the same dollar amount as on the promissory note, which creates a lien against the property until the debt is fully paid. The bank or lender providing the mortgage funds for closing will also receive a promissory note and a trust deed as evidence of their loan. Recording the documents will be arranged by the escrow officer so that the bank's papers (the trust deed) get recorded first, *ahead of any seller's trust deed*. It's the order of recording (time and date) that establishes the loan or mortgage priority—that is, whether it's a first, second, or third mortgage and so on.

There always seems to be a great deal of confusion about recording the documents: which papers get recorded, which ones need to be notarized, and so forth. First, only the documents that will be recorded need to be notarized. Most escrow officers are generally *notaries* themselves, and they perform this function as part of closing. A *notary public* is an official witness who acknowledges that you are who you say you are when you sign the closing documents. Grant deeds, which transfer title to the property, and trust deeds are used to secure the promissory note and are both recorded documents.

A common misunderstanding concerns promissory notes. New investors, and even some not so new, often think such notes are recorded documents. Allow me to emphasize this: **promissory notes are not recorded!** This is one reason it's sometimes difficult to figure out exactly how much money is still owed on a property when you're doing research. A trust deed will show the amount that was owed when the property was last sold. However, only the beneficiary on the *promissory note* can tell you the current balance owing. This is why escrow officers mail out a demand letter to mortgage holders and/or note holders requesting a beneficiary's statement. They want to know how much money is still owed on the note or mortgage.

How to Take Title and Why

When I first started acquiring properties years ago, I remember one of the last questions the escrow officer would always ask me just before he or she typed up the final closing papers, was, "How do you wish to hold title?" I can still remember always being a little confused, but in the interest of time, I always picked "joint tenancy" when I was married, "sole and separate property" when I wasn't, and "partnerships" where others were involved.

Back then, each of these ways of holding title seemed perfectly fine to me—and I might point out that none ever caused me any serious problems! Later on, I would learn some better ways that offered more lawsuit protection and would help me with estate planning. But from a practical standpoint, *I had nothing to protect when I first started out.* Sometimes when I talk about this issue at seminars, it provokes a rather healthy discussion: "Jay, I don't think you fully understand my situation: my house is worth at least $400,000, and I drive a $55,000 Corvette! Can't someone come after my possessions if I get sued over my rental properties?" They certainly can, but what will they get? I then ask my student some details about his $400,000 house: *"Do you have a mortgage?"* "Sure, but it's only $320,000." *"How much do you still owe on your car?"* "Just $35,000 more and it's all mine!"

Friends, I hate to be the bearer of bad news, but in terms of satisfying the judgment in a losing lawsuit, the assets we're talkin' about here don't add up to diddly-squat. A $400,000 house sold quickly at a "fire sale" auction would be lucky to fetch enough to pay all the expenses, plus the mortgage balance. As far as the plaintiff and his or her attorney are concerned, well, they still have each other, but little else! As far as the Corvette's concerned, I suggest you just keep making the payments because no one else will take it with $35,000 debt. Obviously, if you have cash or liquid assets that someone can take without a hassle, we can talk about more protection. However, very few Fixer Camp students seem to be afflicted with having too much cash. As far as I'm concerned, acquiring good properties should be the first order of business. Keep the title in your own name until you figure out a good reason to change it. If you're worried about lawsuits, think about what you own that's free and clear with loads of equity. If the answer is nothing, then you're worried about *nothing*.

How Long Does It Take to Close?

Obviously, there's no single answer for how long it should take to close an escrow. In my years of investing, I've had long escrows lasting 90 days or more with which I was basically stalling, trying to round up the funds I needed for closing. I consider 90 days a long escrow in my business, and I might point out that most sellers who own decent properties won't go for stalling in normal times when properties are selling well. In my particular situation, buying rundown properties, I generally get my way because I'm buying from lonely sellers. Sellers get that way because very few buyers show up looking for dirty rundown properties. As a rule,

I close escrow in 45 days or less, which allows everyone plenty of time for coffee breaks, redoing paperwork, and even taking a few days off for sick leave.

Once in a great while, lightning speed is required. The seller is leaving town, getting divorced, getting married, going to jail—the list goes on, but the big question is, "Can we close right now?" The answer is yes, and it's a whole lot easier when you're calling in a favor from that escrow officer I told you to get acquainted with. Also, do you recall my advice about *loyalty*—doing business and developing a good relationship with the same title company? This is where it pays off big time! A title company can actually close an escrow in a single day with a special afternoon recording. When the escrow officer grabs your file from the big stack on his or her desk and hand carries it through the process, it takes only three or four hours tops to get the job done. Also keep in mind that bribery works quite well if you haven't built up loyalty just yet! A $500 bonus for closing fast can work a whole lot faster than Cialis, believe me!

Writing offers and closing escrows should not be chores unfamiliar to do-it-yourself investors. As long as they remain a mystery, it means you're giving up far too much control to other people. I continually listen to tales of woe from wannabe investors. They're always waiting for their agent to do this or that, waiting for more information about the property, waiting for someone to write an offer. It seems like every chore is wait, wait, wait! Friends, you'll never get anywhere in this business if you don't take charge **and stop waiting**. The sooner you become the doctor and quit being the patient, the more successful you'll be.

18

Sweat Equity Works with Little Money

Quite often, the greatest asset a new investor can have is little or no money to invest with. It forces a person to start thinking creatively right from the get-go! I can still remember my early years. It made very little difference whether a seller was asking $20,000 down or $120,000 because I didn't have either! Having little or no money to invest can actually be a blessing in disguise because it quickly narrows down the types of properties you'll likely be able to purchase. In my case, I realized I'd need to acquire properties with potential to increase my equity quickly. Otherwise, I'd have no money to keep investing. This is where sweat equity would come to my rescue.

Sweat equity offers the greatest insurance plan in the world for investors or wannabes who don't have much money to start with. It insures that there's a way to invest if they have the desire and are willing to work hard. It also levels the playing field economically—a million dollars' worth of equity is still $1 million whether you earned it from sweat or paid $200,000 to get it! The ability to find the right properties with a high potential for increasing the value is a skill that's worth millions but often begins with nothing.

Property Selection Is the Key

Creating equity from thin air may sound impossible, but I've often been accused of doing just that! In my defense, I must tell you, that I've earned every nickel I've made. Still, much of my success can be attributed to the types of properties I've acquired. To say this another way, sweat equity investors must search for the kinds of properties where cleaning and fix-up will significantly boost the value. This will not happen automatically! For example, in most slum areas, you can work your tail off fixing, cleaning, or whatever—you'll lose a lot of sweat all right, but you'll gain very little equity for your efforts. **Property selection is the key.** You'll have poor results working on the wrong properties.

Sierra Boulevard could have been the poster child for sweat equity properties! Driving by, I still remember thinking to myself, "If any of these tenants are even breathing, that will add value." The property was a total pigsty! I counted 4 houses, along with 12 cars in various stages of dismantling. Household garbage had been dumped inside the cars, and all kinds of auto parts were strewn about the property. I'm describing the front yard here; the backyard was even worse! Considering what a mess it was, I still felt there was great potential for quick equity at Sierra. Obviously, this is the kind of property where you'll likely find the serious motivated sellers.

Sweat equity describes a transaction in which the buyer plans to contribute physical work in exchange for a substantial price reduction and very liberal purchase terms—*as in no money down or certainly not very much!* The type of property I'm searching for must have the potential for a quick increase in value, and the location must be good enough to support higher rents. It's nearly impossible to get the price and terms I'm looking for with nonfixer types of properties. Motivated sellers are the folks who make these transactions possible. But don't forget that it's *buyers* who must determine the potential value and profits. The wonderful thing about sweat equity investing is the low risk involved.

It Takes Vision to Spot Value

By using leverage and sweat equity together, investors can earn phenomenal returns and do it rather quickly. My goal is to double the property value and increase the rents by 50 percent within two years. First-year returns exceeding 100 percent are very commonplace. Sierra Boulevard would beat the socks off these numbers, but of course, I had years of experience before this deal came along.

The property consisted of four separate rental houses situated on a large city lot—150 feet Sierra Boulevard frontage by 140 feet deep. When I called the selling agent, I was immediately informed that there were only three houses. However, the lot showed future commercial zoning. The fourth building, she said, was just an old garage being used for storage by the two tenants living there. It turned out that the garage was full of auto parts. The only two tenants living on the property were claiming 12 junk cars between them, and they said they needed a building for more auto parts. Wow! Not exactly the highest and best use of the property, I thought.

The sellers were a recently divorced couple, and they had left the area soon after their split. The two renters left behind were personal friends of the husband, and they had agreed to care for the property in exchange for favorable rents. The agent informed me that "favorable rents" meant paying every three months or so, just in time to catch up the payments on two small mortgages. Both mortgages were several installments behind when I took over the property. Finding both owners was our first challenge, and when we did, they wouldn't speak to each other. This made negotiations quite difficult, even though they were both very anxious to sell—they both needed money! Fortunately for me, they understood that almost every potential buyer would be completely turned off by how the property looked. The agent told me she'd had only one low-ball offer in the nine months since the owners had split.

Figuring the Value of Junky Lookin' Property

The value of income-producing properties like Sierra is pretty much determined by the rental income. In this case, with only two deadbeat tenants living there and no stable income anyone could verify, the investor would have to know what comparable fixed-up units would rent for in order to determine how much to pay for the property. New investors' worst sin is paying too much for *potential value!* **Potential means it ain't here yet!** With the Sierra property, the real estate agent had already tried the oldest trick in the book: *future commercial zoning.* I'm always happy to own commercial zoning, but I'm not willing to pay extra to get it. I'm in the rental housing business so that's what I'll pay for!

The agent's multiple listing information indicated that the large three-bedroom house in the back had been renting for $425 per month; however, it was vacant now. The two small studio cottages were supposed to be renting for $250 each. They were both occupied by the two master mechanics living on the property. According to the agent, the total income was $925 per month, although she couldn't prove it. The sellers had listed the property for $119,000, but they had cut the price twice, the second time to $99,000. That was their *no budge, backed-in-the-corner, bottom-line price,* she told me, *and it's a steal!* In my opinion, the only thing on the property that resembled a steal was the fleet of junk cars scattered around the place!

A price tag of $99,000 might have been somewhere in the ballpark if the income had actually been $925 per month. As it was, even the $250 cottage rents were barely provable. Even so, that would make the gross rent multiplier 16.5. Back then, the most you could get for brand new luxury units with top-notch tenants in my town was about 12 times gross rents.

Poking Around for More Income

When I begin my Lieutenant Columbo style of investigation of a property, I'm always thinking about ways to create additional income. Is there some way I could move a rental trailer on the property and hide it behind the trees or even build a special fence to conceal it? Could I turn a large rambling house into a duplex or perhaps add another bedroom using part of the covered carport or garage? Maybe it's possible to convert an old shed or garage into an income-producing apartment.

Sierra Boulevard had one of the ingredients I was looking for: *a good solid garage* full of junk auto parts! The structure already had a water faucet (hose bib) attached to the building, plus a separate electrical meter.

Obviously, someone had once used the building for a workshop. With approximately 500 square feet of space and a separate electric meter and water, I knew I had all the makings for a cozy one-bedroom efficiency unit, which would easily rent for $350 per month. I estimated it would cost approximately $9,000 to construct interior walls, install a kitchen and bathroom, and hook up a sewer line to the three-bedroom house, just 30 feet away. Having an additional income-producing unit on the property would obviously increase the property value.

Right about now, as I discuss my most intimate cash flow secrets, there may be some who would question my ethics. "Are you not violating the building codes?" you might be asking. Allow me to answer the question this way. I will never advise people to do anything they're not comfortable doing. It may sound like I'm not opposed to being a little bit sneaky, and if that's your opinion, so be it. However, before we drop the issue, let me make it crystal clear that I will never do anything to jeopardize the safety of my tenants. For example, when I install new gas lines or electrical panels, I always obtain the required permits and hire qualified contractors. I might be *a bit sneaky, perhaps*, but I'm always concerned about the safety of my tenants first and foremost.

My Offer: See How High They Jump

At my seminars, I'll often use the tactic *"let's see how high they'll jump."* Naturally an explanation is required. Years ago I was working with a crafty old real estate broker who was helping me figure out what price to offer on a property he had listed. He suggested a price that I thought was way too high, and, of course, my counterproposal was much too low. Silence filled the room for several minutes. Finally, he said, "Okay, let's present your offer *and see how high they jump*." Ever since then, that's what I've been calling my lowball offers on junky looking properties like Sierra Boulevard.

"Okay, you say the sellers are now asking $99,000," I mumbled. The agent sorta wobbled her head around, which seemed like a yes to me. Finally I said, "I'll split the difference with you. I'll offer six times the gross rents, or $66,000, full price." "What split and what kind of difference are you talking about?" she asked.

"With only two units rented for $250 each," I replied, "your total monthly income is $500. That's $6,000 annually, so nine times the gross rents of $6,000 equals $54,000. Obviously, if all three units were bringing in the rents your listing shows, they would add up to $925 per month. It appears that your sellers are asking nine times the gross rents: $925 × 12 = $11,000 gross rents × 9 (GRM) = $99,9000 The big problem is that you don't have $925 income—*all you have is $500!*"

Naturally, I totally agreed with my own calculations, *but I was the only one!* The sellers said some very unkind words to describe both me and my offer. Fortunately, it was just a verbal offer, submitted over the telephone, so the agent wasn't able to see how high the sellers jumped. Unfortunately, it was high enough for them to say no! Even though there were no other offers in sight, both sellers were determined to get the highest price they could—seems like they were holding out for a miracle. They would also turn down my next offer of $70,000, but they finally agreed to accept $75,000. As things eventually turned out, the price would be a superbargain for me:

Full price	$75,000	Third offer accepted
Down payment	11,000	$6,500 cash + Chev half ton
Private first mortgage	21,000	Take over payments
Private second mortgage	11,570	Take over payments
New seller carryback	31,430	Negotiated with sellers

Lemonade Offer Softens Sale Price

I agreed to $75,000 for several reasons, even though the income at closing was only $500 per month. My **first reason** for paying the $75,000 was that the sellers had agreed to accept my *lemonade down payment*. That means *part sugar, part lemons*. The sugar, or $6,500 cash, was the least amount I could get them to accept. Both sellers had used up their overextended credit with friends and desperately needed payback funds. I was able to include my old pickup truck in the down payment because the wife's car had recently quit running. Unbeknownst to me at the time, it was one of the dirty dozen vehicles left on the property I would eventually haul away. The trade, however, paid for all my hauling expenses because the truck had cost me only $2,400.

My **second reason** for paying $75,000 was because I would close escrow with *three private mortgages* on the property, which I felt were all excellent candidates for buying back at a discount. The second mortgage holder had already missed several payments before I came along. In fact, I had to make up the missed payments at the closing. I could tell that he was still extremely nervous about his balance (approximately $11,570). He called me several times right after I purchased the property to inform me that I had to clean up the property. "It's one of the conditions in the deed," he said. Once I sensed how nervous he was, I told him, "I don't have the money right now to do very much! In fact," I said, "after coming up with the down payment cash, I'm just crossing my fingers I'll have enough rent money to is pay all the mortgages. My biggest problem," I explained, "is that I have three mortgage payments totaling $710 every month but only $500 income! All I can do right now is promise that I'll try my very best!"

Two weeks later, shortly before his first $200 mortgage payment was due, he called me again. "I'm about to make you a once-in-a-lifetime proposition," he said. "If you can somehow beg, borrow, or find $6,000 cash before my payment comes due (about two weeks), I'll tear up my mortgage and call the total debt **paid in full**." *My second reason* for paying $75,000 had come to pass much earlier than I ever expected. It took another creative technique (like borrowing from the kids' piggybanks), but I managed to make the payoff. Wow! In a single day, I had already made $5,570 by taking over a private mortgage held by a nervous beneficiary!

My **third reason** for paying $75,000 was perhaps the best one of all: Both the agent and her clients thought they were selling me a three-unit property! In my mind, however, *I was acquiring four separate rental houses*. Obviously, there would be some fix-up work to do (sweat equity) to make the garage rentable, but once completed, it would increase the property's cash flow by approximately 25 percent. The schedule below shows my rental income from the very beginning, 'til recently:

Description	Close of Escrow, $	6 Months, $	24 Months, $	Current Rents, $
3-bedroom unit	-0-	450	625	825
Studio cottage 1	250	295	350	435
Studio cottage 2	250	295	360	435
(Garage) 1-bedroom unit	-0-	-0-	425	645

Rent-to-Value Factor Shows a Winner

Determining value using the *gross rent multiplier* (GRM) becomes a bit confusing when half the property has no income. This is where I depended on my **rent-to-value method**. First, I assigned a *dollar value* to each rental unit, dividing up the $75,000 purchase price. Obviously, each unit would have a different value based on its size and condition. I assigned unit values as follows: $12,500 each for the studio cottages: $20,000 for the garage (one-bedroom conversion); and $30,000 for the three-bedroom house. *These values added up to the $75,000 purchase price.*

Then I divided the monthly rent for each unit by the value I had assigned to it. For example, if the rent for my three-bedroom house was $450 per month, the rent-to-value factor would be 1.5 percent:

$$\frac{\$450}{\$30,000} = 0.015$$

Move the decimal two places right. The studio rent-to-value factor was 2 percent on the day I acquired the property. Any rent-to-value number above 1 percent is a winner; 2 percent and above will make you the first millionaire on your block, *and it won't take very long!*

Earn Big Money by Helping Yourself

Two years after I acquired Sierra Boulevard, it was hard to imagine the way it had looked when I made my first visit to the property. Somehow it looked much bigger with all the cars gone! Just doing the cleanup work increased the value a great deal. The reason I mention this is because shortly after towing away all the cars and hauling the junk from the yard, I was offered $55,000 more than I paid, and I hadn't even started painting the exterior yet. This is very important for sweat equity investors to understand. People will pay big money for plain old unskilled grunt work! *Based on $55,000 more than I paid,* two people (me included) doing plain old cleanup work for 60 hours (120 hours total) each earned $458 per hour. I don't mind telling you that I've worked for a whole lot less!

My rent-to-value ratio for the studio cottages was approximately 2.8 percent at the end of 24 months. Each unit was rented for $350 per month, *or $4,200 annually!* As you recall, the purchase value I assigned to each cottage was $12,500. That meant that just three years' worth of rental income would completely pay the total cost for each cottage, assuming I used the rents for that purpose. For the sake of comparison, a $200,000 house that rents for $1,000 per month would take $16\frac{1}{2}$ years to pay off using all the rent money. Obviously, there are other financial considerations to think about, but as any investor can tell you, **no measurement ranks higher than being free and clear of debt in the least amount of time.**

Location and Desirability

Sweat equity investors must be extremely careful when considering location. I've already made it clear that slum investing doesn't work very well because it's almost impossible to push up the value no matter how much time and money you spend making improvements. The reason is because the tenants can't pay higher rents (they live there because it's cheap). Also, investors will expect to pay fire sale prices when they buy properties in higher-risk locations.

Personally, I have two main reasons why I stay away from slum locations. The first has to do with safety—**my safety!** I don't want to get killed working on my property with only a paintbrush to defend myself. The second reason is strictly business. I can tell you right now that I would not like the tenants who show up to rent houses in slum areas. The customers I'm looking for are afraid to live in the slum locations for the same reasons I'm afraid to work there.

Sierra Boulevard was located in what I call the older residential area of town, one of the two locations I recommend for equity investors who need quick improvements with fast results. To jog your memory about the five location choices, I've listed them below. Obviously, you'll find some overlapping and combinations, but if you think about where you live, I'm sure you'll recognize each one of these locations (See also appendix A):

1. *Snob Hill*. Where the wealthiest folks in town reside
2. *Downtown commercial*. Mostly businesses and acres of concrete and blacktop
3. *Older residential*. Surrounding downtown area, generally 50 years and older
4. *Dense slums*. Downtown or pocket areas, often older, plus government housing projects
5. *Suburbia*. Sprawling subdivisions, tract houses, mostly owner occupied

For the most part, I purchase properties in just two locations: **downtown commercial** and **older residential**. These are the two locations where you'll find the older rundown types of properties you're reading about. Sometimes it's not easy to distinguish the difference between the two locations. However, to get the idea, try to picture the stump of a recently cut tree. You'll notice growth rings in the wood as the tree grew larger in diameter each year. Folks claim you can tell how old a tree is by counting the growth rings in the stump. Towns and cities have similar growth patterns as they grow outward from the center, or the city core. First there are the stores and businesses, surrounded by the older houses. Referring to my five different locations, *downtown commercial* represents the city's commercial core, and it's the older houses mixed with commercial buildings that are of interest to me.

Today, these houses are older, and many are rundown and neglected. Most are functionally obsolete. With a reasonable amount of upgrading, however, these older houses and small multiple-unit properties make excellent rental units. Most are now sitting on commercial land or land that is zoned for potential commercial use in the future. This pretty much describes my Sierra Boulevard property. Sometimes people will ask me,

"Is it legal to operate residential rentals on commercial land?" *The answer is yes*, as long as the residential use was there in the past and continues. The houses and tenants are what is called *grandfathered*, meaning that they can stay there for as long as the residential use continues and the properties are kept in good repair.

Sweat Equity Builds Value Quickly

The main reason sweat equity investors enjoy **much faster profits** and **cash flow** is because appreciation is not the primary growth ingredient. It's the **investors' sweat** that drives up the values! When you can purchase rundown properties for substantial discounts and then contribute your own sweat and labor to bring them up to snuff, the value of your equity grows very quickly.

Unlike *appreciation growth*, which comes and goes with the times or economic cycles, *sweat equity is much more dependable*. It's also available any time and any place you're willing to roll up your sleeves and get started! Several wealthy investor friends of mine started this way, then gradually transitioned into more expensive properties as their bank accounts grew. Sweat equity is still the best game in town for average working folks who are serious about changing careers but have very little money to start with. That pretty much describes my own situation when I quit my telephone company job. Knowing there would be no more paychecks, I was fully aware that properties like Sierra Boulevard would have to pay my grocery bills.

Most income-producing properties will eventually forgive an investor who overpays a few dollars if enough time passes by and the investor can just hang on long enough. *Paying too much*, **underestimating expenses**, and *agreeing to pay excessive mortgage payments* (debt service) are the most common investor mistakes. These are buying errors that will keep you from having cash flow. And much like two angry hands squeezing around your neck, these buying mistakes can strangle you almost as quickly. I don't know of a single investor who hasn't miscalculated his or her cash flow when negotiating the purchase price—*and, of course, that includes me!* However, I can promise you this much, that if you keep making miscalculations, you'll end up dead broke and without any properties.

One of the major reasons for lack of cash flow is just plain ignorance. *Folks simply don't know what it costs to operate income properties.* It is much better to learn this lesson before you sign the closing papers *than afterward*. In Figure 18-1, you'll find my **income and expense chart** for the first 10 years of operation at Sierra Boulevard. Study the numbers very carefully; the chart will help you get a good handle on what things really cost *and, equally important*, where you can save big bucks by doing things yourself.

When you examine my expenses, you'll notice I've allowed 5 percent of the gross income for vacancies, and also an equal amount for credit losses. You should never estimate less than these amounts even when all the units are rented. Rental properties do not stay 100 percent rented all the time, and no landlord is exempt from getting "stiffed" occasionally. A 5 percent allowance for each of these categories is very reasonable. However, as your tenant management skills improve and you're able to keep all the units rented to customers who pay their rents as scheduled, guess what happens? You may pocket the vacancy allowance and credit the loss allocations to yourself. After all, your skillful management techniques should be rewarded!

The value of my income and expense chart (Figure 18-1) is that it shows you where all the expense money goes. Most investors have little difficulty figuring out what the total income should be. *It's expenses that cause all the problems!* At my House Fixer Camps, I teach students to avoid *negotiating or agreeing* to accept mortgage payments that require more than 55 percent of the total monthly income. As you can see, the mortgage payments on my Sierra property were far less than that amount, but don't forget that I was able to purchase the second mortgage for a substantial discount shortly after closing escrow. That purchase eliminated a monthly mortgage payment of $200.

Do-It-Yourself Investors Pocket More Money

Sierra Boulevard generated much more cash flow than my income and expense chart might suggest. The main reasons were that I got the property up and running quickly and I rarely had any vacancies. As for loss of

	Years of Ownership										
	End of First 6 Mos.	1	2	3	4	5	6	7	8	9	10
Income (Rents)	6,240	17,220	21,120	21,120	21,900	22,200	23,040	24,900	25,200	25,640	26,040
5% Vac. Allowance	312	860	1,056	1,056	1,095	1,110	1,152	1,245	1,260	1,282	1,302
5% Credit Losses	312	860	1,056	1,056	1,095	1,110	1,152	1,245	1,260	1,282	1,302
Net Rental Income	5,616	15,500	19,008	19,008	19,710	19,980	20,736	22,410	22,680	23,076	23,436
Expenses											
Taxes	405	805	800	820	825	870	895	925	905	925	940
Insurance	465	855	850	850	860	815	865	850	850	840	869
Management	315	1,722	2,100	2,100	2,190	2,200	2,305	2,490	2,520	2,564	2,604
Maintenance	312	1,720	2,000	2,065	2,190	2,175	2,300	2,460	2,500	2,550	2,604
Repairs	510	860	1,050	1,005	1,060	1,100	1,152	1,245	1,260	1,280	1,300
Utilities	1,305	2,406	2,400	2,445	2,485	2,465	2,490	2,515	2,510	2,545	2,580
Acctg. and misc.	275	410	400	385	200	310	250	310	345	422	390
Total Expenses	**3,587**	**8,778**	**9,600**	**9,670**	**9,810**	**9,935**	**10,257**	**10,795**	**10,890**	**11,126**	**11,287**
Operating Income	2,029	6,722	9,408	9,338	9,900	10,045	10,479	11,615	11,790	11,950	12,149
Mortgage payment 1	3,000	3,000	3,000	3,000	3,000	3,000	750*				
Mortgage payment 2	Pd. Off	Before	First	Pymt.							
Mortgage payment 3	3,120	3,120	3,120	3,120	3,120	3,120	3,120	3,120	3,120	3,120	3,120
Annual Cash Flow	(4,091)	602	3,288	3,218	3,780	3,925	4,359	7,745	8,670	8,830	9,029
Accumulated Cash Flow	**(4,091)**	**(3,489)**	**(201)**	**3,017**	**6,797**	**10,772**	**15,081**	**22,826**	**31,496**	**40,326**	**49,335**

* First mortgage paid off after first three months.

Figure 18-1. Income and expense chart, Sierra Boulevard Property

rents (credit losses), I was stiffed only twice during my first 10 years of operation. Regarding the management, you might be thinking to yourself, "Why in the world does Jay show *10 percent of the gross income* going out for property management? Doesn't he manage the property himself?" Yes, I do manage my own properties, *but I don't do it for free!* When I managed properties for others years ago, my standard fee was always 10 percent of the gross rents. I see no reason to manage for any less because I'm the owner.

Maintenance and repairs are property expenses no matter who owns the property. Someone must perform the labor and purchase materials. As an owner, it's always my choice to pay someone else or handle those chores myself. At Sierra Boulevard, *I was my own maintenance man and also my own repair service.* Naturally, owners are not allowed to pay themselves, but they can save the money that would have otherwise been spent had they hired the work out. By not paying someone else the amounts shown on my chart for maintenance and repairs, the money simply stays in the pot and increases the bottom line (cash flow). Obviously, monies not spent for hiring outside help ends up in the owner's pocket!

Can you begin to see that buying small properties like Sierra Boulevard can be a good start toward financial independence? At Sierra, not only did I benefit by quickly adding value to the property but I also created a respectable monthly income (cash flow) for myself as well. By keeping the houses fully rented (managing well) and providing all the maintenance and repairs, my actual cash flow was at least twice the amount shown on my income and expense chart in Figure 18-1.

My rental records show that for years 5, 6, and 7 (as shown on the chart), I had no vacancies or uncollected rents at Sierra. That means that the more than $2,200 set aside for vacancies and credit losses for each of those three years wasn't needed. Can you guess who gets to keep that $2,200? The same goes for the management fees, which averaged about $2,300 for each of the same three years since I was the manager. Also, approximately 70 percent of all the money allocated (shown on the chart) for maintenance and repairs was spent for labor! *In this case, it was my labor!* By not hiring outside help, I saved roughly $2,400 each year.

Obviously, my cash flow was improved by the same amount. When you add these amounts (approximately $6,900) to my actual take-home earnings for each of the three years, you can begin to see why small-time start-out investors who are willing to take on rundown properties like Sierra Boulevard can build wealth and financial security rather quickly.

Asset Accumulation Plus Cash Flow

Rich folks understand that income by itself won't make you a millionaire. The woods are full of high-salaried people who live from payday to payday. They earn a ton of money, but they don't save much! They don't spend their money to acquire appreciating assets like Sierra Boulevard. In his bestselling book *The Millionaire Next Door*, author Thomas J. Stanley explains what it takes: "Millionaires," he says, "understand that **building personal net worth** is what made them that way—*earning a high income is not enough!*"

Several years ago, Sierra Boulevard was appraised by a local Member of the Appraisal Institute (MAI) for the purpose of acquiring a 12-foot right-of-way strip for a street improvement project. Both the comparable properties (comps) method and the standard income value method were used by the appraiser to determine the value. Obviously, the potential commercial zoning added some extra value, but I was pleasantly surprised and naturally quite pleased that the new appraised value was $550,000! I can promise you this: it won't take many properties like Sierra Boulevard to get you a personal interview with Mr. Stanley when he writes his next millionaire book.

19

Financing Comes in Two Flavors

When you talk about financing with most folks, it's generally a discussion about various ways to structure a new loan, or *debt*, in order to acquire a property. The new debt might take the form of a traditional bank mortgage using the property as security or it might take the form of seller financing.

Both of these methods are called *debt financing*, and both generally require a lien to be recorded against the property as security for the debt. Debt financing is the most commonly used method for financing real estate transactions. *However*, it's not the only method.

Equity financing offers another option for acquiring properties without adding debt. Instead of using debt and creating additional liability, this method gives away ownership instead. Like debt financing, equity financing can be set up to fit most any transaction, but perhaps the simplest way is to give away part of the deal at the time of acquisition.

Equity Financing

Let's say, for example, that you are blessed with a unique ability to "sniff out" good deals and negotiate superdiscount prices. Let's assume that while applying your talents, you've located a rundown, ugly looking six-unit property that you can purchase at a discount of roughly 25 percent.

The property is worth $300,000, as is, but you've negotiated to buy it from the motivated sellers for $225,000. The sellers had been asking for 10 percent down, but they have finally agreed to accept $20,000, which will take every nickel you can get your hands on. Since fix-up will be required and several obnoxious tenants must be persuaded to leave, it's quite apparent that more money will be needed to complete the project. Financing $205,000 worth of mortgage debt, even at a modest interest rate, plus borrowing an additional $45,000 to complete the fix-up job, seems totally out of the question! Besides that, the sellers have been unwilling to carry financing (provide terms) for any longer than five years.

When I'm negotiating *financing*, or *terms*, 10 years is pretty much my bottom-line position. I start with 30 years before I even think about retreating. In my opinion, five years is barely long enough to ferment the wine. I can still remember how fast I aged when I once signed a five-year promissory note. Time just flew by! For a buyer who's completely "tapped out" after struggling to find a small down payment, there's simply too much risk involved.

What's needed here is a plan that doesn't require borrowing additional money. This is where equity financing comes to the rescue. It's accomplished by giving away a portion of the ownership or equity in exchange for not having any mortgage payments to worry about. It also eliminates the added stress of having negative cash flow, along with the more serious problem of running out of money altogether.

Sharing the Action

Giving away a piece of the deal is far better than having no deal at all, but only if it's done right. That means getting the benefits you need to make it profitable. There is no right or wrong way to share the risk and rewards.

It's strictly an agreement between you and the *share-ee*. Obviously, benefits have different weights, or values, to each party.

In my transactions, I'll always insist on being able to generate monthly cash flow. That means keeping the monthly expenses and mortgage debt reasonable so that the property can afford to pay them from the rental income. I see many deals in which the mortgage payment requires 70 to 75 percent of the income before ever spending a single dime for expenses! That's a disaster waiting to happen. Any time the debt payment exceeds 55 percent of the gross income, you'll quickly discover that you're working for nothing.

In this example, I'm looking for a well-healed investor who can put up the balance of funds needed to close ($205,000), plus the estimated funds for the fix-up costs ($45,000), in exchange for half the deal. He or she will become a 50 percent owner and will share 50 percent of the future profits, as well as half the tax write-offs generated by the property. The monthly payments in return for his or her investment will be half the cash flow from the property, less the operating expenses. Included in the operating expenses will be a 10 percent management fee for yours truly. Well, I can't work for nothing, can I? This can be a very lucrative deal for both parties in the long term.

The Search for the Right Investor

Most do-it-yourself investors who think about sharing investments usually end up with people who look and think the way the investors do. This is not who you want! The person you want to share your investment will more than likely be a professional of some sort—say, a doctor, a CPA, your dentist, or someone who won't miss a meal investing his or her money in the deal. You're looking for a *passive* type of investor who can benefit from the tax write-offs and is eager to double his or her investment in a short (two-year) period of time, as you've explained it. You have clearly pointed out that his or her monthly returns (receivables) will be small at first but they will gradually increase as you fix up the property and raise rents during the first couple of years. The investment person you're seeking should want nothing to do with the property or tenants; he or she will be happy to leave that job up to you!

You might be thinking to yourself, "Where does Jay expect me to find these professionals?" One suggestion is, talk to your tax preparation person if you have one. Tax preparers often advise their clients about investing in real estate to lighten their tax burden. They also recommend investing for growth by taking advantage of real estate appreciation. Another way to find these professionals might be mumbling something about real estate investing to your dentist while he or she is drilling your teeth. Be prepared to explain exactly how your deal works *step by step* to your potential "moneybag" investors. You won't get one thin dime until they believe you can do exactly what you say you can. You must clearly explain how their investment money will earn a profit, and *how much and when!*

I do not recommend taking money from passive investors until you've proven to yourself that you can make your promises come true. I often counsel wannabe investors who must still rely on fee appraisers to tell them property values: if you don't know the property values in your area *forward and backward*, you're not ready to take other people's money just yet. You also need to know what properties will rent for and how to effectively estimate what the fix-up costs will be. Using other people's money can make you a wealthy investor 10 times faster than you can do it alone, but only if you keep your promises. If you don't, you'll have the shortest investment career in town. *Believe me*, your credibility and track record count for everything!

Jay's Basic Investment Model

If I am the investor in the example above, I'm searching for someone who can pony up $250,000 for a period of two to three years. For fixer-upper units, my plan is to acquire properties with low gross rent multipliers (GRMs) and improve them by at least two GRM points. In this example, I'm acquiring a property valued at eight times the gross rents for a discounted price of $225,000. The current annual income for the six small houses on the large residential lot is $37,800. However, one unit is vacant, and two tenants are lagging behind with rent payments. Figure 19-1 shows the estimated values and rental incomes for my particular area. The GRM figures on the left side represent the amount (or rent multiplier)

GRM	Rent, $	No. Units	Per Month, $	Annual Rents, $	Est. Value, $
15X	900	6	5,400	64,800	972,000
14X	875	6	5,250	63,000	882,000
13X	840	6	5,040	60,480	786,240
12X	800	6	4,800	57,600	691,200
11X	750	6	4,500	54,000	594,000
10X	685	6	4,110	49,320	493,200
9X	600	6	3,600	43,200	388,800
8X	525	6	3,150	37,800	302,400
7X	475	6	2,850	34,200	239,400
6X	395	6	2,370	28,440	170,640

Figure 19-1. Jay's investment area: Multiunits

buyers are willing to pay for multiunit properties based on the location and condition of the property within my buying area.

I've explained to Dr. Bob that I estimate the cost of fixing up the six rundown houses to be about $7,500 each, which would include new landscaping and fencing. Fixed-up two-bedroom houses should easily rent for $700 per month—maybe more! In short, I will have no problem increasing both the income and value of the property to at least a 10 GRM level. I've also explained to Dr. Bob that two years from now, our property will be worth $500,000—or almost double the price we paid ($225,000), plus $45,000 for fix-up.

Should we elect to sell the property after two years for $500,000, Dr. Bob and I will both receive our initial investments back first—$20,000 for me and $250,000 for Bob. The remaining balance of $230,000 will be split 50–50 between us. In my co-ownership agreement with Dr. Bob, I have included an option for extending our ownership period by mutual consent. This way, if the selling market tanks in two years, we can elect to keep the property and enjoy the tax shelter, appreciation, and cash flow benefits. Assuming our rents are $700 per unit at the end of two years, Dr. Bob and I will share $4,200 gross income per month. The net income for each of us will be about $13,000 annually.

You might look at these dollar numbers and conclude, "Jay's making a killing on this deal. He has only $20,000 invested, and he's receiving monthly management fees! After two years he will make a profit of $115,000. It sounds like a license to steal!" I will certainly agree that I'm being rewarded quite handsomely, but that's why I'm in this business to begin with. You mustn't forget that my paydays don't come from the amount of money I have invested. They come from my investment skills—putting these deals together and making them work.

Reducing Mortgage Debt with Equity

One of the slickest ways to improve your cash flow is to trade debt for equity when you own seller-financed properties. In my case, nearly 70 percent of all my debt has been seller carryback financing. On some properties I've had as many as four different seller carrybacks, or private mortgages, on the same acquisition. When I purchased the property, I simply took over the private mortgages subject to the existing terms. These notes or private mortgages are all excellent candidates for trading debt for equity, especially during times of inflation when dollars are rapidly losing their buying power.

One of my favorite techniques is to offer the mortgage holder a percentage of my ownership in the property in exchange for the remaining balance of the mortgage debt I owe. For example, let's say I own a property worth $420,000. My mortgage balance is $100,000, requiring monthly payments of $1,000 for the principal and interest. I might offer the mortgage holder 33 percent ownership in my property for the balance of what I owe on the mortgage ($100,000). That means he or she will receive an appreciating asset valued at $140,000, plus the depreciation (tax write-off) and 33 percent of my $1,500 monthly operating income ($500).

What I get is freedom from mortgage debt **and an immediate cash flow increase of $500 per month.** I also get a 10 percent management fee for 33 percent of the property's $3,000 monthly gross income. That will add another $100 per month to my cash flow. The following table shows my financial position before and after this transaction:

	Before, $	After, $
Jay's value	420,000	280,000
Mortgage debt	100,000	-0-
Gross monthly income	3,000	2,000
Expenses	1,500	1,000
Operating income	1,500	1,000
Mortgage payment	1,000	-0-
Monthly cash flow	500	1,000 + $100 management fee

With this transaction, I've doubled my cash flow immediately by using equity that would never benefit me unless I sold the property or borrowed money against it. I'm not very fond of either choice! Obviously, these transactions create a good deal of safety for property owners by eliminating mortgage debt and turning equity into income production. There is no right or wrong way to exchange debt for equity. It's whatever both parties can agree to. So be creative, be fair, and you'll get results.

For investors like me who value the peace of mind that comes from having less debt and more jingle in their pockets every month, the idea of financing a lifestyle with equity rather than taking on additional debt is a winning proposition. From an income tax standpoint, trading debt for equity can be much less expensive than buying extra properties in order to sell off a few so that you can pay off the debt on what's left. One final note: Eliminating debt shuts off the interest cost, which is one of the biggest expenses for all owners with mortgaged real estate.

20

The Harper Houses: A Model Money Machine

It's a good bet that no one you know has more faith in real estate than I do! Back in the days when I had a legitimate job—the 8 to 5 kind—but moonlighted with real estate, many close friends thought my faith was blind. I stayed positive even when the market turned sour, *always believing it was only temporary*. Some of the best deals I ever put together were during the Jimmy Carter presidency. Interest rates soared to 21 percent, and the banks quit lending money for houses. Looking back now, that period of time probably taught me more about the business of investing than I could have ever learned otherwise. *Notice I said* **business**. Business skills are what many investors tend to ignore.

I have always believed that investors, *especially the rich ones*, think differently from most wage earners. Some say that both businesspeople and real estate investors are big risk takers and when they guess wrong, everything they have is gone! I don't fit that description at all. In fact, I believe my real estate investing is much safer than most regular wage earner jobs, *once you learn the ropes!*

Understanding Risk and Reward

Knowing the ropes is not a catch. I don't know of any profession in which you can earn big money if you don't know what you're doing. And as far as risk is concerned, it's greatly diminished with knowledge. Comparing what I do, making money fixing house to deer hunting, real estate investing and fixing up houses might be equivalent to finding a big four-point buck tied to a tree with a six-foot rope. Certainly, I could miss the shot, but the odds are quite heavy in my favor! *Learning the ropes*—like how to invest, how to select which properties to buy, and how to pay for them—has effectively removed almost all the risk for me.

For 25 years or so, my properties have taken very good care of me. I have never once had to beg for food or stand along the freeway exit with a cardboard sign. Early on in my career, I'm almost certain that my cash flow might have been better had I held a sign at the exit. *But even back then*, I was building a solid financial foundation that would eventually earn me freedom from money worries. When you start out on a shoestring, the road ahead is a great deal longer than what's behind! Had I lost everything I owned back then, my loss would have not been as much as losing a single free and clear duplex today.

Real estate investment success does not require a 3.5 grade point average from an Ivy League university! In fact, some skills are found more abundantly in reform schools. Discipline most certainly would qualify as one. Investment success is not determined by the amount of money you have to start with either. In my case, I had to borrow my first down payment or at least part of it. I've found that as a real estate investor, having more money than your competition, especially when you're first starting out, is of no particular advantage. The only difference I can see is that *the more you have, the more you can lose!* Skills and money tend to grow together, *side by side*. Seldom do you end up with one without the other!

A Realistic Financial Plan

Most investors are dreamers, and most have a positive vision. In the early learning stage, investors must become *disciplined* and *realistic* in order to achieve success. Being realistic means having a financial plan that you can write down on paper that makes sense and that you can most certainly explain to someone! Simply telling your wife, husband, or significant other that *"someday,* we're all gonna be rich if we just keep chuggin' along" is not a very good explanation as far as I'm concerned. I believe you need to pencil in a time frame and some dollar numbers to make your case.

In my Fixer Camps, I often use the following real-life situation as an example to help students focus on *when and how much!* Let's say that in the bank, I have $10,000 cash to invest. *I am willing to invest,* or tie up, my $10,000 for 10 years' time. Naturally, I'm seeking the highest and reasonably safest return on my money. What amount of interest, or *return,* should I expect to receive?

The answers will differ from almost everyone, but the majority of my students will suggest around 15 percent. Admittedly, that's an excellent rate of return today. However, it's not nearly enough to change anyone's lifestyle. Fortunately for my students, it's enough so that they can pay for my seminar where, hopefully, they'll learn how to do a whole lot better.

For my class example, I will generally toss out the rate of return of 25 percent. But obviously, the students don't believe they can earn that much, *short of selling dope* (which I don't teach). If you were able to invest $10,000 for 10 years and earn 25 percent compound interest, *how much would you guess you would have in 10 years*? The answer, my friends, is $93,000. You would have earned slightly more than nine times your initial investment, *so how do you feel about that?* Most students will say, "Wow, that's great!" But not the teacher! *Most certainly I'll agree that* 25 percent compound earnings are nothing short of sensational. But to me, as a real estate investor, it's simply not very exciting. "Ten years ago I had $10,000, *and now I have $93,000.* My life hasn't changed, I don't feel rich, *and I'm still workin' at my old job.* Where's the beef?" I would ask. Waiting around for 10 years of my life to earn $80,000 profit does not work for me. I agree, it's a good return, but I'm almost positive I can do much better.

Where's the Beef?

The truth is that I want my $10,000 to work a lot harder and earn more. I'm looking for a little Hamburger Helper here. Even if I could spare $10,000 to invest at 25 percent for the next 10 years of my life, *it's just not enough money for me!* I don't see my life changing all that much, and I'm certainly a long way off from being rich! Most certainly I agree that compounding must be a major ingredient in my recipe for becoming wealthy, but I'll definitely need to add a large dose of leverage to the mix.

Real estate investing, the kind I'm recommending for you, requires both **leverage** and **compounding** for fast results. It works when you combine the **four main types of investment returns** as I show you below. By using these **high returns**, maximizing the best you can, you'll be able to "gas up" your investments and achieve much higher leverage. *Higher leverage* coupled with *compounding* will make you rich in the *shortest period of time.*

Type of Return	Percentage Range
Cash flow	5–40%
Equity Build-Up	10–30
Tax benefits	5–50
Appreciation	20–30
Total	40–250

Some folks may have a few doubts about my numbers, but I can assure you that those numbers are quite reasonable. In fact, for the period of the past several years during which many parts of the country experienced a runaway sellers' market, I'd be willing to bet that my minimum range percentages are probably on the low side. Don't forget that I'm talking about *investment types of real estate* here, even though a few of my numbers might also apply to personal-use properties.

The rate-of-return percentages are important because they help you calculate an estimate of time—*as in, how long before you'll be rich*. I don't know about you, but the thought of ending up rich after I've already left the planet has very little appeal to me. Also, I've never been one to be satisfied with statements like, "Jay, someday I'm sure you'll end up very rich!" Obviously, it's a little hard to pin the time down exactly. *Still*, I'd like to think we could at least pick the right decade!

In the example above, I used 25 percent compounding for a 10-year period of time to arrive at $93,000. If I had used 50 percent instead, my earnings in 10 years would be more than 6 times as much—**approximately**

$587,900. If I were somehow able to double that figure to 100 percent, my 10-year earnings would grow approximately 17½ times more *to slightly over 10 million!* About now, *I think we can all agree that's enough!* Unfortunately, there are very few investment vehicles that will earn money that fast! However, fixing up rundown houses as I suggest can at least put you in the right neighborhood.

Are We Rich Yet?

The magic of real estate investing is that it allows skilled investors to use money they don't have *to earn extremely high investment returns!* For example, let's say I purchased a $300,000 rundown investment property, paying the sellers only 10 percent down, or $30,000. *Then one year later*, after cleanup and fix-up, my new appraisal comes in at $420,000. Just look at what my $30,000 has accomplished! In a single year, **it has multiplied itself four times** (400 percent)! Can you see why $10,000 earning just $93,000 after waiting 10 long years is getting a measly return? Using my investment percentage numbers, it becomes much easier to calculate how you can actually become wealthy during your lifetime on this planet.

Earning 100 percent returns is quite easy during the first several years of ownership. But then the rate of return gradually declines. That's why during your "gung-ho" high-five investing years, you need to aggressively keep acquiring new properties. In johhny lunch bucket jargon, you need to keep kickin' butt 'til you achieve your goals! For most of us, that means getting rich. At least half the students who have attended my Fixer Camps and have followed the strategies I'm discussing here are already rich or well on their way. Many are working for themselves full-time or doing whatever else wealthy people do!

If anyone should ask you, "Is investing $10,000 at 25 percent for 10 years a good deal?" Obviously, your answer should be yes! However, by now, I'm hoping you realize that investing in real estate in the way I'm suggesting is a whole lot better. If I had stuck my $20,000 down payment in the bank instead of using it to purchase my Harper Avenue houses, I'd still be working days at the phone company. Harper Avenue consisted of eight boxy little houses—*two bedrooms, one bath each*—located on an oversized city lot about a mile from my home on the river bluffs. By the way, it's boxy little houses like those on Harper Avenue that pay for my unobstructed view of the annual salmon run!

The Harper Avenue Rentals

Buying properties from sellers who are in the same business as I am and who are successful too takes a whole different strategy. For one thing, money is usually not what motivates them. More often it's about lifestyle or retirement—*selling out after a successful run.*

That pretty much describes what the veterinarian seller was doing when he approached my broker, Merv, at a local Rotary meeting. He had owned several other properties much like the Harper houses but he had sold all of those and now had only the eight Harper Avenue houses. The houses were exactly the kind I teach my students to look for! They were separate units (detached), situated nicely in a newer residential neighborhood. They were rented for at least $100 under the market value. It's the kind of property I lust and crave for. Harper Avenue, for me, was love at first sight! Although Merv and the local pet doctor were good Rotarian brothers, they weren't nearly as chummy when it came time for sharing real estate secrets. It wasn't 'til after all three of us sat down together for a serious heart-to-heart chat that asbestos suddenly popped up in the conversation! Seems that the vet had opened escrow twice before during the past 12 months, only to see both buyers back out after being shocked by expensive cost estimates for removing the asbestos siding.

Confessions Are Beautiful Things to Hear

Obviously, I now understood why the vet still owned the Harper Avenue houses when all his other properties had sold off rather quickly—mostly to his buddies, as I later found out. The only reason my broker, Merv, had been told about the Harper Avenue houses was because of *asbestos*. I'm certain, looking back now, that the vet was fully aware that by tipping off Merv, "*Jay would automatically become an interested buyer.*" See how cagey these experienced owners can be! Had it not been for asbestos, I'm almost certain that neither Merv or I would have heard anything about Harper Avenue!

Finding out about the asbestos siding was about as close as I ever expect to come to winning the lotto jackpot! "Why is that?" you ask. Because then I knew the seller's "hot button." *I knew what was motivating him*, and I also knew that he was likely to have a very difficult time selling the property with its asbestos siding to so-called normal investors. After a little Lieutenant Columbo detective work, Merv learned that the cost estimates (actual bids) for removing the asbestos siding were approximately $4,000 per house. Eight houses at $4,000 each and that did not even include the replacement siding and labor to install it.

It was my guess at the time that the total job cost would be in the neighborhood of $50,000 for the siding replacement work. That was nearly one-third the total cost of buying all eight houses. My initial offer for Harper was $150,000, although I did pay a little more as you shall learn. I'll tell you why when I show you the final terms we agreed to. But first, let's talk about *asbestos shingles*.

The first thing you need to know is that no law requires removal of these shingles if they are not cracked, damaged, or falling off or if you are not planning to modernize the units with HUD grants or loans. What the failed escrow buyers didn't realize was that all they were required to do was replace the broken shingles and renail the loose ones and paint over them. That's what is normally required to abate the problem in most areas. Since the houses needed painting, *regardless* of the shingles, I didn't consider paint as an extra expense. My extra costs were only $250 per house. *Here's what I did.*

Abatement Combined with Beautification

Asbestos shingles are not sold anymore, *so how could I replace the damaged shingles?* I removed the shingles from the worst side of one or two houses; then I resided them with T1-11 panel siding. As a result, I had a big pile of undamaged shingles to work with. Next, I replaced the bad shingles on all the other houses from my stockpile before caulking and painting. This technique saved me approximately $48,000, when compared to the cost of removing all the shingles. **Knowledge is power,** *and when you have it*, you'll leave your competition in the dust!

Negotiating with the veterinarian required several trips back and forth, mostly to ask questions about the property. Merv and I both understood the vet was by no means planning to give his property away. I'm almost certain he would have taken $150,000 cash if he thought that was our last offer. However, he had already explained to Merv that *he would much prefer to carry paper*. From a tax standpoint, he was much better off with an installment sale. Besides, the only way I could have produced $150,000 cash back then was to rob an armored truck. An installment sale would work perfectly for both of us, and the $20,000 in my piggy bank was perfectly agreeable for the down payment. The vet had asked Merv for a 10-year payoff on his carryback note, but he finally agreed to 20 years when I offered to pay $160,000 total price. What I was really after was easy payback terms. By paying a little extra and waiving the asbestos card, *that's exactly what I got*.

When I write my offers to purchase real estate, they don't look much like regular offers written on the standard forms used by most real estate agents. My offers are written on just plain 8½-by-11 letter-sized white paper. I like to start from scratch where I can utilize my vast knowledge—some say *half vast*—putting transactions together. Boilerplate terms and drip-dried clauses for backside protection are not really needed. My offers demonstrate the free spirit of creativity, and they're written with a great deal of thought toward achieving my goals—namely, *very few changes and hardly any counteroffers*.

Designer Offers Are Powerful Buyers' Tools

As you read, you must keep in mind the kind of properties I'm interested in acquiring. Most are rundown, ugly to look at, and older, and they generally have management problems. Naturally these are the kinds of properties that have motivated sellers, which are absolutely essential to make my offers work. All older properties have a variety of things wrong with them, and it's *these things* that I design my offers around. In other words, my offers don't accentuate the positive but, rather, the negative! This was the kind of offer I designed to acquire my Harper Avenue houses. I employed the three apocalyptic conditions that plague nearly every older property— namely, asbestos, lead-based paint, and black mold growth.

Terms in My Offers That Discourage the Sellers' Counteroffers

Item no. 7

Buyer is aware that all Harper Avenue houses have asbestos siding. Buyer agrees to abate problem with no additional costs or liability to seller. Buyer agrees to waive all tests regarding asbestos abatement normally paid by seller.

Item no. 8

Buyer agrees to waive lead-based paint inspection report and eliminate any hazardous problems at no cost to seller.

Item no. 9

Buyer is aware of dangerous mold levels in at least 4 of the Harper Avenue houses. Have confirmed with property manager, ABC Management, Inc., that mold abatement has been helpful but not very successful. Buyer will accept houses in as-is condition without further testing and additional expense to seller. Buyer agrees to hold seller harmless for existing mold conditions for all houses afflicted.

You may be thinking to yourself, "Jay must be smokin' those funny-looking cigarettes again! Why in the world would he take on these kinds of problems?" The short answer is, this is what I do! I specialize in older fixer-type properties. Most older properties have these problems, and when you learn to fix 'em, you can earn the big bucks for your skills. Remember Red Adair: he quickly snuffed out oil well fires that no one else would touch, and it made him a millionaire. *Become a specialist; you'll be very well paid for your efforts.*

Now bear in mind that the veterinarian seller was no dummy who just fell off a turnip truck! He had owned several older properties similar to Harper Avenue, and he was quite successful as a rundown property investor. However, the doc was not a hands-on guy like I am. I seriously doubt if he knew asbestos shingles from Swedish rye toast. Obviously, *mold* was not a new word in his vocabulary nor was *lead-base paint*. Several of his renters were HUD-subsidized tenants requiring annual inspections. Even so, the ABC Management Company more or less insulated the vet from the dirty little secrets of day-to-day management.

My offers are designed to have a chilling or intimidating effect on sellers and most certainly their agents. Licensed real estate agents are already aware of the seriousness of the "failure to disclose." My offers are intended to make both the agents and property owners fully aware, in writing, about conditions they would much rather not hear about, and, in their fondest dreams, would much prefer the buyer never find out about. This is the reason I like to address each issue individually, giving a separate item number for each condition as I've shown above—in this case, asbestos, lead-based paint, and mold! These are very powerful bargaining chips to have on the table when you're negotiating to finalize your offer. Sometimes when I feel the need for something a little stronger, I'll toss in another of my favorite terms like this one:

A Term in My Offers That Is Guaranteed to Weaken the Sellers' Resistance

Item no. 10

Buyer is aware that roofs on units 5, 6, and 10 are badly deteriorated and require replacement. Buyer accepts roofs as is and will hold seller harmless for all damages caused by leaks.

Quite often at seminars, students will ask, "How do you know so much about the roofs? Do you hire a professional roof inspector, or do you climb up and look for yourself?" The answer is, neither one. I'm getting way too old to be crawling around on junky roofs. Besides, who says there's any requirement to look any closer than from my kitchen table. After all, that's where I write these offers. Get the picture?

The Human Nature Element

Just for a moment, try and picture the agent as he or she returns to the seller with my offer in hand. How would you guess he or she might feel discussing items 7, 8, and 9 with the client (the seller)? Would you think the agent might be just a little hesitant to suggest that the client counter my offer with a higher price or better terms? Now, pretend you are the seller of a junky property and you desperately want to sell. *"Jay's offer is the only reasonable offer you've had!"* Would you be quick to bump up the price the way that many agents routinely suggest to their clients? My guess is that you wouldn't. In fact, I'm guessing that with all the negative stuff spelled out in items 7, 8, and 9, you'd feel extremely fortunate just to keep the offer alive without losing anything!

Obviously, this is the kind of response I'm looking for from sellers. By clearly pointing out these negative conditions in my offers, it's my hope to discourage any thoughts of a counteroffer in the minds of both the seller and his or her agent. I want them afraid to even think about any changes for fear I might cancel my offer and disappear. When either party, *buyer or seller*, writes a counterproposal of any kind, there's always a good chance the other side won't respond. When this happens, **the deal is dead!**

My offers also tend to poison the well for any competing offers. For example, let's say you're the seller's agent and you receive another offer that mentions nothing about items 7, 8, and 9. Would you feel compelled —in other words, would you feel *legally obligated*—to discuss these items about the property? Obviously, you now have knowledge about them because of my offer, which is more than likely still in your file.

The Pursuit of a Cash Flow Deal

The Harper houses were my kind of property. Neglected, low rents, and managed by the local ABC Property Management Company. ABC did maintenance only when something quit working. By the way, ABC is not much different from any other management company I've found! Their strongest suits are collecting rents and hiring high-priced plumbers.

The veterinarian was a proud owner. But more than that, he was already semiwealthy and successful. My guess is that he was in his early sixties, and from what I could tell, the Harper houses were the only rental units he had left to sell. Repeating what I said earlier, the only reason I was even in the running as a buyer was because of **mold** and **asbestos**!

Several would-be buyers had already passed on the houses before my agent, Merv, was even told the property was available. I thought long and hard about my offer before writing it because I knew the vet would not mess around with any lowball proposal, and I most certainly didn't want to insult him.

My agent, Merv, was fairly certain that $150,000 would buy the houses, and, of course, the doc had already told him he wanted an installment sale. Based on that information, I wrote my offer. Average interest rates at the time were in the 9 to 11 percent range, but I decided 6 percent might do the trick. Rather quickly, I learned my decision was wrong! Merv informed me that my offer sounded okay with the doc, except that he felt my interest rate was not quite up to snuff. Weekly Rotary meetings with the veterinarian gave Merv a special advantage of quick feedbacks.

As always, my biggest concern was cash flow, and my proposed payment of $779 per month on the seller's carryback mortgage was about as high as I could pay. Rents were averaging just $175 per month at Harper Avenue, and I knew that after I coughed up the $20,000 cash down payment, I'd basically be tapped out!

Paying Less Now but More Later On

My revised offer bumped up the selling price to $160,000. *I decided to pay more* and, in turn, ask the doc for help with the payback (terms). Basically, I designed a variable interest rate payment plan that would allow me lower payments in the early years in exchange for higher rates and payments later on. I would pay an average of 9 percent interest on the doc's carryback mortgage of $140,000. *However*, I would do it with interest-only payments during the first 10 years, then 9 percent amortized payments (30-year schedule) for the next 10 years. The entire balance would be due and payable at the end of 20 years. Figure 20-1 shows my customized payment schedule for the $140,000 mortgage at a variable interest rate that averages 9 percent.

My second try was a winner. The vet signed my offer within two or three minutes after Merv handed it to him. Now the Harper houses were mine! Merv later informed me that the doc's personal real estate agent stayed hidden in the background. My (terms) items 7, 8, and 9 had scared

Years	Monthy Payments, $	Interest Rate, %	
1	758	6.5	$292 underpay (neg.)
2	817	7.0	$233 underpay (neg.)
3	875	7.5	$175 underpay (neg.)
4	933	8.0	$117 underpay (neg.)
5	992	8.5	$ 58 underpay (neg.)
6	1,108	9.5	$ 58 overpay (plus)
7	1,167	10.0	$117 overpay (plus)
8	1,225	10.5	$175 overpay (plus)
9	1,283	11.0	$233 overpay (plus)
10	1,342	11.5	$292 overpay (plus)
11–20	1,126	9.0	Amortized 30 years

Figure 20-1. A payment schedule for a $140,000 mortgage with a variable interest rate that averages 9 percent

the heck out of him! Even though he had prepared formal disclosure documents, which I signed, he was totally relieved to see the deal approved without his being in the room.

Dealing directly, *one-on-one* with sellers is always much easier when it comes to disclosure rules. Agents are always concerned about lawsuits, so they feel duty bound to fess up to everything they know about the property. On the positive side, agents will more likely advise their clients, that they would be "smart to take Jay's offer and dump this dog; there are just too many problems! Besides, we may never get a better offer." Don't ya just love it when the seller's agent starts working on your side!

The Value of Good Terms

Harper Avenue was a winner almost from day 1. The rents were even a little bit more under the market value than I'd originally thought. My earlier estimate of $100 per house turned out closer to $150. Harper would soon become one of my best cash flow properties because of the favorable mortgage terms the veterinarian had given me. The only comment Merv ever heard from the doc regarding the negative terms in my offer was, "Boy, I certainly wasn't aware of all those things. Apparently my management company took care of everything themselves."

Saving nearly $400 per month on the initial mortgage payments—$1,126.47 at 9 percent amortized *versus* $758—equaled $368.47 **in savings**, or *$46 per house, in cash flow to me*. The easy payback mortgage payment schedule allowed me to pay much less in the early years when my fix-up costs were the highest, *then* make up the underpayments later after the houses were fixed up and painted *and, of course, earning much higher rents*.

In the short period of 14 months, all the Harper houses were renting for $300 and $325 per month—*$2,500 total monthly gross!* Debt service (mortgage payments) was only 33 percent of the total monthly income. Having mortgage payments of 50 percent or less of gross income is like finding gold in the street. It will never happen unless you take the upper hand and control the financing. Compare single-family-house investing where the rents are $1,000 per month with mortgage payments of $725. Can you see why properties like the Harper houses are exactly what the doctor ordered for investors suffering from the "cash flow blues"!

A Long-Term Money Machine

The Harper Avenue property was the first stopping point for Fixer Camp students visiting my properties in Redding for a dozen years or more. The property was ideally located in the fastest-growing part of town. And even though the houses were all situated on a large single lot, each of the eight detached houses had its own separate yard with a small lawn area. Driving time from my seminar location is less than three minutes in the slow lane!

During my ownership (over 20 years), the property was always a top income producer. And because affordable two-bedroom one-bath houses are somewhat scarce in my town, *the turnover rate was always far less than comparable apartment units*. Year after year, rent adjustments increased my net earnings, and eventually, before I sold Harper, my mortgage payments consumed only 25 percent of my annual income. Anyone can make money with this kind of income/payment ratio! Naturally, this is why I was always proud to show Harper Avenue to my students! It was a *model money machine*

The Harper houses sold for three times what I paid, and the buyer felt *he'd struck the deal of a lifetime.* Fixer Camp students often ask me, "Don't you have to be a good manager and do a little more maintenance to operate Harper types of properties?" Yes, you do! With landlording, doing it right is the key to success for Harper types of properties, *but just look at the benefits I get!* Once again, I'll repeat what I've told you already: I'm probably the highest-paid do-it-yourself plumber you've ever met, *and it's rare that I stop a leak on the first visit!*

Many people have asked me, "Why would you pay $10,000 extra for a property with mold and asbestos?" The answer is that I wanted the vet to give me **soft payback terms** on his carryback mortgage. I felt the extra $10,000 was an excellent trade-off. Let me say this as loudly and clearly as I possibly can: By far, **the most important part of any noncash real estate transaction is the way you're allowed to pay off the mortgage debt.** In less than five years, I had all my money back, including my down payment and initial fix-up costs. After that, *my net-net earnings*, year after year, exceeded my down payment. Quite frankly, learning to handle asbestos and mold is hardly too much to ask for this kind of reward— wouldn't you agree?

21

Working for Tax-Free Income

Rich folks get that way in part because of how they earn their income. You've no doubt heard the old adage "It's not how much you make that counts. *It's how much you get to keep for yourself.*" Taxes inhibit the ability of most working folks to become rich because as their earnings go up, so do their taxes. Our progressive tax system goes in only one direction and that's up! Unless you can somehow control or eliminate having your taxes increase as your income increases, it's almost impossible to rise above the working class, which, of course, ain't rich.

W-2 wage earners pay the lion's share of income taxes. In fact, if the government should ever decide to pass out gold medals to the real tax heroes, all the regular working folks who swap their time and energies for W-2 earnings would surely get one. I haven't quite figured out exactly where they should pin them, however!

One of the important lessons the superrich learn from the very start is that their income must be invisible to taxing authorities. Okay, now don't throw up your arms and get all nervous thinking I'm talking about something illegal. I promise you, I'm not! What I'm discussing here is all perfectly legal, and, in fact, it's your right. But you must decide because the choice is ultimately yours to make!

Invisible Income

About now, you might be thinking to yourself, "Jay's been watching too many reruns of that ancient radio-television show called *The Shadow*!" The Shadow was a completely invisible man. Obviously, if you're not a senior citizen like me, you probably missed all those exciting episodes of yesteryear. The Shadow was a very cool guy. He could suddenly appear out of nowhere and hit you in the mouth, and you wouldn't see a thing. That's exactly how you need to earn your income so that the IRS and state taxing authorities never see it. Stay with me here—you might discover this is easier than you think!

In my business of buying properties and adding value to houses, I'm constantly looking for properties that I can acquire for substantial discounts. "What's that?" you ask. To me, substantial discounts range anywhere from 20 to 50 percent below the true market value of a property. Let's say, for example, I find a house that I believe has a true market value of $250,000. Using my creative negotiating skills, I convince the owners to sell their property for $150,000. That's a substantial discount (40 percent).

Let's assume for a moment that it took me 50 hours of my time or labor to put this deal together. How much am I getting paid? If you divide my 50 hours into the $100,000 discount, the answer is, way too much: $100,000 divided by 50 hours equals $2,000 per hour. Obviously, there will be many other expenses to bring the property up to its market potential ($250,000), but as you can clearly see, my pay will still be substantial! More importantly, whatever the amount is, it's totally invisible to everyone, including IRS. Suddenly, I've become "The Shadow," as far as my earnings are concerned. Keep in mind here, that we're talking about personal income taxes (those nasty deductions taken from your paycheck if you happen to be a W-2 wage earner).

It's obvious that if you purchase an asset for $100,000 less than its true market value, you've somehow got to be a little richer, even if there's additional expenses to make the property market ready. The point is that my $100,000 discount feels like I'm earning $100,000, but it's tax free to me. You won't find a line on a 1040 federal tax form to report one nickel of my $100,000. In fact, the government is not asking me to report any earnings from this activity. As far as it's concerned, the full $100,000 I earned using my negotiating skills is a total freebie. This is what I call "working for my personal net worth"! I'm *building*, or *increasing, my equity*, which in turn will earn more rental income for me. Rental income (passive income) for the most part is sheltered by my depreciation expenses, leaving little or nothing to pay for personal income taxes.

Earning Payroll Wages Is Much Different

If you're an upper-class wage earner making $100,000 in W-2 wages, your payroll earnings will receive a far different treatment. Obviously, **you're not the least bit invisible.** Everyone knows exactly how much you earn, and they plan to share it with you. Depending on your marital status, number of dependents, and so on, your tax deductions will vary somewhat. Still, you'll end up with substantially less money than the amount you actually earned. Federal income taxes, state taxes, and your FICA deductions (Social Security taxes) will gobble up at least 35 to 40 percent of your paycheck in my state, leaving you much less than you thought you were making.

Payroll wages are very easy to track since employers are required by law to keep perfect accounting of every nickel you earn. Your annual W-2 form shows exactly what you earned—naturally, a copy must be sent to the IRS and state taxing authorities with your regular tax forms. If you should toss it in the garbage by mistake, no need to worry—your company has already provided the tax folks the very same information on its payroll reporting forms. After all, that's how the company proves its expense deduction for the wages it pays. If you are a W-2 wage earner, you're trapped! You can't hide one thin dime of your earnings from anyone, especially the tax folks who stand ready with open hands, eager to grab their share!

Keeping as much of the money you earn is just as important to your financial well-being and overall wealth as earning it to begin with. Many moons ago, while toiling at the telephone company, my average tax deductions would automatically trim about $15,000 each year from my paychecks—before I even received them! I say *automatic* because my employer withheld the money without ever discussing it with me. That's the beauty of payroll deductions. If somehow I had been allowed to keep my annual tax deductions and invest the money for my own benefit, my combined tax deductions invested at a piddly 5 percent in a government certificate account would have made me a millionaire in a normal 30-year telephone career. Since I quit after 23 years of service, I would have had to settle for a measly $700,000. Still, that's a big wad of dough compared to the worthless pile of paycheck stubs I received.

It's Not What You Earn—It's How You Earn

Everyone gets to choose how they will earn income! Obviously, knowing a little something about the way taxes work can greatly influence the decision! Three different people can be earning exactly the same amount of income and yet be paying different amounts of personal income tax on their earnings.

Without a full-blown discussion on revenue Tax Code 469, let me simply say that all income is divided into three different categories. As you might have guessed, each of these categories gets taxed differently. Let's take Billy Bob, for example. He's single and earns $35,000 annually selling T-shirts and popcorn at the local county fair. He has a special trailer he tows around to operate his mobile business. When tax time rolls around, he takes the standard deduction of $4,000, plus another $3,000 or so for a single dependent. This reduces his taxable income to $28,000. He now pays 15 percent federal taxes, plus another 15 percent for Social Security taxes: 30 percent of $28,000 equals $8,400 in taxes. This means Billy Bob gets to keep only $26,000 of his total earnings.

Slick Willie has a $35,000 income, just like Billy Bob. The only difference is that Slick Willie earns his income from promissory notes and mortgages. He's single so, like Billy Bob, he gets the standard deduction of $4,000 and also $3,000 for one dependent. Slick Willie's taxable income, like Billy Bob's, is $28,000. His federal tax bracket is 15 percent, but since his income is called **portfolio income**, he doesn't pay Social

Security taxes: 15 percent of $28,000 equals $4,200 in taxes, which means that Slick Willie gets to keep $30,800 of his earnings.

Landlord Louise earns $35,000 a year, just like Billy Bob and Slick Willie. Her income comes from rents, which is called **passive income.** Like the others, Louise is single, and therefore she takes the standard $4,000 deduction and also $3,000 for one dependent. Her taxable income is also $28,000. However, Louise owns $700,000 worth of income-producing real estate, which nets her 5 percent annually. Louise, just like the others, is in the 15 percent tax bracket. But first, she has $600,000 worth of depreciable assets, which generates $28,000 annually in depreciation write-offs: $28,000 taxable income less $28,000 depreciation equals 0 taxes. Therefore, Louise gets to keep every single nickel she earns!

As you can see, the three separate taxpayers are earning exactly the same amount of income and are in the same tax bracket, but there are substantial differences in what each one gets to keep. Landlord Louise's income is earned from the assets she owns. Because of the depreciation expenses she's allowed to take, her $35,000 income is pretty much invisible to taxing authorities.

Acquiring assets like rental houses that produce income and depreciation is a much more efficient method of acquiring wealth than working as a W-2 wage earner because you don't have to share with others. In this example, Landlord Louise has kept $8,400 more of her earnings than Billy Bob and $4,200 more than Slick Willie. Should Louise decide to reinvest her $8,400 tax savings to buy more real estate each year, she could reasonably expect those funds to earn her a million dollars or so during the next 10 years.

The Awesome Power of Keeping What You Earn

After I quit my job, I can still remember how frightened I was about giving up my dependable income to become a full-time real estate investor. Although my gross rents far exceeded my telephone paychecks, I had tons of expenses and mortgage payments. For the first several months or so, I constantly worried about whether there would be enough rent money left over for me. But somehow there always was, and eventually my worries were gone.

After a year or so of being on my own, I began to realize that there's a huge difference between gross income and net income—that is, the amount you get to keep. I also became aware that many of my personal expenses could now be paid by my real estate business. The accountants call these expenses *above-the-line deductions*. In other words, items I use for my business like my automobile and transportation expenses are now paid by my rental properties. Back at the phone company, those kinds of expenses were paid from my after-tax, *net earnings*; in other words, they were *below-the-line deductions*.

So working full-time in my own business allows me to treat many of my personal expenses as business expenses, and the few personal expenses that remain, such as the cost of new suits for work just sorta fade away. I often refer to myself as a walking, breathing expense account. What became quite obvious to me when I had been on my own for a while, working for myself, was that many of my normal out-of-pocket expenses were actually business expenses; most of the other miscellaneous expenses such as the cost of lunch every day, five days a week, with my telephone buddies simply disappeared altogether.

Generating Tax-Free Money to Live On

A question frequently asked is this: "How do I get money for groceries if I keep making improvements to my properties but never sell them? My rental income is simply not enough to support my living expenses after paying the mortgage payments and operating costs." The quickest method is to pledge equity or borrow money against the property. Borrowed money is not taxable income; therefore, the taxing authorities could care less about what you do with the money. Perhaps equally important, you still own the appreciating asset, and you still enjoy the income from rents, which provides an excellent hedge against inflation. The temptation to sell a well-performing income property should be avoided when you're in the wealth-building stage.

In my book *Investing in Fixer-Uppers* (McGraw-Hill, 2003), I wrote about fixing up the Haywood houses. I calculated my earnings to be approximately $8,000 per month for doing the major share of the fix-up work myself. Most would agree that those were fairly decent earnings

30 years ago, but my big mistake was selling the property to create my payday. Twenty years later, the 12-unit property was valued at over $1 million. Pocketing $8,000 a month for my 12 months' worth of fix-up work, paid for by selling the property, turned out to be one of my dumbest decisions. I could have very easily borrowed the same amount against my equity and still owned Haywood today!

Balancing Income and Depreciation

Pocketing real dollars from rents while at the same time reporting zero income to the taxing authorities is at the heart of living tax free with real estate investments. The statement in Figure 21-1 shows you what I mean.

	Cash Flow	Tax Flow
Annual Income	$12,000	$12,000
Annual Expenses	$ 5,000	$ 5,000
Prop. tax $1,200		
Insurance 600		
Utilities 460		
Maintenance 1,400		
Management 1,000		
Services 340		
Total Expenses	$ 5,000	$ 5,000
Net Operating Income	$ 7,000	$ 7,000
Depreciation		$ 4,000
Mortgage Payments	$ 5,000	
Interest $5,000		$ 5,000
Amortization -0-		
Cash Flow, Spendable	$ 2,000	
Taxable Income		($ 2,000)

Figure 21-1. Income and expense statement for Fixer Jay's Shangri-la duplex

From a cash flow standpoint, Jay's Shangri-la duplex is generating $2,000 annually in real spendable dollars. However, when tax time rolls around for reporting the income to the IRS, we've pitched a total shutout! There is no taxable income to report. In fact, the $2,000 loss can be used to offset positive income on another property or carried on the books to be used against positive income in the future. Working on your own properties to produce **invisible, tax-free income** is how poor working folks become rich real estate tycoons. The challenge, of course, is to earn enough personal income without selling the assets that produce it.

Getting Bigger and Bigger Properties

Section 1031 of the Internal Revenue Code is the investor's ultimate tool for pyramiding real estate wealth. This provision allows investors to grow bigger investments by exchanging their smaller properties for bigger properties without paying one dime of income taxes on the gain!

Unlike selling a property and paying taxes on the profit or gain, 1031 exchanging allows investors to simply move their total equity from a disposed property to a new and bigger property, provided that a few simple rules are followed.

Section 1031, tax-deferred exchanging, is designed to preserve the investors' capital as long as they keep investing in what the tax code calls "like-kind properties." The idea of keeping all your investment dollars intact for reinvestment is a powerful incentive to trade properties rather than sell them.

Appendix A

Five Investment Locations

Most duplexes and multiunit properties recommended in this book can be found in almost any sizable town or city in two locations: **downtown commercial** and **older residential**.

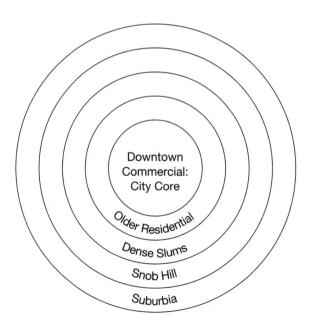

Figure A-1.

Appendix B

Charts Showing Typical Rents in My Town

Figures B-1 and B-2 show typical rents for single-family houses and multi-unit properties in my town. As shown in Figure B-1, a single-family house that costs $250,000 will rent for $850 per month. The rent-to-value ratio is 0.34, which I consider very low.

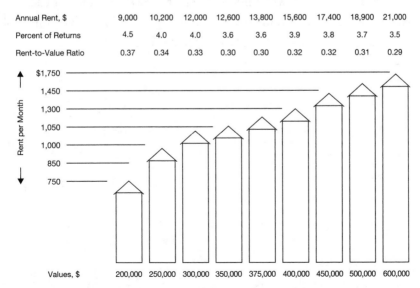

Annual Rent, $	9,000	10,200	12,000	12,600	13,800	15,600	17,400	18,900	21,000
Percent of Returns	4.5	4.0	4.0	3.6	3.6	3.9	3.8	3.7	3.5
Rent-to-Value Ratio	0.37	0.34	0.33	0.30	0.30	0.32	0.32	0.31	0.29

Figure B-1. Typical rents from single-family houses in my town

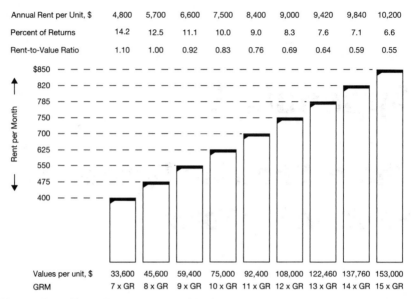

Annual Rent per Unit, $	4,800	5,700	6,600	7,500	8,400	9,000	9,420	9,840	10,200
Percent of Returns	14.2	12.5	11.1	10.0	9.0	8.3	7.6	7.1	6.6
Rent-to-Value Ratio	1.10	1.00	0.92	0.83	0.76	0.69	0.64	0.59	0.55

Values per unit, $	33,600	45,600	59,400	75,000	92,400	108,000	122,460	137,760	153,000
GRM	7 x GR	8 x GR	9 x GR	10 x GR	11 x GR	12 x GR	13 x GR	14 x GR	15 x GR

Figure B-2. Typical rents from multiunit properties in my town

Figure B-2 is calculated based on values for a typical six-unit property in my town. Remember, I'm talking about rundown properties (fixer-uppers). Based on Figure B-2, I would expect to pay approximately $273,600 for six rundown units that rent for $475 per month each, or $34,200 annually. The rent-to-value ratio equals 1.00, which is almost three times more than the ratio for a typical single-family house.

Appendix C

Gross Rent Multiplier Charts for Income Properties in My Town

- Figure C-1. Gross rent multiplier (GRM) chart for my town.
- Figure C-2. Likely description of property based on its GRM.
- Figure C-3. How difficult to acquire a property in terms of down payment, likelihood of trades, and motivation of the sellers based on the property's GRM. Note: The lower the GRM, the easier to acquire the property.
- Figure C-4. Handyperson skills required based on the GRM and the condition of the property. The lower the GRM, the more rundown the property is; therefore, a six times GRM property will require the most skills to fix up.

Typical Small Income (Six-Unit) Properties: Two Bedrooms, 750 Square Feet, in Jay's Investment Area					
GRM	**Description**	**Rent, $**	**Rents (6), $**	**Annual, $**	**Value, $**
15X	Snob Hill	900	5,400	64,800	972,000
14X	Premo	875	5,250	63,000	882,000
13X	Deluxe	835	5,010	60,120	781,560
12X	Desirable	795	4,770	57,240	686,880
11X	Average plus	725	4,350	52,200	574,200
10X	Average	675	4,050	48,600	486,000
9X	Rough	595	3,570	42,840	385,560
8X	Rundown	525	3,150	37,800	302,400
7X	Pigsty	450	2,700	32,400	226,800
6X	Falling down	375	2,250	27,000	162,000

Figure C-1. Gross rent multiplier (GRM) chart for use in establishing rent-to-value ratios

Typical Small Income (Six-Unit) Properties: Two Bedrooms, 750 Square Feet, in Jay's Investment Area		
GRM	**Description**	**Likely Location**
15X	Snob Hill	Best area in town
14X	View plus	Special, near water, hilltop
13X	Premo	Best apartment location
12X	Deluxe	Rentals with frills: pools, etc.
11X	Desirable	Near schools, residential areas
10X	Average	Decent areas, apartment areas
9X	Blue collar	Near factories: plants, sawmills
8X	Rundown	Anywhere
7X	Trashy	Anywhere
6X	Pigsty	Anywhere
5X	Falling down	Slum, intercity, rural
4X	Condemned	Slum area, "OK Corral"

Figure C-2. Likely description of property based on its GRM

GRM	Description	How Difficult to Acquire
\multicolumn{3}{} **Typical Small Income (Six-Unit) Properties:** Two Bedrooms, 750 Square Feet, in Jay's Investment Area		
15X	Snob Hill	All cash, no deals
14X	Premo	All cash to existing loan
13X	Deluxe	All cash to existing loan
12X	Desirable	Likely: all cash or tough terms
11X	Average plus	Big down payment, terms possible!
10X	Average	Sellers want average price
9X	Rough	More cash, better terms
8X	Rundown	Trades likely acceptable
7X	Pigsty	Expect good terms
6X	Falling down	Easy seller, very flexible

Figure C-3. How difficult to acquire a property in terms of down payment, likelihood of trades, and motivation of the sellers based on the property's GRM

GRM	Description	Do-It-Yourself Skills Required
\multicolumn{3}{} **Typical Small Income (Six-Unit) Properties:** Two Bedrooms, 750 Square Feet, in Jay's Investment Area		
15X	Snob Hill	Professional manager-owner
14X	Premo	Professional manager-owner
13X	Deluxe	Likely professional manager-owner
12X	Desirable	Maintenance and management
11X	Average plus	Maintenance and management
10X	Average	Not much to do
9X	Rough	Improve looks mostly
8X	Rundown	90% cleanup with some fixin'
7X	Pigsty	Fixin' and cleanup
6X	Falling down	Journeyman skills

Figure C-4. Handyperson skills required based on the GRM and the condition of the property

Appendix D

Typical Fixer Jay Offer to Purchase

Figure D-1 is an actual offer; only the names have been changed. Remember that this offer is typical for the kind of properties I buy—ugly and run-down. This is not the kind of offer you would use to purchase a property in top condition or to purchase a home.

Refer to Chapters 17 and 20 for more details on how I structure my offers and the reasons why I write them the way I do.

Appendix D

APN: 005 390 013 & 005 390 012

ADDRESS: 1120–1124 Easy Street North, Shasta Lake, CA 96019

FROM: Jeb Owens and Sharon Owens, Husband and Wife

TO: Gerald A. Brown and Kelley Brown, Trustees of Brown Family Trust

Purchase Price:	**$300,000**
Cash Down Payment:	$ 50,000
Seller to Carry Financing:	$250,000
Terms:	Interest Only 6%
Monthly Payments:	$1,250
Term:	10 Years, Then All Principal and Interest Due and Payable

Terms and Conditions

1. Seller warrants there are no outstanding "fix-it" letters or letters of demand for repairs, code violations, hazardous conditions, or red tags from city, county, or any other government agency.
2. Offer is contingent upon Buyer being able to obtain standard fire and liability insurance policy.
3. Buyer agrees to waive standard lead-based paint and asbestos tests required for older properties. Years built 1938 and 1952.
4. Seller warrants all dwellings are "hooked up" and serviced by city/county water and sewer providers (Shasta Lake).
5. Buyer has observed marginal condition of roof on structure 1124 Easy. Buyer will waive roof inspection and hold Seller harmless for leaks in house.
6. Buyer is aware that only two apartments are rented. Buyer will accept empty units in "as-is" condition.
7. Buyer has observed drainage problem at several units and apparent flooding in lower level of structure 1124 Easy. Buyer will waive further tests and will repair as needed.
8. Buyer has observed black mold at 3 locations. Buyer will waive standard tests. Seller will abate mold growth as required.
9. Seller will furnish list of existing tenants, rent amounts, and deposits held by Seller.
10. Buyer agrees to waive standard termite inspection and home inspection. Buyer will accept property in "as-is" condition.
11. Seller warrants there are no unpaid utility assessments or undisclosed debts or liens, recorded or unrecorded, secured by property.
12. Buyer shall have the right to inspect and approve property (inside and outside) with Seller or his or her agent within 10 days after acceptance of this offer.
13. Upon acceptance of this offer, Buyer or his or her agent will open escrow at Placer Title (Hartnell office) and deposit $5,000. Closing shall be set for 60 days or sooner. Balance of down payment will be paid at closing.

BUYERS: SELLERS: Acceptance

_____Date   _____Date

_____Date   _____Date

Figure D-1. Offer to purchase real estate

Appendix E

Example of an Installment (or Promissory) Note

Figure E-1 is a sample 10-year *installment note* (also called a *promissory note*) secured by a deed of trust. The fixed payments are $800 or more per month. The terms are 120 months, at which time all the remaining balance—principal and interest—is due and payable.

Often I will offer an extension if the buyer pays well! For example, I might offer a five-year extension with an interest rate increase to 9 percent. Or I may ask that payments be increased from $800 to $900 per month. Notice the due on sale clause and late-fee charge described at the bottom of the note.

DO NOT DESTROY THIS NOTE: When paid, this note, with
Deed of Trust securing same, must be surrendered to Trustee for   Escrow #
cancellation before reconveyance will be made.   12345

INSTALLMENT NOTE

Amount: <u>$100,000</u>   Location: <u>Redding, California</u>   Date: _____

In installments as herein stated, for value received, I, the undersigned, promise to
pay to   <u>TYCOON FIXER JAY</u>

or order, at place designated by payee, the sum of <u>100,000</u> DOLLARS,
with interest from <u>June 1, 1999</u>, on unpaid principal at the rate of
<u>8.5</u> percent per annum; principal and interest payable in installments of
<u>Eight-Hundred and 00/100th (800.00)</u> DOLLARS or more on the
<u>1st</u> day of each <u>and every</u> month, beginning on the <u>1st</u> day of
<u>July 1999</u>, and continuing thereafter until <u>June 1, 2009</u>, when
the whole of the unpaid principal and interest shall immediately become due and
payable.

Each payment shall be credited first on interest then due, and the remainder on
principal, and interest shall thereupon cease upon the principal so credited.
Should there be default in payment of any installment of principal or interest when
due, the whole sum of principal and interest shall become immediately due at the
option of the holder of this note. Principal and interest payable in lawful money of
the United States. If action be instituted on this note, I promise to pay such sum
as the Court may fix as attorney's fees. This note is secured by a DEED OF
TRUST TO <u>ABC TITLE COMPANY</u>, a corporation.

The whole of the unpaid principal and interest on this note shall, at the option of
the Beneficiary, immediately become due and payable upon sale, agreement to
sell, or transfer to another party of the property described in the Deed of Trust
recorded as security for this Note.

Maker herein agrees to pay a late charge of <u>$48.00</u> for each
payment received more than 10 days late.

Buyer: <u>Investor Ivan Smith</u>

Buyer: <u>Investor Sally Smith</u>

Figure E-1. Example of an installment (or promissory) note

Appendix F

Resources for Real Estate Investors

Books

Autry, Gene, with Mickey Herskowitz, *Back in the Saddle Again*, (Doubleday, 1978).

Brangham, Suzanne, *Housewise* (Clarkson Potter, 1987).

DeCima, Jay P., *Investing in Fixer-Uppers*, (McGraw-Hill, 2003).

———, *Start Small, Profit Big in Real Estate: Fixer Jay's 2-Year Plan for Building Wealth—Starting from Scratch* (McGraw-Hill, 2004).

Kroc, Ray, *Grinding It Out: The Making of McDonald's* (Contemporary Books, 1977).

Nickerson, William, *How I Turned $1,000 into Five Million in Real Estate* (Simon & Schuster, 1984).

Reed, John T., *Aggressive Tax Avoidance for Real Estate Investors* (Reed Publishing 1993).

Robinson, Leigh, *Landlording: A Handy Manual for Scrupulous Landlords*, 10th ed. (ExPress Publishing, 2006).

Schaub, John W., *Building Wealth One House at a Time* (McGraw-Hill, 2004).

Sprouse, Terry, *Fix 'Em Up, Rent 'Em Out* (Planeta Books, 2007).

Newsletters

Readers may obtain a free copy of these newsletters by writing to the addresses given below.

Trade Secrets Newsletter   (monthly)

>Jay P. DeCima
>KJAY Publishing
>P.O. Box 491779, Ste. C
>Redding, CA 96049
>1-800-722-2550

The CommonWealth Letters   (monthly)

>Jack Miller
>P.O. Box 21172
>Tampa, FL 33622
>1-813-286-8478

Strategies and Solutions (six issues annually)

>John Schaub
>2677 S. Tamiami Trail, Suite 4
>Sarasota, FL 34239
>1-800-237-9222

Seminars and Workshops

Jay P. DeCima	House Fixer Camps
1-800-722-2550	Managing Tenants & Toilets
www.fixerjay.com	
Jack Miller	Various Wealth Building Seminars
1-888-282-1882	
www.crewealth.com	

Peter Fortunato   Acquisition Techniques
1-727-397-1906
www.peterfortunato.com

John Schaub   Making It Big on Little Deals
1-800-237-9222
www.johnschaub.com

 **Index**

Index

Index

About the Author

"Fixer Jay" DeCima is a seasoned real estate investor-landlord with nearly 50 years' experience and 200 rental houses to show for his efforts. Jay is also a successful career changer having worked more than 20 years for the telephone company.

Twenty-five years ago, Jay began teaching others his high-profit fixing and adding-value techniques. Jay's popular House Fixer Camps are taught several times each year in his hometown of Redding, California. Jay is widely regarded as the undisputed king of fixer-uppers on the national teaching circuit!

Trade Secrets, Jay's monthly how-to newsletter, is the only national newsletter specifically written for the do-it-yourself, start-out investors and career changers. Jay writes about practical techniques and strategies with special emphasis on cash flow investing. For a free copy write to Fixer Jay, P.O. Box 491779, Ste. C, Redding, CA 96049.

To see Jay's bimonthly tips and information blog for do-it-yourself investors, visit www.fixerjay.com.